Satanta

Kiowa Chief Satanta (White Bear).
Photo by William Stinson Soule, Fort Sill, Oklahoma. (Courtesy Archives &
Manuscripts Division of the Oklahoma Historical Society)

SATANTA

The Life and Death of a War Chief

by
Charles M. Robinson III

foreword by
William H. Leckie

STATE HOUSE PRESS
Austin, Texas
1997

Library of Congress Cataloging-in-Publication Data

Robinson, Charles M., 1949-
Satanta : the life and death of a war chief / by Charles M.
Robinson III ; foreword by William H. Leckie. — 1st ed.
p. cm.
Includes bibliographical references and index.
ISBN 1-880510-55-3 (hardcover : alk. paper)
ISBN 1-880510-56-1 (pbk. : alk. paper)
ISBN 1-880510-57-X (deluxe ltd. : alk. paper)
1. Satanta, Kiowa Chief, ca 1815-1878.
2. Kiowa Indians—Biography.
3. Kiowa Indians—History. I. Title.

E99.K5S29 1998
973'.049749'0092—dc21   97-37009
[B]

Printed in the United States of America

FIRST EDITION

cover design by David Timmons

STATE HOUSE PRESS
P.O. Box 15247
Austin, Texas 78761

Table of Contents

List of Illustrations vii

Foreword ix

Acknowledgements xiii

Introduction xv

Chapter One: Satanta and the Kiowas 1

Chapter Two: The Making of a Raider 15

Chapter Three: "This Fiend Satanta" 31

Chapter Four: Bloodshed and Politics 45

Chapter Five: Medicine Lodge:
"My Heart Feels Like Bursting" 59

Chapter Six: The Winter Campaign 77

Chapter Seven: "Peace on the Reservations;
War Off of Them" 97

Chapter Eight: The Warren Massacre 113

Chapter Nine: Arrest 125

Chapter Ten: The Trial 141

Chapter Eleven: Prison 153

Chapter Twelve: Parole 167

Chapter Thirteen: The Red River War 181

Chapter Fourteen: Death and Immortality 193

Chapter Notes 201

Bibliography 223

Index 231

List of Illustrations

Satanta . . . . frontispiece
Dohasen the Elder 5
Satank 10
Satanta 11
Satanta's Medicine Shield 25
Fort Larned, Kansas 30
Kit Carson 37
Stumbling Bear 40
Kicking Bird 42
Lone Wolf 43
Jesse H. Leavenworth 44
General W.S. Hancock 50
Henry Morton Stanley 58
Medicine Lodge Treaty 66
General Philip H. Sheridan 78
Colonel William B. Hazen 79
George A. Custer 85
Battle of the Washita 87
Lawrie Tatum 105
Colonel Benjamin Grierson 106
Fort Sill, Oklahoma 107
Big Tree 117
Warren Wagon Train Massacre 120
General William Tecumseh Sherman 121
Fort Richardson, Texas 121
Ranald S. Mackenzie 121

Satanta's Boastful Harangue 128
Samuel W.T. Lanham 143
Fort Richardson Guardhouse Ruins 151
Satanta and Big Tree in Prison 154
Governor Edmund J. Davis 171
Satanta in prison 176
Satanta 182

Foreword

Set-t'ainte (White Bear), commonly called Satanta, was a noted Kiowa chief, orator and diplomat. Born a few years prior to 1820, Satanta's rise to prominence came comparatively late in his life, and not until the 1860s did his colorful personality and relentless raiding command national attention. Although he never achieved the status of a Red Cloud of the Sioux, Joseph of the Nez Percé, Cochise of the Chiricahua Apaches or even that of Victorio of the Warm Springs Apaches, he nevertheless became one of the best known Indian leaders of his time.

He commanded the attention of President Ulysses S. Grant and the concern of generals William T. Sherman and Philip Sheridan as well as field commanders George A. Custer, Benjamin H. Grierson and Ranald Mackenzie. His exploits were chronicled in the national press, and distinguished photographers and artists were eager to provide the public with portraits of the burly Kiowa. Among his own people, however, his contradictory character often led to distrust, and the Texans both hated and feared him due to his merciless raids on the state's frontier.

Satanta's fame, or ill-fame, reached a peak in May 1871 when he participated in an attack west of Fort Richardson, Texas, on a ten-wagon train owned by Captain Henry Warren. Seven teamsters were killed, their bodies badly mutilated, and about forty mules driven off. The raid coincided with an inspection tour of Texas frontier posts by General Sherman, who received the news while encamped at Richardson and immediately ordered Colonel Mackenzie, with a battalion of his Fourth Cavalry regiment, to march to the site of the strike and pursue the raiders. Sherman then moved on to Fort Sill in Indian Territory to inspect the post and visit with his old friend Colonel Grierson.

When Sherman reached Fort Sill he interviewed the Indian agent, Quaker Lawrie Tatum, and informed the horrified agent of the attack on the wagon train. Soon thereafter the Kiowas arrived at the agency for rations and Tatum questioned them about the raid. Satanta loudly and boldly announced that he had led the war party and named others who had accompanied him. Tatum forwarded this information on to Sherman and Grierson and, in a dramatic confrontation at Grierson's quarters, Satanta and chiefs Big Tree and Satank were arrested and imprisoned. A few days later Colonel Mackenzie and his column arrived at Fort Sill. The Kiowas were turned over to him with orders to transfer them to Texas for trial, but Mackenzie was barely underway when Satank managed to free his hands from shackles and attack his bodyguards. He was shot and killed and his body thrown by the roadside.

Satanta and Big Tree were brought without further difficulty to Jacksboro, Texas, where they were tried and sentenced to be hanged. The Warren Wagon Train Massacre and its aftermath attracted national attention. Pressure, largely from eastern humanitarians, caused Governor Edmund J. Davis to commute the sentences to life imprisonment, to the great disgust of General Sherman.

Satanta's history did not end here. His people became increasingly incensed at the imprisonment of their chiefs, and there was fear at Fort Sill that the tribe might resort to war. When even President Grant became involved, a sorely tried Governor Davis at last agreed to set both Satanta and Big Tree free.

Satanta's freedom was short-lived. With the outbreak of the far-flung Red River War of 1874-1875 he was charged with taking part in the hostilities, arrested, and returned to the state penitentiary at Huntsville, Texas. The next three years of confinement broke the chief's spirit, and on October 11, 1878, he took his own life by leaping from an upper porch to the ground below. In contrast, Big Tree converted to the Baptist faith, lived a long and constructive life among his people, and died in 1929.

Much was written about Satanta during his lifetime, and the

published flow of information has continued after his demise, but the portraits of him to date have been largely one dimensional. Charles Robinson's *Satanta* places the chief in the setting of his time and is, therefore, as much a history of the Kiowa people as it is the biography of one of their leaders. Satanta's life story here portrayed is also the history of a clash of cultures and of a way of life threatened with extinction. Here is a definitive work on the subjects both of Satanta and of the Kiowa nation's unhappy fate destined by American westward expansion.

—William H. Leckie
Winter Springs, Florida
August 1996

Acknowledgements

I first became aware of Satanta more than ten years ago while working on *Frontier Forts of Texas*, a general guidebook subsequently released by the Gulf Publishing Company of Houston. The story of Satanta and the Jacksboro Trial, which I included in my entry on Fort Richardson, fascinated me, but because *Frontier Posts* was basically a guidebook covering the entire state, Satanta and the trial received very little space.

Once *Frontier Forts* was released, however, I began researching the trial of Satanta, and the result was *The Indian Trial*, released in 1997 by the Arthur H. Clark Company. *The Indian Trial* is the story of a massacre, the subsequent judicial proceedings, and their relationship to the decline and fall of the Kiowa nation. Although Satanta loomed large in the story, he was only one character among many, and his own life was beyond the scope of the work. Yet he is a central figure in the history of the Southern Plains, deserving of his own biography, and with that in mind I gathered my unused material on Satanta and began filling in the gaps. This book is the result.

Many people and organizations assisted in this project. Although the completed work and the conclusions drawn are entirely my own, I feel that some recognition is in order.

This book would have been impossible without Betty Washburn of Apache, Oklahoma, Satanta's great-great-granddaughter, who gathered tribal lore from the Kiowa elders, as well as material handed down through her own family, and shared it with me. To her and all her people I owe a debt that can never be repaid.

Towana Spivey, director of the Fort Sill Museum, first put

me in contact with the Kiowas on this project.

Dr. Robert Pierce, director of the Texas Prison Museum in Huntsville, filled in many small details not only of Satanta's imprisonment but of many other aspects of his life.

Special appreciation goes to William H. Leckie for reviewing and offering his assistance with the manuscript, and for writing the foreword.

Robert M. Utley reviewed the manuscript, endorsed the project and offered sound advice.

The University of Oklahoma Press was gracious enough to invoke its fair use policy and allow extensive quotes from Wilbur S. Nye's *Carbine and Lance: The Story of Old Fort Sill*. Thanks also to Henry Holt and Company for permission to quote from Dee Brown's 1970 *Bury My Heart at Wounded Knee*.

Others who helped include, in Texas, Judy Rayburn at Jackboro's Fort Richardson State Historical Park; Joan Farmer at Albany's Old Jail Art Center and Archives; Barbara A. Neal Ledbetter in Graham; The Center for American History at the University of Texas at Austin; Thomas A. Munnerlyn, Deborah Brothers and Erik Mason of State House Press; the Interlibrary Loan Service of the University of Texas-Pan American; and the Arnulfo Oliveira Library at the University of Texas at Brownsville. In California, the Phoebe Hearst Museum at the University of California-Berkeley, and the Henry E. Huntington Library and Art Gallery in San Marino. In Kansas, the Kansas State Historical Sociey at Topeka. In Montana, Kitty Belle Deernose of the Little Bighorn Battlefield National Monument at the Crow Agency. In Oklahoma, the Oklahoma State Historical Society in Oklahoma City, the Thomas Gilcrease Institute at Tulsa, and John Joerschke in Stillwater. In Washington, Robert A. Clark of the Arthur H. Clark Co. in Spokane. In Washington, D.C., the Library of Congress.

Portions of Chapters One and Two originally appeared as "Young Satanta: The Making of a Kiowa Leader" in *Old West*, Winter 1993, Western Publications, Stillwater, Oklahoma.

Introduction

If a citizen of the late 1860s or early 1870s had been asked to name a plains Indian, as likely as not the answer would have been Satanta. Although later overshadowed by often greater chiefs, Satanta was one of the best known Indians of his time. An accomplished war leader, a wily and gifted diplomat, an orator of note and philosopher of sorts, his activities and statements appeared frequently on the pages of the great New York newspapers. In Charles Schreyvogel's famous painting, "Custer's Demand," Satanta is near the center, his famous medicine lance in hand, face daubed in red and observing Custer from the corners of his eyes. In Washington, his very existence often worried the generals and bureaucrats; in Texas, where his name symbolized all the Indian depredations which the settlers had come to expect on their frontier, he was thoroughly hated.

This contemporary fame—or infamy—is odd when one considers the character of the man. He did not inspire, as did Cochise, nor was he a great tactician like Geronimo, Victorio or Red Cloud. He was not a leader in the mold of Crazy Horse, nor did he draw the universal admiration of Chief Joseph. The society of his people, the Kiowas, almost seemed to have been structured to prevent such outstanding figures from rising.

Satanta was, however, a charismatic figure who drew attention wherever he went. His mercurial temperament kept both friends and foes continually off balance. In treaty conferences, his skillful diplomacy sometimes bordered on brilliance. Even his enemies acknowledged his gift for oratory, and all listened when he spoke. He never forgot a favor nor forgave a slight.

He seems to have had associates rather than friends. When drunk he became mellow and would laugh and joke with his drinking companions, but even then he left an impression of reserve, of never allowing himself to become overly familiar. This complicated warrior once caused a New York *Times* correspondent to write:

> It must be remembered that in cunning or native diplomacy SATANTA has no equal. In worth and influence RED CLOUD is his rival; but in boldness, daring and merciless cruelty SATANTA is far superior, and yet there are some good points in this dusky chieftain which command admiration. If a white man does him an injury he never forgives him; but if on the other hand the white man has done him a service, death alone can prevent him from paying the debt.[1]

The strengths and weaknesses of men seem to have been exaggerated in this one man, intensified in a Kiowa living in the nineteenth century among a people and in an era in which he did not belong. He possessed a towering intellect within a society which did not prize intellectual ability, a Machiavellian society with cruel and duplicitous attributes toward which his intellectual accomplishments were directed.

Satanta was nevertheless capable of human feelings. He began his family late by Kiowa standards, and even the accounts written by his white enemies leave no doubt that he loved his children and appeared to respect his several wives. Stories still circulate among the Kiowas about his kindness to children in general. He always seemed to have time for them and would teach them tribal handicrafts.[2]

In 1863 a cattleman named Evander Light met Satanta without realizing who he was. Light and his bride had joined a military wagon train for protection during a trip from Denver, Colorado, to Fort Leavenworth, Kansas. Near the Arkansas River in central Kansas, they heard the sound of gunfire and knew a fight was underway somewhere over the hills ahead. Presently a lone Indian came riding toward the train from the direction of the fighting. Decades later, Light recalled:

The warrior, half-naked from the waist up, sat bare-back on a paint pony, his buck-skin covered legs dangling lower than the animal's belly...but an eye less practiced than a physician could readily see that the man was wounded in several places. The more experienced among the travelers appraised him carefully and then knew him for what he was—a Kiowa, and to all appearances, a head-man of his tribe.

"Tough lookin' hombre, ain't he?" the sergeant of the train commented, then added while nodding toward the sound of the fighting in the hills, "But that ain't ary [sic] picnic out yonder."

The Indian looked the group over, then rode up to Light. "Peace, friend," he said in broken English. "We are Kiowa...on warpath. We fight Pawnee. But my gun...I have lost him."

Without a second thought, Light pulled out his revolver and handed it over, grip first. The Indian stared at him very closely for a minute or two, then kicked his pony and rode back toward the sound of the guns.

Light forgot the incident until a couple of years later when he joined a trading expedition heading south into the plains from Fort Larned, Kansas. Not long after leaving Larned they were overtaken and captured by a band of Kiowas and Cheyennes en route home from a dispute, with their agent, which had left them in a foul mood. The whites were carried to the Kiowa village and taunted by young warriors who fired arrows at their feet before taking them to the head chief of the village—Satanta.

Light and Satanta stared at each other, each trying to decide where he had seen the other before, then Satanta rushed forward and shouted "Arkansas!" as he threw his arms around his white prisoner. Light realized this was the Kiowa to whom he had given the pistol. Satanta restored the whites' wagons and property to them, and told them to go in peace.[3]

Another beneficiary of Satanta's gratitude was C.F. Doan, a Quaker who operated a store at Fort Sill. Apparently referring to the Red River War of 1874, Doan wrote:

I was warned during that time by Satanta that the
Indians liked me and they wanted me to leave the
country because they intended to kill every white
man in the nation. I rather think that the friendly
warning was given me because I often gave crackers
and candy to the hungry squaws and papooses and
of course Satanta's family received theirs.[4]

No one was neutral about Satanta, either during his lifetime
or after his death. Even among his own people, he remains an
enigma; to the modern Kiowas he is a hero and, like heroes of
all races, his achievements have been magnified by time and
legend. The Kiowa elders have many stories about him which
may or may not be true but which, after more than a century,
can neither be verified nor refuted.

The Kiowas who knew him were divided into numerous
political factions and rent by the great social upheavals brought
on by the whites. Among them he was detested as often as he
was admired, and the dissenting views create special problems
for anyone attempting to learn about him. He engendered such
passions that there are often conflicting, indeed irreconcilable,
accounts of the same incidents. A biographer must sort through
these events to eliminate those least likely to be factual and to
draw conclusions from the remainder, while hoping that the
end result approximates the now-lost historic fact.

In the 1930s Colonel W.S. Nye, whose definitive history of
Fort Sill, Oklahoma, is equally a history of the final years of
Kiowa independence, commented:

Satanta was that type which today makes gangster
leaders. He was brazen and impudent, shrewd at
times, yet, naive, addicted to violence and boasting.[5]

In 1970, after those who knew him were dead and the
passions of the Indian Wars had calmed, author Dee Brown
took a kinder view:

Satanta was a burly giant, with jet black hair reaching
to his enormous shoulders. His arms and legs were
thickly muscled, his open face revealing strong con-

fidence in his power. He wore brilliant red paint on his face and body, and carried red streamers on his lance. He liked to ride hard and fight hard. He was a hearty eater and drinker, and laughed with gusto. He enjoyed even his enemies.[6]

Somewhere, amid these portrayals, is a man. He lived in a time when the Kiowas produced many notable chiefs. As a warrior and a leader he was perhaps equal to other chiefs, but no greater, yet he alone became the physical embodiment of everything that was Kiowa. He was famous in his own time, and remembered in ours, not so much for who he was but for what he represented.

Chapter 1
Satanta and the Kiowas

Satanta enters history suddenly, as an adult of distinction as if he sprang from the plains fully grown, his talents as a diplomat and warrior fully developed. His abrupt emergence is due to his extensive training, as a warrior and leader, which lasted far longer than normal for a Kiowa youth. Satanta was the oldest son of Red Tipi [*To-quodle-kaip-tau*], the ranking Kiowa priest of his time. The Kiowas say Red Tipi was so proud of his son that he kept Satanta under strict supervision long after most young men would have gone out on their own. When his father finally released him into the world, Satanta was thoroughly prepared for his role in the Kiowa nation.[1]

The Kiowas had no written records. Their formal history is confined to pictographs illustrating key events of only two generations in the middle of the nineteenth century. The little that is known about Satanta's early life comes from oral traditions passed down by the Kiowa elders. Even his age is disputed but, based on general agreement among his white contemporaries as well as modern genealogical research, it may be safely assumed that he was born between 1815 and 1818.[2] His birth probably occurred on the plains, somewhere in the vast landscape between the North Platte River in western Nebraska and the Canadian River which flows through North Texas and Central Oklahoma; this was the range of his people at that time.[3] Although Satanta's descendants believe he was Kiowa on both sides, he may have been of mixed blood and once indicated that his mother was Arapaho. Another possibility was raised in the 1850s by two Mexicans, recently escaped from Kiowa captivity, who told a corporal at Fort Chadbourne, Texas, that Satanta's mother was also a Mexican captive who spoke to them in Spanish when they were alone and assisted them in escaping. Kiowas, however, practiced polygamy, and the tribal elders believe this Mexican woman was Red Tipi's number-two wife, the mother of Satanta's four half-brothers and his half-sister.[4] If Satanta was of mixed blood, from whatever source, this was not unusual among the Kiowas.

Soon after his birth Satanta was given the baby name Big Ribs [Gauton-bain], apparently referring to the massive physique for which he was known throughout his life. Since Kiowa parents did not participate in the naming of their children, he probably received the name from a grandparent or other relative. His permanent name, which translates into English as "White Bear," would have been acquired later, perhaps from a dream or from some sort of merit gained in war, hunting or in council. The Kiowa word for White Bear, Set-t'ainte, is virtually unpronounceable to English-speaking whites, and by the 1870s the English corruption "Satanta" was often used by the Kiowas themselves.[5]

The Great Plains on which Satanta was born were a vast, rolling, unending prairie extending from horizon to horizon, unbroken except for small clumps of timber near rivers and streams. Winter brought bitter winds sweeping down from the arctic with blinding snow or rain mixed with sleet. Temperatures could fall more than thirty degrees within a single hour. In the summer the sun beat baked the plains in visible heat waves which radiated back toward the sky. Spring snow melts from mountains hundreds of miles to the west turned the rivers into raging torrents. When the meltwater was spent the rivers became sluggish, choked with mud until, by the middle of summer, they dried out to mudflats with treacherous quicksand. This harsh land of the Kiowas bred a proud, suspicious, self-reliant people.

By modern white standards there appears to have been little to admire in Kiowa society, a warrior society built on raiding against other tribes and, later, against whites. Young men gained wealth by plunder and acquired merit by their proficiency with a scalping knife. Ethnologist James Mooney lived among the Kiowas for several years, probably knew them better than any other nineteenth-century white and genuinely liked them, but he was forced to admit:

> In character the Kiowa are below standard [of other tribes]....They have the savage virtue of bravery, as they have abundantly proven, but as a people they have less of honor, gratitude, and general reliability than perhaps any other tribe of the plains. The large infusion of captive blood, chiefly Mexican, must undoubtedly have influenced the tribal character, but whether for good or evil the student of heredity must determine.[6]

Lieutenant James Will Myers, an officer of the Tenth Cavalry at Fort Sill who knew Satanta personally and whose writings reflect a definite sympathy toward the Kiowas in their conflict with the whites, nevertheless observed that the Kiowa's

> language is as rough as his manner, and his heart is as cruel as it is fearless. His women are his slaves whom he can starve or beat to death unrestrained by any law of God or man known to him.[7]

Although generally associated with the Southern Plains, the Kiowas were not indigenous to the region. Originally a mountain people who emigrated from the area of western Montana when forced southward under pressure from more powerful tribes, particularly the Lakota Sioux and Cheyennes, they acquired horses and absorbed cultural aspects of the earlier plains tribes such as the Sun Dance and the formation of warrior societies. On the Southern Plains they eventually confederated with the Comanches and a small Athapaskan group which became known as the Kiowa-Apaches or Plains Apaches.[8]

By Satanta's time the Kiowas were organized into six major groups, one of which was actually Apache. These were not distinct tribal groups such as the Oglalas and Hunkpapas of the Lakota Sioux, or the Chiricahuas and Mescaleros among the Western Apaches. The Kiowa nation at its height was never large enough to support such distinctions; their groups were administrative units, often bound by blood ties, each with its own political chief who was, in turn, subject to a paramount chief. When the entire nation gathered, the bands formed a camp circle with the *K'at'a*, the most important, in the east and the others to their left in order of importance around the circle.

K'at'a means *"Arikara,"* a northern plains tribe also known as the *Rees* through whose territory the Kiowas probably migrated in the early eighteenth century. The use of the name by the Kiowa band probably indicates an early trading relationship with the Rees rather than blood ties. These Kiowas sometimes called themselves *Ga'i-K'at'a* [Kiowa Arikara] to distinguish themselves from the true Rees. It was an aristocratic band numbering among its members Dohasen the Elder, the most powerful of all paramount chiefs who headed the Kiowa nation for well over thirty years.

Second in importance was the *Ko gui* [Elk] band, to which Satanta belonged, which led the nation's war ceremonies. After them came the *Ga'igwu*, or Kiowa Proper, perhaps the original band from which all others originated. This was a priestly band, custodian of both the *Taime*, the sacred medicine symbol of the Sun Dance, and of the medicine tipi used during the Sun Dance ceremony. To the left of the *Ga'igwu* was another priestly band, the *Kinep* [Big Shields], keepers of the idol which was placed in front of the *Taime* during the Sun Dance. Fifth in the circle were the *Semat*, the Kiowa-Apaches. The sixth and last were the *Konta'Iyui* [Black Boys], the significance of whose name has been lost.[9]

The six major bands were divided into smaller sub-bands whose populations were fluid, with people sometimes moving from one to the other according to the prestige of a particular chief. At any given time there might be ten to twenty of these bands, some with as few as ten lodges and others with as many as fifty. Each sub-band was headed by a political chief who exercised a degree of authority over the band as a unit. The paramount chief of the Kiowa nation was elected in a council of all the political chiefs. James Mooney speculates that before the coming of the whites, the power of the paramount chief must have been "almost despotic" and that he was feared as well as respected by his people. By the time the whites came to know the Kiowas well, however, the system had altered so that the chiefs led more by prestige than position. Consequently

*Dohasen the Elder, the most powerful of the Kiowa's paramount
chiefs. (Painting by George Catlin,* Letters and Notes on the
Manners, Customs and Conditions of North American Indians.*)*

Dohasen, whose name means "Little Mountain," was the only
man in recorded history with enough power to give real
meaning to the term "paramount chief." An autocrat, he ruled
the tribe through force of character from 1833 until his death
in 1866.[10] George Catlin, who accompanied a military expedition through the midwest in 1834, met Dohasen early in his
career as paramount chief and described him as "a very gentle-
manly and high minded man, who treated the dragoons and

officers with great kindness while in his country."[11]

Dohasen never seemed to grasp completely the power of the new forces he faced; whites neither frightened nor impressed him. As more of these pale strangers came into his territory, he no doubt participated in raids against them and is known to have been in several fights against U.S. military troops. He did not make a career of attacking soldiers or settlers, however, and as time passed he assumed an attitude of grudging tolerance. As he grew older he leaned more and more toward moderation, and Kiowas later said he advised them "to take the white man by the hand, and clear above the elbow."[12]

Although Dohasen ruled the Kiowas during most of Satanta's adult life, he never became a role model for the younger man. Satanta was a warrior and a raider, and the role of moderate fell to a much younger chief, Kicking Bird,[13] who understood the power of the whites and realized the survival of his people depended on accommodation. Their different philosophies caused Kicking Bird and Satanta to become bitter enemies.

War chiefs such as Satanta were chosen by their followers according to bravery and wisdom, and they had to maintain their followers' confidence in order to continue leading. In addition to their duties as planners and leaders of battles, they also supervised the Ya'pahe, the camp police who enforced regulations, punished violations, organized buffalo hunts and led in tribal ceremonies.[14]

Elementary education was the responsibility of the medicine man who, in Satanta's case, was probably his father, Red Tipi. Unlike the shamans of the Eskimos or the sorcerers of some African tribes, the Kiowa medicine man was not a dreaded figure but a respected friend, wise, kind and generous, a counselor and oracle. He taught children religion and tribal lore as well as good manners and respect for their elders.[15]

Sex roles were emphasized from early childhood. Girls were little more than servants, since that was the position they would have as women who gathered wood and water and performed household chores. Boys, however, were prized as future warriors who might someday become the great men of the nation. They learned to care for ponies and were taught to use bows and arrows. Most of the time they were allowed to

do much as they pleased and seldom were disciplined. Outstanding achievement was announced publicly, and the boy
being honored was given a reward, generally ponies. Thomas
Battey, superintendent of schools at the Kiowa-Comanche
Agency at Fort Sill in the 1870s, wrote that

> They may tyrannize over the girls, and, as future lords
> of the tribe, are seldom chided in any respect. If any
> one of them, however, becomes unbearably inso-
> lent, on some occasion when the principal men are
> together, and he is present, he becomes the subject
> of cutting sarcasm, to which he cannot utter a word,
> and from which he may not withdraw; he must
> endure until he most heartily abhors himself. Even-
> tually he learns to conduct himself with more becom-
> ing dignity and decorum.[16]

At the age of eight or ten a boy joined the Rabbit Society,
the first stage of his military training and the lowest of six warrior
societies through which he ultimately might rise. The old men
drilled the boys and taught them the dance of the society, which
imitated the jumping of a rabbit. After showing proficiency as
Rabbits, the boys were promoted to the next society, the Young
Wild Sheep, followed in succession by the Horse Headdress
Society, the Black Legs, and the Skunkberry or Crazy Horse
Society,[17] with each promotion based on merit or the necessi-
ties of war. The greatest warrior society was the *Koiet-senko*,
the Real or Principal Dogs, restricted to the ten bravest men of
the tribe.[18]

The Koiet-senko carried great honor but heavy responsibility as well, with duties and obligations similar to those of the
samurai of old Japan. According to Mooney, they "were
pledged to lead every desperate charge and to keep their place
in the front of battle until they won victory or death." Each
Koiet-senko composed a death song which he would try to sing
when he knew the end had come.

When a vacancy occurred in the Koiet-senko ranks, either
through death, retirement, or degradation due to cowardice,
the society waited until the annual Sun Dance to initiate a new
member. As vacancies were not frequent, Mooney observed,

"the event was always a matter of considerable importance."
The high point of the ceremony was the new member's inves-
titure with the sash of the order. The leader's sash was made of
elk skin dyed black; three of the sashes were of red cloth, and
the remaining six of elk skin dyed red.

Members of the Koiet-senko had youthful associates, apparently apprentice warriors such as squires were to the knights of
medieval Europe. If a Koiet-senko did not choose to go on an
expedition, he might lend his sash to the associate and could
also allow this associate to wear the sash in camp. If, however,
a major war party was planned, the Koiet-senko was obliged to
wear the sash and participate himself or else be pronounced a
coward and stripped of his sash. When he became too old for
war, he would formally retire and give his sash to a younger
warrior whom he deemed worthy. The young warrior, in turn,
presented gifts to the retiring Koiet-senko. A sash might also be
publicly removed from a Koiet-senko grown too old for war,
but this was again retirement and no stigma was attached.[19]

Little is known of Satanta's advancement through the warrior societies. The modern Kiowas say only that he was a
member of the Black Legs Society and a Koiet-senko [see
footnote 18], and presumably he went through the intermediate
order of the Crazy Horses, as well as the minor orders preceding
his appointment to the Black Legs. His Koiet-senko death song
was

> No matter where my enemies destroy me,
> Do not mourn for me,
> Because this is the end all great warriors face.[20]

As a Koiet-senko, Satanta often associated with Satank
[Sitting Bear], the leader of the society. Born sometime between
1798 and 1800, Satank was a true Kiowa of the plains, having
grown to manhood in a world free of white influence. He was
cruel and ruthless, with a vindictive nature. Although a warrior
rather than a priest or medicine man, he nevertheless was a
practitioner of the occult and was said to use his sorcery to
dispose of those who had offended him. Satank was feared and
disliked by his own people; as the whites came to know him,
they shared that opinion.[21]

As head of the Koiet-senko, Satank was the foremost warrior in a nation of warriors. He carried a ceremonial arrow and wore the broad elk skin sash which crossed his chest from his left shoulder and trailed the ground. The lower end of the sash had a hole, and his duty when lining up for a charge was to dismount in front of the warriors and thrust the arrow through the hole, pinning himself to the ground. There he remained until the Kiowas either carried the day or, in retreat, freed him by pulling the arrow from the ground. Throughout the fight he would remain stationary, making no attempt to avoid danger. If, in retreat, the Kiowas failed to pull the arrow from the ground, the Koiet-senko chief stayed in place until he was captured or killed. Since the Kiowas did not sacrifice their bravest men needlessly, this ceremony was performed only in a fight to the finish against their bitterest foes.[22]

Because of the similarity of their names, both derived from the Kiowa word *set* [bear], and their nearly simultaneous careers as leaders, many writers confuse Satanta with Satank. In 1906 Percival G. Lowe, who had been a soldier in the 1850s, recalled meeting a warrior whom he identified as Satanta during treaty negotiations at Fort Atkinson, Kansas, half a century earlier.

> He was a man about five feet ten, sparely made, muscular, cat-like in his movements—more Spanish than Indian in his appearance—sharp features, thin lips, keen, restless eyes, thin mustache and scattering chin whiskers that seemed to have stopped growing when one to three inches long.[23]

Lowe was, however, remembering Satank, as a photograph of that chief confirms. Another soldier, Captain Richard T. Jacob, positively described Satank as

> a small man and decidedly insignificant but he was generally regarded as a man of superior ability. In appearance, he might have been a mixed-blood or of Mexican descent.

Satanta, on the other hand, "was a man of magnificent

Satank, after the death of his son, showing his left little finger amputated at the joint in mourning. He wears the sash of the Koiet-senko Warrior Society. (Courtesy National Archives)

This photograph of Satanta, one of the most famous which was extensively reproduced in the 19th Century, shows him with military jacket and peace medal. (Courtesy National Archives)

physique, being over six feet tall, well built and finely propor-
tioned."[24] New York *Herald* correspondent DeB. Randolph
Keim remembered Satanta as a very large-framed man "with a
tendency toward obesity." And the African explorer Henry
Morton Stanley, who knew Satanta in the late 1860s, wrote that
he was "large, and very muscular, showing great strength...."
He was also clean-shaven. Intelligent, with a forceful personality, he was arrogant and boastful. Anyone reading the contemporary accounts is struck by Satanta's theatrics and oratory, but
his posturing concealed a very real ability as a warrior and
leader. At the height of his prestige in the late 1860s no one,
white or red, questioned his bravery.[25]

Although Kiowas generally married when they were old
enough to assume independent responsibility, the girls at about
fourteen and the boys at about sixteen, Red Tipi's close supervision delayed any marriage plans Satanta may have had. When
he finally did marry he was old by tribal standards, probably in
his late twenties or early thirties. Like his father he had multiple
wives, but the exact number is unclear. In 1868 Lieutenant
Colonel George Armstrong Custer counted four wives, all much
younger than Satanta. The modern Kiowa elders, however,
believe he had only two. In 1850 one of his wives, Zone-ty,
gave birth to Satanta's oldest child, a boy named Gray Goose
[*Tsau-lau-te*] who, in addition to being his heir, was also his
favorite.

More children followed, but again the number is uncertain.
In addition to the teenaged Gray Goose, in 1868 Custer
counted four infants, one carried by each of the four supposed
wives. Records at the Smithsonian Institution say Satanta had
only four children, two sons and two daughters. Modern Kiowa
accounts give a total of eight, three sons and five daughters.
Some lists, however, give an additional daughter, Kills-them-at-
the-door, who was probably the daughter of Satanta's half-
brother Black Bonnet. Her inclusion, and possibly the inclusion
of some of the others, may be due to an old Kiowa custom of
referring to nieces and nephews as sons and daughters. Regardless of how many there actually may have been, the story of
Satanta's relationship with his children centers primarily
around Gray Goose.[26]

One reason for Kiowa polygamy was the surplus of single

women created by male casualties suffered in their continual warfare. The Kiowas also had a low birth rate and high infant mortality rate, which accounts for the large number of captive children adopted into the tribe.[27] Because of the shortage of children and the attrition of natural aging, disease and war, by the late 1870s the tribe faced what modern demographers call "negative growth" with a death rate often out of proportion to the total population. The Kiowas, therefore, generally attacked their enemies only when they had overwhelming numerical superiority or when the opportunity for gain outweighed potential losses; they simply could not afford heavy casualties. As General W.S. Hancock pointed out to Satanta during a council at Fort Larned, Kansas, in 1867,

> If we lose soldiers we don't have to wait for them to grow up. Your Great Father will send us more—a great many more. You know very well that when you lose a man you cannot send another but you must wait until your young men grow up.[28]

Lieutenant Myers had a similar observation.

> Knowing the loss of a company of soldiers would only infuriate the government without materially weakening it, while the extinguishment of such a number of well armed soldiers . . .would involve the sacrifice of many good warriors, they refrain from attempting it [even] when the opportunity is all they could wish; not from cowardice though but from economy.
>
> Two or three well armed men will head off a considerable party of Indians under certain circumstances—but one thousand men cannot prevent five Indians from stampeding their stock if the Indians want it. Why? Because while in trading parlance it will "pay" to lose two or three warriors in exchange for a fine herd of horses; it will not pay to sacrifice several warriors in obtaining two or three scalps.[29]

The economics of raiding—the lives of three warriors in exchange for about forty mules in an incident known to history as the Warren Wagon Train Massacre—was to be the key factor which ultimately removed Satanta from his people, confined him to prison and, by extension, ended his life. But that was decades into the future.

Chapter 2
The Making of a Raider

Satanta's world was undergoing one of the greatest upheavals in history—the final subjugation by the races of the Old World of the territory that was to become the United States. The Revolutionary War and the Industrial Revolution accelerated a process which had begun on the eastern seaboard almost three centuries earlier, and whites were now entering the plains at a massive and alarming rate. When Satanta was born, many plains tribes had never seen a white man. Within a decade of his death, however, the plains were entirely settled by whites whose rule was virtually complete.

At the same time Indian civilization, never sedentary, was in a constant state of change and development; but with no sense of past beyond a generation or two, the Indians did not fully perceive their development. Instead, they tended to view their current way of life as one they had always maintained, and the arrival of the whites meant the demise of what they imagined to be ancient traditions and perhaps even the demise of the people themselves. Describing the Indian's predicament, Lieutenant Myers of the Tenth Cavalry wrote:

> Trails are just beginning within his haunts and...are to him the precursors of the march of that irresistible civilization which has doomed alike his fellows of the eastern seashore, and of the broad savannahs of the Missippi [sic].
>
> Occasionally his wrongs impel him to make a stand against the great tidal wave which threatens to

overwhelm him—for a season its volume is broken
as it dashes against the solid front of his resistance
but the white spray soon breaks over and his is
ingulfed [sic], as he nobly but with futile effort com-
bats the flood.[1]

White pressure, Indian defense of traditional indigenous
values, and the Kiowas' warrior culture made conflict inevitable. Each spring when the snows melted, while the grass grew
tall for their ponies and the nights were clear and moonlit, the
Kiowas and Comanches prepared for their annual raiding
season. It was also the season of the Kiowas' most sacred
ceremony, the *Skaw-tow* or Sun Dance. The ceremony was
not necessary for the raids to begin; indeed by the time the
dance was held about the middle of June, raiding may have
already been underway for several months. It served, however, as a major communication with the gods—as thanks-
giving for the safe return of a war party, recovery from illness,
beseeching of blessings for individuals or families, or for any
major endeavor.

Satanta's great-great-granddaughter, Betty Washburn,
whose Kiowa name is *At-me-ponyah Sankadota*, writes:

> Kiowas are summer people, and during our an-
> cestor's time the annual Sun Dance was one gather-
> ing that they all looked forward to because this was
> one time that the Kiowas all gathered and took part
> in this four-day event. It kept their ties strong as a
> tribe.[2]

Despite their confederation with the Comanches, the Sun
Dance essentially was a Kiowa event. A secular and pragmatic
people, the Comanches had little interest in formal religion and
did not practice the ceremony although, when the Sun Dance
was a prelude to raiding, they usually attended through courtesy, waiting in exasperation while their more-mystical Kiowa
allies invoked the world of the gods.[3]

In many ways, the Kiowa Sun Dance resembled the Sun
Dance of the Lakota Sioux and Cheyennes. The women held a
procession to cut down a central pole for the medicine lodge,

and the men fought a sham battle for possession of the pole. The medicine lodge was built, and the tribe danced, fasted and abstained from sleep for four days. Lakota and Cheyenne warriors often tied themselves to the Sun Dance pole by leather thongs attached to skewers through their flesh, but the Kiowas never practiced self-mutilation during the dance. Even the accidental shedding of blood was an ill omen to the Kiowas, and if it occurred the dance would be abandoned. Voluntary laceration, practiced at other times, was never done during the *Skaw-tow*.[4]

The Sun Dance was the only time that the *Taime*, the sacred image which symbolized the Sun's power, was exposed to public view. Sacred sun shields owned by a chosen few warriors were hung in front of the image. Describing the dance, Mrs. Washburn writes:

> During the Skaw-tow, the Ten Sacred Medicine Bundles were also brought into the medicine lodge with the Shield. The Tai-may priest (medicine man) fanned while praying for good health, long life, success on the warpath and other requests by the people....
>
> The owners of the [sun] shields and medicine men danced at times during the four days of the Skaw-tow dance. They did their sacred songs and ceremonial rituals during the dance. The shield owners who danced were painted with yellow or green designs representing the moon and sun.
>
> The medicine men who danced were also painted white, wore white buckskin skirts with breechclouts outside and carried eagle bone whistles. They puffed smoke toward the four corners of the earth, east, south, west, and north, and finally toward the Sun that gave the Kiowas light, and then they prayed....
>
> At the end of the dance, thanks for the Tai-may's protection was shown first in the form of a gift, possibly a blanket and other items. The next morning the camp circle was broken and raiding parties were organized by leaders. They say Set'-tain-te [Satanta] always went on raids after each Skaw-tow.[5]

Much of the raiding during Satanta's time occurred in Texas, an ironic situation because the initial contacts between Kiowas and Texans appear to have been peaceful with little indication of the bloodshed which would tear the country apart for more than two decades. One of the earliest official records of Kiowa dealings in Texas occurred in the fall of 1836 when the provisional government of the republic dispatched a trading commission to the tribe.[6] The outcome of this commission was not recorded, and the next mention of official contact appears in 1844 when a Kiowa named Good Shirt attended a council between representatives of the government and the various tribes on Tehuacana Creek in east-central Texas. Pledges of friendship were exchanged, and the Kiowa was given about five dollars worth of goods.[7] Not long afterwards, however, skirmishing was reported between Kiowas and Texas Rangers, and thereafter the relationship seesawed back and forth between war and uneasy truce.

Aside from fighting whites, like most plains Indians the Kiowas were involved in almost continual warfare with other tribes. This grew more acute as white pressure from the south and east forced unrelated tribes into continually smaller areas, creating general population stress and putting traditional enemies in close proximity to each other. Satanta undoubtedly received his first taste of war in this intertribal strife. David Lavender, in his history of Bent's Fort, names Satanta as the Kiowa leader in an 1837 massacre of warriors from the Cheyenne Bow String military society. Lavender, however, erroneously believed that Satanta and Satank were the same person; nineteenth-century naturalist George Bird Grinnell, who possessed more accurate information, wrote that Satank was the leader in this fight.

This incident, which is noted on the Kiowa Calendar as the "Summer that the Cheyenne were massacred," occurred in the early summer when the Kiowas, Comanches and Apaches were camped on a tributary of the North Fork of the Red River in the Texas Panhandle near the present town of Mobeetie. In his interpretation of the calendar, Mooney described the Kiowas as preparing for the Sun Dance when a young man, sitting alone straightening arrows, saw two men slipping toward him with grass hung over their faces. Thinking they were Kiowas camouflaged for a deer hunt, he was going out to meet them when they opened fire and wounded him. The young Kiowa ran back to camp to give the alarm, and the strangers fled as the Kiowas and their allies rushed out in pursuit, overtaking a small Cheyenne party and killing three. Several more were killed in a running fight which led into the main Cheyenne camp where the Cheyennes dug rifle pits and fought until their ammunition ran out. The Kiowas and their allies overran the positions and killed all except one Cheyenne who committed suicide to avoid capture. The Cheyennes were scalped, stripped and laid out in a row. Trophies included a medicine lance in a feathered case and a Dog Soldier staff, similar to the Kiowa's Koiet-senko arrow, which was carried by Cheyennes pledged to die at their posts. Six Kiowas were killed, but the losses did not cancel the Sun Dance.[8]

The following summer the Cheyennes staged a vengeance raid and killed several Kiowas. Fighting continued back and forth until the winter of 1839-40 when smallpox ravaged the plains tribes. Weakened and exhausted by the disease, the Cheyennes and Arapahos, and the Kiowas and their allies, held a peace council on the flats of the Arkansas River three miles east of Bent's Fort in what is now eastern Colorado. Here, again, Lavender confuses Satanta with Satank; it was undoubtedly Satank who, as Grinnell states, accompanied Dohasen to parley with the Cheyennes and Arapahos and make a permanent peace with them. If Satanta was present when these fights and the peace council occurred, his role was probably that of a minor subchief or spectator.[9]

By the 1850s, however, Satanta was appearing more frequently in accounts of tribal battles and dealings with the whites, and there remains no question of identity. Historian Donald Worcester has even suggested that, by the 1850s, Satanta's influence already rivalled Dohasen's, but there is no evidence from any other source that Dohasen would have tolerated competition from the much younger man. The suggestion that Satanta was a rival, however, does reveal the extent to which his image was already being crafted; he was on the scene and highly visible whenever something important occurred.[10]

After the peace council the Cheyennes and Arapahos were no longer enemies of the Kiowas, but white pressure had forced the Pawnees and Osages westward into the Kiowas' home ranges, and eastern tribes were beginning to move out onto the plains from their settlements in eastern Oklahoma where they had lived after being driven from their homes east of the Mississippi. The arrival of these tribes forced the Kiowas to roam farther west toward the mountain areas of Colorado claimed by the Utes. The Kiowas' conflict with the Pawnees and Osages from the east, and with the Utes to the west, was fairly constant for more than a decade. The Kiowas also raided regularly into Mexico and increased their depredations against the American whites, although not on the scale which would be reached during the ten years from 1864 to 1874.

In 1852 several prominent Cheyennes were killed in a fight with the Pawnees, and the following spring the relatives of the dead warriors asked the Cheyenne soldier bands for a vengeance raid. Messengers were sent asking the Burnt Thigh Sioux, Arapahos, Kiowas and Apaches to join on the raid against the Pawnees. In June 1853 the various tribes, including Satanta among the Kiowas, gathered around the Cheyenne medicine lodge on the Republican River in western Kansas. Scouts found a fresh Pawnee buffalo kill and determined the location of the main enemy camp before returning to the Cheyenne gathering. After going through the various preparations for war, the Cheyennes, Kiowas and other allied tribes began marching toward the Pawnee camp. Two Cheyennes, scouting ahead, slipped up to the main enemy camp and recognized Shawnees among the Pawnees.[11]

The next day the Cheyennes and their allies charged the position their scouts had seen but found only the ashes of fires. The Pawnees had spotted the allied tribes and moved their camp, sending their women, children and horses to a secure spot while the warriors dug in behind the banks of a nearby stream. Again and again the allies charged the breastworks, exhausting themselves against an enemy who would not come out and fight. They were about to give up when the Shawnees, who had earlier left the Pawnee camp, returned to the scene with their long rifles gleaming in the afternoon sun.

Acquainted with Shawnees, the Kiowas held back the Cheyennes and asked for a parley, but the Shawnees opened fire and killed a Kiowa. The allied tribes retreated and the

Shawnees, unfamiliar with the plains Indian tactic of luring an enemy away from support, gave chase. When the Shawnees were far enough away from their Pawnee friends, the allies turned and charged. Fighting seesawed back and forth over the plain until both sides stopped and eyed each other across the field. Two Shawnees finally dismounted, but Satanta dashed in on horseback and lanced one of them, and the fighting again ensued until the Pawnees arrived and gave the Shawnees the upper hand. Badly mauled, the allied tribes finally broke off and left the field to the Shawnees and Pawnees.[12]

As the 1850s progressed, the Kiowas and Comanches expanded their warfare against the whites, although the Indian leaders always contended the raids were independent actions without tribal sanction. "There was no active war," Private Percival Lowe wrote. "Every day some of the head men of the tribes came into [the military] camp to talk with the 'white chief,' always expressing regret that they could not 'control their young men.'"[13] Although the Kiowas raided in Colorado, Kansas and New Mexico, most of their depredations were directed against Texas and Mexico. The annexation of Texas by the United States was beyond Kiowa comprehension. Having first dealt with the state during its period as a sovereign republic, they viewed Texans as a distinct people, a notion that the Texans' own proud, independent attitude did nothing to dispel. Having no particular quarrel with the United States, the Kiowas could not understand why the federal government was concerned about their raids into Texas. Comprehending even less the treaties with Mexico by which the U.S. government had obligated itself to prevent Indian raids from the United States, they likewise did not understand why they could not cross the border at will nor why they were expected to return Mexican captives. The Kiowas reasoned that because they had remained neutral in a recent conflict between the U.S. government and the Osages, the United States should not interfere with Kiowa raids into Texas and Mexico.[14]

The federal government saw things differently, and in 1853 it convened a treaty conference at Fort Atkinson, Kansas, hoping to impress the Kiowas with the situation. By now Satanta was becoming a power in his own right among the Kiowas. Lowe recalled his frequent visits to the military camp while

waiting for the conference to begin, and from his descriptions
there can be no doubt that this time Lowe meant Satanta and
not Satank.

Satanta always arrived on a "handsome horse" with Spanish equipment and carrying a cavalry sabre. Reaching the sentry
line he would leave his horse with his servant, whom Lowe
described as a Mexican Indian, to be escorted into camp where
he was received by the commanding officer, Major Robert Hall
Chilton, a career soldier from Virginia who had been graduated
from West Point sixteen years earlier. Satanta spoke Spanish,
which the major understood although he often used an interpreter who conversed with the Kiowas in sign language. "Usually," Lowe wrote,

> the conversations between the Major and Satanta
> were apparently pleasant, though sometimes the
> latter became somewhat emphatic. He complained
> of the treatment of the Indian received from the
> whites, the manner in which they overran the coun-
> try, destroyed the game and ignored the Indians'
> rights, and his eyes flashed as he jammed the end of
> his saber scabbard into the ground.

Major Chilton, who sympathized with many of the Indians'
problems, acknowledged their grievances and outlined steps
the government was taking to correct the situation. According
to Lowe, he

> always tried to be pacific and just, admitting many
> wrongs complained of, but never permitting a threat,
> even by innuendo, to pass without an emphatic
> rebuke. He felt that Satanta was a superior, intelligent
> man, and treated him as such. There was a good deal
> in common with these two men. Both had tempers
> easily excited, unbounded energy, boldness and
> courage. Educated and civilized, Satanta would have
> been a match for the Major anywhere. In cunning,
> Indian duplicity and shrewdness he was a full match;
> but the Major was not a man to be trapped, flattered,
> coaxed, driven or bluffed....[15]

During one of these discussions, an argument broke out and Satanta apparently threatened several wagon trains that were on the road. Chilton looked straight at him and told him the army would wreak havoc among the Kiowas if they interfered with the trains. He was so blunt that the interpreter, a mountain man named Pyle, hesitated to translate. Assuming by Satanta's indifference that Pyle had not repeated his comments, Chilton had the interpreter tied to the wheel of a cannon until a correct translation had been made. Learning what the major had actually said, Satanta sulked off and did not return until Agent Thomas Fitzpatrick arrived to begin the treaty conference.[16]

The conference itself proceeded rapidly. An ox train drew up with presents for the Indians, and Fitzpatrick stated the government's terms. The Kiowas, Apaches and Comanches were to maintain peace with Mexico and the United States, including Texas. As part of this peace, the Indians were to return Mexican captives. The Indians also were to acknowledge the government's right to establish roads and military posts within their territory. In turn, the government promised $18,000 worth of annuities for ten years, with a five-year renewal option.

Although the tribes resented the roads and military posts, it was ironically the peace with Mexico and the return of Mexican captives which created the greatest controversy.[17] The Indians greeted this proposal with a flat refusal. Fitzpatrick, noting the impact this provision would have on the tribes, which replenished their livestock from raids on Mexican herds and built up their population with captives, wrote,

> so intermingled amongst these tribes have the most of the Mexican captives become that it is somewhat difficult to distinguish them. They sit in council with them, hunt with them, go to war with them, and partake of their perils and profits, and but few have any desire to leave them.

In the end the best the agent could get was assurance from the Indians that there would be no future raids for livestock and captives,[18] but the Kiowas never had any intention of returning Mexican captives or ending their raids into Mexico or Texas.

Within a year Fitzpatrick was forced to acknowledge the depredations were continuing. "They deny ever having consented
not to war on the Mexicans," he wrote. "They say that they
have no other place to get their horses and mules from."[19]

By the time of this treaty Satanta was a noted warrior almost
forty years old. His father, Red Tipi, had taken his own name
from his heraldic lodge, painted red and decorated with red
streamers, and now he passed this lodge on to Satanta. The
Kiowa elders say that when Satanta departed for battle, the
whole camp turned out to see him off, and his wives chanted
war cries as they followed him to the outskirts of the village. In
battle he wore red paint on his upper torso, face and hair, and
a buckskin vest painted red on one side and yellow on the other.
Among his associates was the ancient medicine man Black
Horse who, along with Red Tipi, appears to have been a
mentor. In 1897 the warrior Taybodl, who at eighty was
considered the oldest living Kiowa, told Captain Hugh Scott of
the Seventh Cavalry's Kiowa L Troop, "Neither Black Horse nor
Tsait-an-te [Satanta] ever stayed at home long. They went to war
with every tribe and with Mexicans, Texans, and white men."

It was Black Horse who provided Satanta's most important
piece of battle equipment, one of the sacred sun shields hung
before the *Taime* image during the Sun Dance. In the 1790s
Black Horse had made a set of six shields all endowed with
powerful medicine. Many years later, recognizing Satanta's
potential as a warrior and leader, the aging Black Horse gave
him one of the shields. Before he could accept it, however,
Satanta had to sacrifice his own flesh to the sun in ritual
laceration. Normally four gashes cut on each side of the chest,
Satanta's four gashes were cut into the back of each shoulder,
just above the joint with the arm, and were a more painful and
enduring sacrifice.

The shield's two sides, both covered with buffalo hide,
represented the dual purposes of fighting and ritual. The sun
painted in the center had two rings around it, representing the
halos which often appear around the moon. One side was
decorated with red cloth strips and the other with yellow cloth.
The head of a crane, apparently one of Satanta's animal totems,
was tied to it, and when he took the shield into battle, he wore
the longest wing feather of a crane in his hair. In camp, he kept

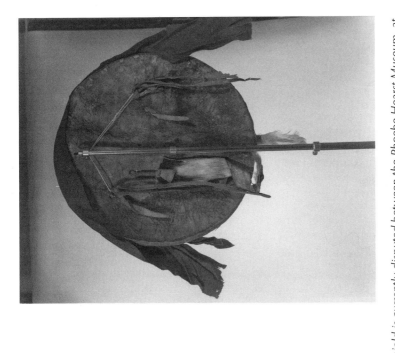

Satanta's medicine shield, made in the 1790s. Ownership of the shield is currently disputed between the Phoebe Hearst Museum, at the University of California at Berkeley, and Satanta's descendants who claim it was illegally obtained. (Courtesy Phoebe Hearst Museum of Anthropology.)

the shield on a tripod about two hundred yards from his lodge.[20] A woman who lived at Fort Chadbourne, in Texas between what are now San Angelo and Abilene, remembered Satanta's riding into the post in 1857 with the long, wavy, brown hair of a white woman's scalp hanging from the shield. A corporal at Chadbourne told essentially the same story.[21]

The Kiowas had several stories about Satanta and his shield. Old Taybodl told Captain Scott about an incident he had personally witnessed during a raid near Durango, in northwestern Mexico.

> The Mexicans came out to fight us with ropes. One roped Tsait-an-te—tied the rope to the horn of his saddle—jerked Tsait-an-te off his horse and was dragging him off at a gallop—Tsait-an-te bounding along first on one side then on the other. Frizzle Head [a Kiowa warrior] rode up to kill the Mexican with his spear but the Mexican got scared, turned the rope loose and got away. Tsait-an-te was saved but both legs and sides were skinned from this dragging and he was very sore for a long while. He had that shield on him then.

In other raids, Taybodl recalled, Satanta was carrying the shield when he lanced a Mexican, again when he killed a Sauk north of the Arkansas, and yet another time when he lanced a Ute during a night fight near Fort Lyon, Colorado.[22] The death of the Ute may have been the same incident recorded in the Kiowa calendar for the fall of 1859 when Satanta and Satank raided into the same Ute territory, in Colorado along the upper South Canadian River, and attacked a lone tipi, killing one man and wounding several others.[23]

The Kiowas viewed the sun shield as Satanta's most important possession, but among the whites his best-known trademark was the bugle which he blew to signal an attack, announce his presence, or for whatever other purpose he might decide.[24] The Kiowas say he captured the bugle during a fight with federal troops after observing the soldiers' responding to the different bugle calls. Fighting his way through the lines, he killed the bugler and took his instrument, then celebrated by blowing into the horn and making enough noise to cause general confusion among the soldiers. Eventually, he learned to play "Charge" and "Retreat," and henceforth used the bugle to signal his warriors in battle.[25] Although other Indians, most notably the Cheyenne Dog Soldiers, also carried bugles and signaled warriors with army calls during fights, whites came to associate it most often with Satanta and automatically assumed he was present if they heard the sound during an Indian fight.

Compared with the next two decades, the years 1850-60 were a period of relative peace between Indians and whites on the Southern Plains. Indian fights nevertheless occurred, even as the whites of North and South prepared for their own bloody conflict. On July 11, 1860, during the last full year of peace in the United States, a scouting detachment of First Cavalry under Lieutenant J.E.B. Stuart, who would attain a general's stars in the Confederate Army, clashed with a group of Kiowas under Satank near Blackwater Springs, Nebraska. Two warriors were killed and sixteen women and children captured; one officer and two enlisted men were wounded in the fight. Three separate reports of the clash positively identify Satank. Captain William Steele correctly spelled the name "Satank," but Major John Sedgwick called the chief "Sitanki" and Stuart wrote "Sotanko."[26] In a *Civil War Times Illustrated* article on the fight in which the reports were reprinted, however, author Don Russell again confused names and said it was Satanta.[27]

The Indians became a key issue with the breakup of the Union in 1861, as North and South struggled for influence on the plains. For the Confederacy the area was particularly critical, since the South nominally controlled the Indian Territory of Oklahoma, the gateway to Confederate Texas. Southern leaders in the Territory knew that the Texas settlements would be only lightly defended, with many of the state's men fighting in the east. On May 4, 1862, Brigadier General Albert Pike, commanding the Confederate Department of the Indian Territory, wrote that a group of the Comanches and Kiowas

> has sent to me to know if they can be allowed to send
> a strong party and capture any [federal] trains on their
> way from Kansas to New Mexico, to which I have

no objection; To go on the warpath somewhere else is the best way to keep them from troubling Texas.[28]

Such cooperation between the South and the plains tribes was short-lived, however, for on July 31 of the same year Pike advised President Jefferson Davis that the Comanches and Kiowas had turned against the Confederacy and were "preparing to enter and devastate the Texas frontier."[29]

Far from being pro-Union or anti-Confederate, the Kiowas were merely opportunists. According to Mooney, they later "distinctly stated that they had been told by military officers of the [federal] government to do all the damage they could to Texas, because Texas was at war with the United States...."[30] Based on faraway events about which they knew nothing and which were too complex for them to understand, the North's federal policy only reassured the Kiowas that Texas was a separate nation against which they had carte blanche to raid as they pleased.[31]

In general the Kiowa attitude toward the federals remained peaceful during the first two years of the war. In July 1862 Percival Lowe, who had left the army and now was a civilian employee of the U.S. government, was ordered to take six hundred horses and 120 six-mule wagons from Fort Leavenworth to Fort Union, New Mexico.[32] Autumn was approaching by the time the train was finally ready for the main leg of the trip from Kansas along the Arkansas River and then down into New Mexico. Since the Indians would be going into winter encampment along the Arkansas, Lowe requisitioned as many troops as he could obtain from the posts along the way, but the number of men available was not adequate to prevent a major attack.

> I knew . . . that I would have to pass through the whole Kiowa and Comanche Nations, camped along the Arkansas in the vicinity of where now stands Dodge City, and the sight of 600 fine horses passing close would be a great temptation to possess themselves of some. . . . Be it remembered that an Indian's weak point (or strong point) is horses; horses, scalps, and squaws are what contribute to his happiness and make life worth living.[33]

Several days out of Fort Larned, the federal train came upon the Indian encampments spread for miles along both sides of the river. Lowe made a strong camp two miles below the Indians, and Lieutenant Richard Irving Dodge, who had joined the train at Larned, ordered pickets on the high ground around it. Sentry lines were established and no Indian was allowed to cross without Lowe's permission, but hundreds of Indians crowded the line and had to be held back by the soldiers. Fortunately they were only curious; if they had wanted to force their way in, the soldiers could not have done much to stop them.

Satanta soon arrived with Lone Wolf, another important chief who one day would become his rival for control of the Kiowa war faction, and Lowe invited them in for supper. Lowe realized that the Indians might make some attempt at the horses if they knew how few soldiers actually were with the train. To give the impression of more strength, Lowe ordered each teamster to position his musket so that it stuck out from under the wagon covers. Both chiefs spoke Spanish to some extent, and Lowe explained through his Mexican interpreter Jose Armijo that most of the soldiers escorting the train were asleep in the wagons; those they saw were only a few of the troops available. He said he did not believe the Indians meant any trouble, but added that curiosity might draw them too close and frighten the horses. Because the train was large enough to see at a distance, he suggested the Indians remain a few hundred yards off. The chiefs, apparently fooled by the bluff, "promised [me] that all of their people would observe my wishes and I need feel no uneasiness about it."[34]

The next day Lowe broke camp and headed west, amazed at how the hundreds of Indians observed the promise of Satanta and Lone Wolf. "For more than ten miles these people trudged on foot, or cavorted about on ponies on either side of the train, never approaching more than 200 yards." After twenty miles most of them had dropped behind, but Satanta, Lone Wolf and a few others remained. Finally the two chiefs rode up, shook hands with Lowe and said good-bye. Through Armijo, Lowe thanked them for their cooperation and gave them a barrel of hardtack and a sack of sugar.[35]

Fort Larned, Kansas, 1869. (Courtesy Kansas State Historical Society)

Chapter 3
"This Fiend Satanta"

When Lowe's train passed through their territory, the Kiowas were recovering from a smallpox epidemic which had devastated the plains tribes during the winter of 1861-62.[1] To combat further outbreaks, the federal government sent a physician who arrived at Satanta's camp about forty miles up the Arkansas River from Fort Larned in April 1864. In his report, he stated:

> I was four days in Satana's [sic] or White Bear's village....He is a fine-looking Indian, very energetic, and as sharp as a brier. He and all his people treated me with much friendship. I ate my meals regularly three times a day with him in his lodge. He puts on a good deal of style, spreads a carpet for his guests to sit on, and has painted fireboards 20 inches wide and 3 feet long, ornamented with bright brass tacks driven all around the edges, which they use for tables. He has a brass French horn, which he blew vigorously when the meals were ready.[2]

The doctor also commented, "A body of Kiowas and Comanches and some Cheyennes intend to make another raid into Texas in about five or six weeks." He speculated that if this raid was successful, the Indians would raid farther north in Union territory.[3]

The physician's forecast proved well-founded, for 1864 was one of the bloodiest years in the history of the Southern Plains. Satanta began by leading a raid into the vicinity of

Menard, in west Texas, where he and his warriors killed several whites and captured a Mrs. Dorothy Field.[4] Returning to Fort Larned, the Kiowas held a scalp dance to celebrate the raid. When it ended, the Koiet-senko leader Satank and another Indian wandered over to the post, where they were warned away by the sentry. Not understanding, they continued on. The soldier raised his rifle, but before he could fire Satank shot two arrows into him and the other Kiowa fired a pistol. Soldiers and Indians both panicked; the Kiowas jumped on their horses, and the garrison rushed to prepare a defense. As they rode away, the Indians came upon the military horse herd grazing outside the post, stampeded it, and made off with most of the animals. The now-dismounted troopers were unable to pursue. A few days later, Satanta insolently sent a message to the post commander, complaining about the poor quality of the horses and hoping that in the future the army would provide better ones.[5]

Like many events in Satanta's life, this incident, isolated enough in itself, became a major issue. The frustrated agent at Fort Lyon, Colorado, S.G. Colley, wrote Territorial Governor John Evans, "I have done everything in my power to keep peace. I now think a little powder and lead is the best food for them."[6] Over the next several years, the so-called "attack" on Fort Larned would be resurrected from time to time in white-Indian confrontations, particularly when Satanta was involved.

After taking the horses at Larned, the Kiowas moved west into Colorado and left devastation in their wake. On July 30 Major General Samuel R. Curtis, commander of the U.S. Army's Department of Kansas which included the Colorado Territory, wrote Governor Evans that the raids reached across the department from Comanche Crossing, on the Arkansas River eighty-five miles west of Fort Larned, to Six-Mile Creek only twenty-two miles from Council Grove. Although Curtis considered the Kiowas, Comanches and Arapahos primarily responsible, he added, "some stragglers from all the prairie tribes join in the villainy." The Indians were even attacking military posts and stations in the region. Thus far, losses were limited to twelve people killed, six wounded, and 150 head of government stock stolen, but the general expected matters to grow worse.[7]

The same day Curtis sent a letter to Colonel John Chivington, commander of U.S. troops in Colorado, reporting that the last wagon train from the west had been attacked at Cimarron Crossing and two men killed and scalped.

There is no doubt that Satanta was involved in the raids. On the morning of August 7 he rode with Dohasen the Younger, son of the paramount chief, and two other Kiowas to Bent's Ranch, about twenty-five miles up the Arkansas from Fort Lyon, to discuss the problem with William Bent, whose family of traders was well-known to the Indians. Satanta and Young Dohasen admitted they were members of a war party and, as Bent reported in a letter to Colley, the Kiowas told him:

> when they first left their camp . . . there was a very large party of them, and on the Cimarron they killed five whites, and most of the party turned back from there.

Young Dohasen said his father had sent them to see if Bent could make peace with the whites. Bent replied he could not answer until he had discussed it with the proper authorities. "I then told them that General Curtis was at Fort Larned, and that he was a big chief, and that he was the man that they would have to talk to." When Satanta and Young Dohasen asked about Colley, they were told they would find him at Fort Lyon. Bent commented that Young Dohasen "appeared very anxious for peace, but it may all be a suck-in."

Despite their assurances to the contrary, Bent suspected this handful of Kiowas was part of a much larger band waiting on the other side of a hill from his ranch; Satanta and Young Dohasen were too important to lead such a small group. He also believed they might have killed his neighbors, a family named Rood. For his part, Bent said he planned to leave the area. "The women are alarmed, and I don't think it is safe here."[8]

Because Bent did not deem it safe to send a rider to Fort Lyon during the daylight hours, Colley received Bent's letter shortly before midnight and forwarded it on to Governor Evans with a cover letter stating the Kiowas had also attacked a Mexican train camped a few miles upriver from the fort. One man was reportedly killed, and coffee, sugar and other supplies taken. In addition, Colley wrote that shots were heard across the river from the post while Major Edward W. Wynkoop was preparing to take two companies of First Colorado Cavalry in pursuit of the Indians.[9]

Wynkoop wasted no time. By a forced march he reached the deserted ranch of Bent's neighbors, the Roods, and observed signs of a fight, including an unsuccessful attempt to burn the house from the outside. He later learned the ranch had been attacked by fourteen Kiowas, but the house "had been gallantly defended by four men....[who] had finally driven them off, killing one of them."

From Rood's, Wynkoop continued as far as Bent's Ranch. Although he saw no Indians, evidence showed a large band had hurried past toward the Cimarron. After two days and nights in the saddle, his men were exhausted so he returned to Fort Lyon. Reaching the post, he reported:

> I am well convinced that Satanta with 1,000 or more warriors of the Kiowas and Comanches is located over on the Cimarron or in that vicinity. I have also received information that four white men have been murdered by these same Indians near the Cimarron Crossing. The available troops that I have in this garrison will not warrant me in attacking Satanta at present, not being able to take more than fifty men into the field, after leaving what would barely suffice for the absolute protection of the post. If it is possible I would respectfully recommend that I receive some re-enforcement, so that I may take a sufficient command in the field to punish this fiend Satanta and his murdering crew.[10]

In the wake of reports from Bent, Agent Colley and Wynkoop, General Curtis assessed the situation to his subordinate, Major General James G. Blunt, commanding officer of the District of Southern Kansas:

> It shows that the Kiowas moved west, and no doubt they are the same parties who have subsequently given us trouble on that line. Their lodges must be somewhere west of Larned, probably not far from

Bent's Fort or Bent's Ranch. Before any peace can be granted, the villains who have committed the crimes must be given up, and full indemnity in horses, ponies and property must be granted [as much] as Indians can indemnify. Something really dangerous must be felt by them.[11]

Unfortunately for the whites on the frontier, the federal government's primary energies and resources were directed toward the war in the East, and it was powerless to prevent the raids in the western territories. Frustrated at his inability to keep peace on the plains, Colonel Chivington personally led Colorado troops in one of the most disgraceful actions in U.S. military history—the senseless massacre of a friendly village of Southern Cheyennes under the prominent chief Black Kettle. These Indians were camped at Sand Creek, near Fort Lyon where they had been ordered by Colley for a roll call. Initially Chivington was hailed as a hero, but as details of the massacre emerged, including the fact that Black Kettle flew the U.S. flag over his tipi to indicate he was under government protection, praise turned to outrage and Chivington was publicly condemned.[12] Major Wynkoop, who had helped convince Black Kettle to come in, softened his belligerent attitude toward Indians and instead developed a strong suspicion of the military. The attack not only failed to punish any of the hostile bands, it alienated the friendly tribes and for years ruined the government's credibility among the Indians.

The United States was not alone, however, in its Indian problems; 1864 was a bad year for the Confederates as well. In October the Comanche Chief Little Buffalo led between 350 and 400 Kiowas and Comanches into Texas for one of the bloodiest raids in the state's history. After badly mauling a detachment of the Border Regiment of Texas Cavalry, they raided the settlements along Elm Creek in Young County, seventy miles northwest of Fort Worth. Eleven whites were killed and seven women and children taken prisoner.[13]

Several years later, when all the captives had been recovered except an infant girl who was never seen again, Elizabeth Ann FitzPatrick recalled that the Indians had tied them astride ponies, then one of the warriors, whom she called "Satine," blew a bugle and the Indians carried them away toward the northwest. They continued onward for two nights and a day, not pausing for any length of time until they reached the Pease River in the Texas Panhandle.[14] It is generally assumed that "Satine," the warrior with the bugle, was Satanta.

Most of the Young County captives were taken to the Kiowa and Comanche winter camps scattered along the Canadian River in the northernmost part of Texas, near the ruins of a long-abandoned trading post known as Adobe Walls. During the last week of November most of the younger men went out raiding, leaving the aging Dohasen in charge of the Kiowa camps. Many of the Indians who remained with him were suffering from trachoma, a chlamydial infection of the eyelid lining which was widespread in the camps, and in this condition they were located on November 24 by Ute and Jicarilla Apache scouts serving with New Mexico territorial troops under Colonel Christopher Carson.

Despite his diminutive size (he was just over five feet tall), Kit Carson was regarded as a giant among frontiersmen. As a youth he had run away from an apprenticeship in Kentucky, joined a band of mountain men, and became famous as an explorer, mountain man, trader, scout and Indian fighter. When the war broke out he sided with the Union and became a colonel of the First New Mexico Volunteer Cavalry, one of the few successful Indian campaigners of the period. Now, exactly one month short of his fifty-fifth birthday, Carson was hoping to find and destroy the Kiowas and Comanches responsible for the year's depredations.

Carson's force consisted of 14 officers, 321 enlisted men and 75 Indian scouts, a sizable wagon train with enough provisions to last until the end of the year, and two mountain howitzers under Lieutenant George Pettis. On November 5 this force left Fort Bascom, New Mexico, two hundred miles to the west. From a camp thirty miles away from Adobe Walls, the Utes and Jicarillas scouted ahead and returned about sundown with news of the Kiowa-Comanche camps. Carson started his men forward on a night march.[15]

Shortly after 8:00 a.m. on November 25 some of the Kiowa men remaining in camp went out to round up their ponies, saw the troops creeping up, and dashed back to give the alarm. The troops followed them in formation and attacked the western-most camp of about 150 lodges, where the women dropped their preparations for breakfast, grabbed their children and ran. The men jumped on their ponies and rode to meet the troops while Dohasen, despite his age, leaped on his pony and galloped downstream to warn the other camps. The soldiers made their way inside the first camp while the Utes charged ahead to stampede the Kiowa pony herd.[16]

The Kiowas were forced out of their camp, and several

Colonel Christopher (Kit) Carson, shortly after the Adobe Walls Fight of 1864. (Courtesy Museum of New Mexico)

ancient warriors, blinded by trachoma and unable to escape, were killed by the Ute women who were searching the tipis for plunder. Although the Kiowas had abandoned the first camp, Carson noted they "hotly contested" the four miles from their camp to the ruins of Adobe Walls. Reaching the Walls they turned and made a stand, assaulting the leading companies several times before Carson arrived with the main body and the two howitzers. The guns were wheeled into position, and the Indians broke off and retreated, leaving the soldiers in possession of the ruins.[17]

Carson halted his troops at the Walls to rest his exhausted horses and have breakfast. About three miles downriver, however, Dohasen had arrived at the main camp of about 350 lodges. While the women of that camp fled eastward to escape the troops, the men mounted their ponies and started toward the ruins. Carson later estimated there were "at least 1,000 warriors, mounted on first-class horses." Seeing them coming, he immediately ordered his own horses saddled, but by the time this was done the soldiers were surrounded and a desperate fight began.

"The Indians charged so repeatedly and with such desperation that for some time I had serious doubts for the safety of my rear...," Carson reported. His men, however, remained calm and returned a steady fire which, together with explosive shells from the howitzers, kept the Indians at bay.[18] Lieutenant Pettis, who commanded the howitzers, noted:

> About 200 yards in the rear of their line, all through the fighting at the Adobe Walls, was stationed one of the enemy, who had a cavalry bugle, and during the entire day he would blow the opposite call that was used by the officer in our line of skirmishers; for instance, when our bugles sounded the "advance," he would blow "retreat," and when ours sounded the "retreat," he would follow it with the "advance;" ours would signal "halt," and he would follow suit. So he kept it up all day, blowing as shrill and clearly as our very best buglers. Carson insisted that it was a white man, but I have never received any information to corroborate this opinion.[19]

Perhaps it was a white man. But Mooney believed the mysterious bugler "was most probably a Kiowa, possibly Sett'ainte himself...."[20]

Unable to approach close to the Walls, the Indians set fire to the grass. Carson, however, moved his command to a rise where he opened fire with the two howitzers and pushed back the Indians. The prominent Kiowa chief Stumbling Bear led a rear guard action until the rest had time to escape. Capturing the camps, Carson destroyed about 150 lodges, with stores and munitions, and captured "a buggy and spring wagon, the property of Sierrito or Little Mountain [Dohasen], the Kiowa chief of the Indians which I engaged." Commenting on the Indians themselves, Carson wrote:

> The principal number were Kiowas with a small number of Comanches, Apaches, and Arapahoes [sic], all of which were armed with rifles, and I must say that they acted with more daring and bravery than I have ever before witnessed.[21]

After destroying the Kiowa camp Carson withdrew, deeming it unsafe to remain in the area. Government losses were listed as two soldiers killed and twenty-one wounded, several mortally. One Ute scout was killed and four wounded. The government estimate of hostile losses was about sixty killed and wounded, although Kiowa sources put their death toll at five. None of the Young County captives was recovered; Carson had not known about them, and they had been herded into the surrounding brush and concealed when the shooting started. They would remain in captivity for more than a year until ransomed.[22]

Tactically the Adobe Walls fight was a draw. Although Carson had inflicted damages on the Indians, the fight was only a temporary setback for them. Several times during the day Carson had been in serious danger, but he had unnerved the Indians by taking the war into their own domain and attacking them at their winter bases. Ultimately the Kiowas and Comanches asked for peace, and an uneasy calm settled over the Southern Plains.[23]

In response to the Indian request, the government ap-

Stumbling Bear. (Photo by William Stinson Soule, Fort Sill, courtesy Archives & Manuscripts Division of the Oklahoma Historical Society.)

pointed a treaty commission consisting of Thomas Murphy, who was the superintendent of Indian affairs for Kansas, General John B. Sanborn, General William S. Harney, Kit Carson, William Bent, and Jesse H. Leavenworth, the agent for the Kiowas and Comanches.[24] Leavenworth obtained a suspension of military operations to give the Indians a chance to come in and meet with the commission.[25]

Arrangements were made to meet with the Kiowas, Comanches, Apaches, Cheyennes and Arapahos in mid-October 1865, at the mouth of the Little Arkansas River on the site of the present city of Wichita, Kansas. The Cheyenne and Arapaho treaties were signed October 14. Three days later the Apache treaty was signed, and the commission began negotiating with the Kiowas who were represented by Dohasen, Lone Wolf, Heap of Bears, Satanta, Kicking Bird and Stumbling Bear.[26]

The negotiations were aggravated by personal animosity. Satanta disliked Leavenworth, whom the Kiowas accused of cheating on their annuities. Many whites shared the Kiowas' opinion, although in some cases it appears Leavenworth was withholding the goods on government instructions to punish the Indians for raiding.[27] To correspondent Henry Stanley, who met him a few months later, Leavenworth seemed the quintessential bureaucrat who was "devoted to red tapeism. His coat pockets are always full of official documents, and the ends of said papers can be seen sticking out an inch or so, and on each and all will be found legibly inscribed, 'Leavenworth, Indian Agent.'"[28]

The accusations were not one-sided, for Leavenworth considered the Kiowas thieves and murderers. Although he stated he intended to protect his Indian charges from injustice, he felt the Kiowas, as a whole, needed "lead, and plenty of it...before they will behave."[29]

Unlike most Indian treaty councils, the speeches were short and to the point; the cold, biting wind blowing on the blanket-wrapped, bare-legged Indians prompted them to be brief. Nevertheless Dohasen, who did most of the talking, rejected any suggestion for the establishment of an agency, claiming the Kiowas owned the country from Fort Laramie, Wyoming, to Texas, and it was not to be divided among other Indians or given to whites. He was willing to let whites pass unmolested along the Santa Fe Trail, but they were to stay out of other areas.[30]

Their demand, of course, was absurd; the Kiowas had been expelled from much of this territory generations earlier by the Lakota Sioux and Northern Cheyennes. They were forced to share the remaining territory with many other tribes, among whom they were often the minority. Never naive in his dealings with whites, Dohasen no doubt realized the weakness of their

Kicking Bird. (Courtesy Kansas State Historical Society.)

argument because, on October 18, the Kiowas signed the treaty
and agreed to accept a reservation to be established south of
the Arkansas River, with an agency at Fort Zarah, Kansas. The
reservation would include much of the Texas Panhandle and
Oklahoma. The Kiowas relinquished any claims to Colorado,
Kansas north of the Arkansas, and New Mexico, and they and
the Comanches also agreed to surrender five white captives.

     The treaty, never intended to be permanent, was merely to
buy time, primarily for the government.[31] Many plains tribes,
including the more powerful factions among the Southern

Lone Wolf. (Photo by William Stinson Soule, Fort Sill, courtesy Archives & Manuscript Division of the Oklahoma Historical Society.)

Cheyennes, had boycotted the council because of the Sand Creek Massacre. Additionally, though no one bothered to consider it at the time, Texas possessed sovereign control of all public lands in the state, and the federal government lacked the legal authority to assign a reservation in that state.

The Little Arkansas Treaty council was Dohasen's last. Age precluded his participating in raids, and he now spent most of his time in camp. As Dohasen grew older, Lone Wolf rose in prominence. About the same age as Satanta, Lone Wolf was a

Jesse H. Leavenworth
(drawing from Percival Lowe, Five Years a Dragoon*)*

ruthless war leader who sought to be undisputed head of the militant Kiowa faction. This treaty council, however, also signalled the rise of Kicking Bird, who would become a serious contender for leadership among the Kiowas. Younger than either Satanta or Lone Wolf, Kicking Bird (whose Kiowa name *Te'ne-angopte* actually means "Eagle Who Strikes with Talons") was probably the most visionary of all Kiowa chiefs. Although a valiant war leader who was touchy on points of Kiowa honor, Kicking Bird realized the days of the free-roaming Indian were drawing to a close, and that continued existence meant accommodating the U.S. government. Kicking Bird was perfectly willing to let Satanta and Lone Wolf go at each other for control over the war faction; he intended to lead the Kiowas on the white man's road to peace and settlement and thus ensure their survival.[32]

Chapter 4
Bloodshed and Politics

Dohasen's death in late winter 1866 deprived the Kiowas of his leadership at a time they greatly needed it. Despite his sometimes belligerent attitude toward the whites, he was nevertheless a moderating influence, and the raids against the settlers undoubtedly would have been worse without his restraint. With his force of character no longer holding them together, the Kiowa factions began feuding among themselves. The paramount chieftaincy went to Lone Wolf, who openly supported the war faction but lacked Dohasen's ability to enforce his will. Defying Lone Wolf, Kicking Bird and his cousin Stumbling Bear assumed leadership of the peace faction, inaugurating a power struggle which was to last for the next eight years.[1]

Freed from the restraints of Dohasen, Satanta promptly forgot his obligations under the Little Arkansas Treaty and was soon marauding in Texas again. In August 1866 he was leading a raid along the old military road between Fredericksburg and Fort Mason, northwest of Austin, when they spotted a wagon train near the old crossing of the Blanco River. Fearing soldiers might be following the train, the Indians decided to attack immediately before any military help had a chance to arrive. The teamsters saw them coming down a hillside about a mile away, crawled under their wagons and prepared a defense. The Indians began circling the wagons well out of rifle range, drawing the circle a little smaller with each turn but cautiously, because their weapons lacked the range of the teamsters' Spencer repeating arms. Satanta sat on his horse apart from the circling warriors, apparently looking for weak spots in the defense. Occasionally the others would ride up to him, hold a conference and begin circling the wagons again. From time to time he blew his bugle, and the Indians seemed to be responding to various calls.

The Indians finally opened fire with their rifles and bows, accompanied by "demon yells which for weird feature is approached only by the blood-curdling howl of the wolf which on every frontier and for all time has made the human nerve jerk and human flesh quiver," according to an eyewitness to the fight.[2]

The teamsters held their fire as arrows showered down on the wagons and thudded into the trees. Finally, when an Indian rifle shot hit one of the wagons, they opened up with their Spencers. The approximately one hundred warriors were about three times the number of teamsters, and the teamsters realized they could be overwhelmed if the Indians decided to charge.[3]

A Kiowa subchief, whom the teamsters called the Yellow Chief because of his adornment, seemed to be leading the group riding around the wagons. Clarence Wharton heard the story of the attack from his father Frank Wharton, who had been one of the teamsters and who described this warrior as

> a splendid looking fellow...riding a small claybank stallion, often hanging on the opposite side of his horse and firing under the animal's neck. When he sat upright he covered himself and crouched behind a rawhide shield which would ward off a bullet fired at long range....
>
> The dexterity with which the Yellow Chief could manage his high-spirited horse, cover himself with his shield and fire at full tilt would have put the most skillful modern circus performer in the amateur class.[4]

The teamsters were able to kill several Indian horses and wound several warriors. When Frank Wharton and wagon guard Johnnie Jenkins coordinated their shots, Wharton killed the Yellow Chief's horse and Jenkins shot the chief as he fell.

Two other warriors scrambled off to safety when their horses were killed. Satanta gave "a loud blast" on his bugle, and the Indians withdrew to confer. Their losses were becoming too heavy, and they decided to retrieve the body of the Yellow Chief and withdraw.[5]

Several warriors tried to get to the body but were driven back by heavy gunfire from the wagons. Finally Satanta called another conference, then changed horses for a small, fast pony and calmly rode down toward the wagons. Within the teamsters' gun range, he suddenly spurred the pony toward the Yellow Chief's body. Unable to swing down along the side of the pony away from the teamsters because the Yellow Chief's dead mount was in the way, he had to swing down on the side facing the wagons with his full body exposed to the teamsters' rifles. The whites watched in fascination; only one fired and his bullet went wild. Satanta was able to grab the Yellow Chief's arm and swing the body up across the pony in front of him, then ride back to the other Indians.

There was more to his feat than mere bravado. Satanta was not only in a power struggle with Kicking Bird's peace faction but also with Lone Wolf for control of the war faction, and he well knew that this story, embellished and magnified, would be carried back to the Kiowa camps, enhancing his prestige and increasing his support.[6] Regardless of motive, the recovery of the Yellow Chief's body was a remarkable feat of horsemanship and sheer physical strength.

It was now mid-afternoon, and the Kiowas and their ponies were exhausted. They had lost seven ponies and five warriors but had recovered all the bodies except one which had fallen too close to the wagons. Two warriors were badly wounded, one mortally, but the Indians strapped the badly wounded man to his horse and rode on. With the Yellow Chief's body also strapped to a spare horse, they rode until they passed a settler's cabin, where Satanta later claimed they killed the settler's daughter,[7] then they left the road and continued toward the Red River and the Indian Territory as rapidly as possible in case soldiers might be pursuing. About midnight they halted along the San Saba River, where they dug a shallow grave for the Yellow Chief then wrapped the body in a blanket and covered it with stones. What they did with the other bodies was not recorded. The mortally wounded warrior could go no further so they gave him some dried meat, tied his pony nearby, and left him. The other wounded warrior died before reaching the Red River.[8]

Moving north, avoiding the settlements, the Kiowas crossed the West Fork of the Trinity River and arrived on Elm Creek in Cooke County, a few miles from Gainesville, one week to the day after the fight on the Fredericksburg Road. There they came upon James Box, a farmer driving home with his family after visiting neighbors. They killed and scalped Box, mortally wounded his ten-year-old son and carried his wife and four other children into captivity.

Continuing northward across the Indian Territory and into Kansas, the Kiowas finally went into camp near Fort Larned. Satanta went to the post and demanded ransom for the Box family from Agent Leavenworth, who happened to be there at the time. Leavenworth, however, took him to task for violating the Little Arkansas Treaty and demanded the immediate release of the captives without ransom. Satanta replied he would have to consult with the other chiefs and disappeared. Faced with Leavenworth's refusal to negotiate, the Kiowas took the captives to the vicinity of Fort Dodge, about forty miles to the southwest, where the post commander Major Henry Douglass paid a large sum for their release. Satisfied with the conclusion of this latest Texas raid, Satanta remarked that stealing white women was more lucrative than stealing horses.[9]

While the Kiowas congratulated themselves over the success of their raids, they were unaware they would soon be caught up in events unfolding far to the northwest in Wyoming and Montana. In June 1866 the Oglala Sioux had gone to war with the federal government, and in the following months they and their allies wiped out a detachment under Captain William J. Fetterman, the worst massacre by Indians in army history, and placed three forts on the government road into Montana under a virtual state of siege. By early 1867 the war had spilled into the southern plains, where the Sioux now threatened the roads which ran across Kansas, along the Smoky Hill and Arkansas Rivers and into Colorado and New Mexico. Known as the Red Cloud War in the north, here further south the conflict was known as Hancock's War, after Major General Winfield Scott

Hancock, commander of the Department of the Missouri, a military jurisdiction which included Missouri, Kansas, Colorado, the Indian Territory and New Mexico.

The forty-three-year-old Hancock had first gained notice as a young lieutenant when he received a brevet for meritorious service in the Mexican War. He served heroically at Gettysburg in 1863 and still suffered from a serious wound he received there. He was often mentioned as a presidential candidate and would become the Democratic nominee in 1880. Correspondent Henry Morton Stanley of the St. Louis *Missouri Democrat* described Hancock as "a tall stately figure, in the prime of life, with a commanding appearance, [who] excites admiration and respect wherever he goes." But Hancock, with his by-the-book military background, understood nothing about the Indians with whom he was expected to deal on the plains.[10]

Hancock's campaign was not prompted solely by the Sioux conflict but also by the rapidly accumulating reports of depredations by various tribes and nations throughout his jurisidiction. Leaving his headquarters at Fort Leavenworth, he traveled to Fort Larned where he met with several chiefs representing a large village of Southern Cheyennes and Oglala Sioux, thirty miles to the west on the Pawnee Fork of the Arkansas. He demanded the return of any white hostages and told them he intended to inspect their camp. One of the chiefs, Tall Bull, replied that he was welcome to come, but privately implored Hancock to keep away. Only three years had passed since Chivington's massacre of Black Kettle's people at Sand Creek; the memory was still fresh and the Southern Cheyennes, who made up the bulk of the camp on the Pawnee Fork, might panic and flee at the approach of troops.

Ignoring the plea, Hancock marched on the camp. As Tall Bull had predicted, the Indians panicked and fled, so frightened that they left behind all their possessions. The flight convinced Hancock that the Indians were preparing for war, and he determined to burn the village. Agent Edward W. Wynkoop, a former soldier who knew the Indians well, countered that they had fled "by fear alone" and pointedly told Hancock that there would be trouble if the army destroyed the village. Hancock agreed to wait. Meanwhile a detachment of Seventh Cavalry under the young Lieutenant Colonel George Armstrong Custer,

General Winfield Scott Hancock.
(Courtesy Kansas State Historical Society)

on his first Indian expedition, pursued the Indians and found the ranches and way stations devastated along the Smoky Hill Road.

Although it has since been determined that these raids were the work of other Indians, Hancock believed they had been carried out by the Indians who had fled from the village on the Pawnee Fork. On April 18 he ordered the camp destroyed, which infuriated the Southern Cheyennes. Convinced, by both the Sand Creek massacre and now by Hancock's destruction of their village, that they had no other option, the Southern Cheyennes went to war.

On learning of the destruction of the Cheyenne village and believing, in the words of correspondent Stanley, "that discretion is the better part of valor," Satanta and Satank moved their bands far up the Arkansas. Kicking Bird, on the other hand, moved his band close to Fort Dodge to avoid being caught on the plains and mistaken for a hostile. Hancock invited Kicking Bird, his cousin Stumbling Bear, Dohasen's half-brother Man-That-Moves, and several other chiefs to a conference in his camp near Fort Dodge.[11] When the council convened on April 23, 1867, the general stated that he had not come to make war, "but to confirm the good feelings of those who are friendly towards us. We come, however, to fight those who wish to have war with us."

He detailed the recent depredations on the Smoky Hill Road, which he blamed on the Sioux and Cheyennes, and warned the Kiowas that the guilty parties would be punished according to the white man's law. He declared that a state of war existed between the whites and the Sioux and Cheyennes between the Arkansas and Platte Rivers, and then said he wanted the Kiowas, Comanches and Arapahos to serve as scouts. They would receive the same pay as soldiers and would be issued horses, guns, blankets and other equipment.

The chiefs were not enthusiastic over the prospect of scouting against other, more powerful Indians. Skirting the issue, Kicking Bird and Man-That-Moves said they favored peace and promised Hancock he would have no trouble with their bands unless the soldiers started it.

Hancock assured them that there would be no trouble south of the Arkansas as long as they remained peaceful. He said he needed a decision on scouts as soon as possible, and the Kiowas were to advise either him or Colonel A.J. Smith, commanding officer of the Seventh Cavalry and district commander for western Kansas under Hancock, or, in their absence, the commanding officer of Fort Dodge.

Kicking Bird replied they could not give an answer until they had consulted with the head chiefs Satanta, Heap of Bears, Lone Wolf, Black Bird, Satank and Little Heart. He also asked what the Kiowas were expected to do with Black Kettle's Cheyennes who had moved south; Hancock advised them to stay away from the Cheyennes.[12]

At least some of the Kiowas apparently met with Satanta and discussed Hancock's allegations against the Sioux and Cheyennes, because Satanta appeared to have been fully briefed on the general's position when he met with Hancock at Fort Larned on May 1. Among those attending the meeting was correspondent Stanley of the St. Louis *Missouri Democrat*. Although he ultimately gained fame and a knighthood as an African explorer, at this time Stanley was still young and impressionable and somewhat in awe of Satanta who, he noted,

> has made such a terrible name on this road....He is dressed in a captain's regulation coat, with epaulettes to match, leggings ornamented and decorated in the most gaudy manner, with small brass bells attached. He seemed pleased when Dave Butterfield [organizer of the Butterfield Overland Dispatch which had a trading camp near Fort Larned] exhibited some comical pictures representing parlour scenes, but this pleasure was manifested in grimaces on a much painted and vermillionish face.[13]

Several minor chiefs attended, but Satanta did all the talking. Hancock, Colonel Smith, and Agents Wynkoop and Leavenworth were also present, and one can only speculate on their state of mind; shortly before the conference began, interpreters Frederick Jones, John A. Atkin and a man named Kincaid admitted they had been receiving Indian annuity goods and had traded those goods at the Indian camps for buffalo robes, furs and lariats which Agent Leavenworth had sold to a merchant in Leavenworth City for several thousand dollars. They also said Leavenworth had buried several bales of annuity goods for future use.[14] Now Jones, who served as interpreter for the council, opened by stating:

> Before the Council commences I wish to say that I understand that Colonel Leavenworth told Satanta not to talk much to-day, but to go down to Fort

Zara[h] to him tomorrow, and he would make it all right. He may not, therefore, talk as much as he would otherwise have done.[15]

"Colonel Leavenworth is present and can answer for himself," Hancock replied.

Indignantly, Leavenworth said, "All I have to say in regard to that is, that not a word of that kind has passed between us. I did not ask him to come to Zara[h], nor tell him anything about talking."

"That is sufficient now," Hancock told Jones. "If Satanta wishes to proceed, you can let him do so whenever he is ready."

Satanta, in full form, opened with a plea for moderation and pledged friendship toward all men.

> I want the Great Father and all the soldiers and troops to hold on. I do not wish the prairies and country to be bloody, but just hold on for awhile. I don't want war at all. I want peace.

To the best of his knowledge, Satanta said, none of the plains tribes was planning an uprising, but he carefully added that, although his own motives were entirely peaceful, the whites had given the Indians more than enough reason for war. Although Indians normally thought of themselves as members of individual nations or tribes rather than a collective group, Satanta now spoke of them as a single people.

> They are all red men. This country here is old and it all belongs to them. But you are cutting off the timber and now the country is of no account at all....I have heard that there are many troops coming out in this country to whip the Cheyennes; and that is the reason we were afraid and went away. The Cheyennes, Arapahoes [sic] and Kiowas heard that there were troops coming out in this country—so also the Comanches and Apaches, but did not know whether they were coming for peace or for war...They are afraid to come in.

Discussing the overall situation, Satanta showed more understanding than Hancock.

> I don't think the Cheyennes want to fight, but I understand that you burned their village. I don't think that is good at all. To you, General, and to all these officers sitting around here, I say that I know that whatever I tell you will be sent to Washington and I don't want anything else but the truth told. Other Chiefs of the Kiowas who rank before me, have come in to look for rations and look about, and their remarks are repeated to Washington, but I don't think their hearts are good.

"What he means by that is, that the other Chiefs come in to make speeches for nothing else but to get something to eat," Leavenworth interjected.

Satanta agreed, adding that Lone Wolf, Stumbling Bear, Little Wolf and Kicking Bird, all of whom he disliked and sought to discredit, pretended friendship only for the sake of rations. But he said he was speaking sincerely, not only for his own followers among the Kiowas but also for the Cheyennes, Arapahos, Comanches, Apaches and some bands of Sioux, all of whom desired peace and had asked him to represent them. He asked the generals to give him some encouraging sign that they would not destroy the Cheyennes, since all the southern tribes wanted peace. If the government pledged peace, he would repeat it to the Cheyennes. If the Cheyennes went to war after receiving that pledge, the Kiowas would sever relations with them.

After taking another swipe at Lone Wolf, Little Wolf, Stumbling Bear and several other chiefs, none of whom was present to answer back, Satanta urged the officers to make sure his words were taken down correctly before being sent to Washington. Hancock reassured him, "There are two or three interpreters here to witness and prevent mistakes in the translation, so that all will be properly written down."

Satisfied, Satanta said he planned to return to Fort Dodge at 2:00 p.m. and asked the general for a letter of reference so he wouldn't have any trouble with the troops there. Apparently misunderstanding the request, Hancock answered, "As soon as I can get a copy of it I will give you the written proceedings of this Council, but cannot say that I can give it to you as soon as that."

"I simply want a letter when I go into camp, so that I can show it," Satanta explained.

Again, Hancock said he would give him a written copy of the proceedings, and Satanta gave up and moved on to other matters. He said he had no objection to a railroad on the Smoky Hill Road, since that did not directly affect the Kiowas. Likewise, he saw no problems with a wagon road on the Arkansas route but did not want a railroad there; rails brought development which, in turn, depleted natural resources on which the Kiowas depended. Already, he said, the timber had been cut from along the Arkansas.

"There are no longer any buffalo around here, nor anything we can kill to live on," he explained, "But I am striving for peace now, and don't want anything construed to be bad from what I say because I am simply speaking the plain truth."

Satanta added that if other tribes wanted a war, that was their affair; he himself had worked for peace until he had worn himself out but would continue to do so. If whites harassed Kiowas or stole their stock, he would take it up with the legal authorities rather than go to war. In fact, Satanta said, peace would be much easier to maintain if troops were withdrawn from the area.

> If there were no troops in this country, and the citizens [settlers] only lived around here that would be better. But there are so many troops coming in here that I fear they will do something bad to me.

Anyone familiar with Satanta could recognize this reasoning as a gross misrepresentation of his intentions. Certainly the chance existed, and often occurred, that a friendly Indian on the plains might be mistaken for a hostile and killed. But, given his record, it must be assumed Satanta raised the possibility only as an excuse; the withdrawal of troops would allow him to raid the unprotected citizenry at his leisure, as he had done throughout his adult life and would continue to do as long as he was

free. Yet no one challenged him on the statement and he grew
bolder, complaining that Leavenworth played favorites and
gave annuity goods to rival chiefs but allowed him none. His
oration became redundant, mixing grievances with pledges of
friendship until, finally, he concluded.

Hancock replied he was not empowered to make any new
agreements, but only to enforce the existing treaties. To ensure
that both sides observed the treaties, he suggested it was time
the Indians abandon their individual autonomy and that each
tribe select one person as paramount chief to speak for all,
"because we intend to demand that the tribes shall be responsible for the acts of their young men." Then, in a statement
chillingly prophetic of the near future, Hancock said:

> You see you cannot travel in winter. We have
> forage and storehouses, and can move in winter
> when our horses are fat. We may not come down
> south of the Arkansas this month, nor next month;
> but whenever we find out anything is going wrong,
> and who are at home, and who are not at home, we
> shall come, even although we should not come until
> next winter.

He told Satanta that the government did not seek a war but
had the capacity to make one should the occasion arise. He
pointed out he had more troops under his immediate command
than the entire warrior population of the Kiowa nation, and he
reminded them that his losses could be replaced immediately
while it took a full generation to replace a slain warrior.

The general emphasized to Satanta that the government
intended to defend not only travelers on the Smoky Hill and
Arkansas roads, but in the Texas settlements as well. He said
the Texans were no longer at war with the federal government
and were once again entitled to protection. Referring to the
restlessness of the young warriors and the divisions among the
chiefs, Hancock said:

> The Great Father will not permit all these young
> men to run around. And if there is no great chief,
> who can prevent it? The Great Father must do it with

his soldiers....We know that the depredations that were committed last summer and winter, and recently, were by the Sioux and Cheyennes. We know this, and have satisfactory evidence of it. You say the Indians do not want to make war? Is not that war? What do you call war if that is not war?

He described the attack on the Cheyenne village and his plans to continue the campaign, again asking the Kiowas to serve as scouts. Then he became cold-bloodedly realistic about the Kiowas' future, bluntly telling Satanta that there was absolutely nothing the Indians could do about the vanishing timber and the disappearance of game.

> You know very well that in a few more years the game will go away. What will you do then? You will have to depend upon the white man to assist you, and depend upon the Great Father to feed you when you are hungry....You should cultivate the friendship of the white man now, in order that he may be your friend when this time comes. The white men are coming out here so fast that nothing can stop them— coming from the east and coming from the west, like a prairie on fire in a high wind. The reason of it is because the whites are a great people, and they are spreading out and we cannot help it.

Having made his point, Hancock turned to Satanta's complaints about the annuity goods, saying that he had no control over their issue. He would, however, make sure the complaints went to Washington.

When Hancock concluded, Leavenworth responded immediately to Satanta's charges. "These are the men who killed the Box family in Texas," he said, "and my instructions were not to give them any annuity...until all these captives were returned without ransom of which he knows, and we obtained sufficient assurances that no further depredation would be committed....But Satanta has never come in and given any assurances in the matter."

"Stumbling Bear was in that raid, and why should he get so

Sir Henry Morton Stanley, shown here after he became the greatest of all African explorers, was a young newspaper correspondent when he met Satanta during Hancock's War and at Medicine Lodge. (Courtesy Library of Congress)

many goods?" Satanta retorted.

"Because he had come in and given the assurances that had been required of him," Leavenworth snapped.

Satanta started to name other chiefs, but Leavenworth indicated he did not plan to discuss it. For his part, Hancock felt the discussion was becoming too long and tedious (the printed transcript fills eleven pages of his formal report) and decided to bring it to a close. As a parting shot he reintroduced Satanta to Colonel Smith, whom he described as "an old soldier on the plains, and who was here a great many years ago. He commands in this country when I am not here. I wish you to know it."[16]

He then presented Satanta with the coat and yellow sash of a major general. According to Stanley, Satanta "seemed fully aware of the high rank to which he had been elevated." With his new finery, Satanta returned to Fort Dodge.[17]

Chapter 5
Medicine Lodge: "My Heart Feels Like Bursting."

To many, Hancock's War was not a distinctly separate campaign but part of the general conflict that began with Chivington's attack on Black Kettle's people at Sand Creek. The refusal of some of the major plains tribes to participate in the Little Arkansas Treaty emphasized that the conflict was not yet over, and Hancock's destruction of the Cheyenne village was regarded as a prolongation of the hostilities.[1] In addition to the fighting on the Southern Plains, the Red Cloud War was raging in Wyoming where government forces had been brought to a standstill by the Oglala Sioux and their allies.

President Andrew Johnson saw the fighting on the plains as a threat to national development, particularly with construction of the trans-continental railroad underway. "It is of vital importance," he told congress, "that our distant Territories should be exempt from Indian outbreaks, and that the construction of the Pacific Railroad, an object of national importance, should not be interrupted by hostile tribes." Accordingly on July 20, 1867, the U.S. Congress created a new treaty commission consisting of Lieutenant General W.T. Sherman, commander of the Military Division of the Missouri in which all the hostilities were occurring, white-bearded Major General William S. Harney, one of the most experienced frontier field commanders, Kit Carson, John B. Sanborn, Senator John B. Henderson of Missouri, chairman of the Senate Committee of Indian Affairs, Colonel Samuel Tappan of Massachusetts, and Nathaniel G.

Taylor of Tennessee, commissioner of Indian Affairs. Carson, however, was in failing health, and Brevet Major General Christopher C. Augur was named to replace him.[2]

These commissioners agreed among themselves that the Indians should be removed from the vicinity of the western railroads—the Union Pacific and the Kansas Pacific—and concentrated in two gigantic reservations, one south of Kansas and the other north of Nebraska. The Sioux and affiliated bands would be located in the north, and the Southern Cheyennes, Arapahos, Kiowas, Comanches and other southern groups would be moved to the south. They specifically stated that the agreements—not treaties—would provide for the Indians' maintenance and education for ten years until they became self-sustaining. Once self-support was achieved, the two reservations could be organized into Indian territorial governments with governor, council, courts and civil officers. General Harney was to be temporarily assigned to the Sioux, and Colonel William B. Hazen to the southern tribes. However, as Sherman noted, "the patronage of the Indian Bureau was too strong for us, and that part of our labor [the creation of self-governing Indian territories] failed."[3]

Instead, in an effort to end all hostilities, Congress approved a bill authorizing the commission to negotiate treaties with the warring nations in both Northern and Southern Plains. In the Southern Plains the commissioners were empowered to settle Indian claims against the government for the Chivington massacre and for Hancock's attack on the Cheyenne village, to adjust claims for back annuities, and to remove the Indians to reservations out of the path of the new railroad.

One clause in the congressional bill was entirely new to Indian negotiations—the treaties were to establish "a system for civilizing" the Indians. Past efforts had been directed toward pushing them aside and keeping them apart from the white community; now the government would attempt to integrate them into the mainstream of national society. They would be steered away from their nomadic lifestyle and taught to settle down, own real estate, and become farmers.[4]

The commission met first with Oglala and Brulé Sioux and Northern Cheyennes in North Platte, Nebraska, in September 1867, but nothing was settled and both sides agreed to adjourn and meet the following spring at Fort Laramie, Wyoming, with the hope that the Red Cloud War could be formally ended. With negotiations suspended until spring, the commissioners turned their attention to the Kiowas, Comanches, Southern Cheyennes and other Southern Plains nations with whom they would meet at Medicine Lodge, Kansas, in October.

The date and location for the Medicine Lodge Council had been fixed three months before the council was scheduled to begin. In the interim, the government suspended all military operations to give both sides an opportunity to calm down. "All the civil and military authorities, agents, traders, interpreters, half-breed scouts and friendly Indians at or near the theatre of war, were put to work to carry out the plans of the Commission," according to A.A. Taylor, Commissioner Taylor's teenaged son who served as assistant secretary for the peace commission.[5]

The commission arrived at Fort Larned, eighty miles northeast of the Medicine Lodge Council site, on October 12. It had been joined en route by Governor Samuel Crawford and Senator Edmund G. Ross of Kansas. Crawford and Ross made their positions clear. As the *Cincinnati Commercial* noted:

> In case treaties adequate to the security of absolute peace can not be made, they will use all their influence to have a large number of troops stationed on the Plains, and sufficient aid extended to the railroad to complete them. With the railroads finished, they say the game will disappear, and with it the Indians.[6]

To the relief of the news correspondents, General Sherman was absent, having continued on to Washington to advise the government of the progress so far, and in his stead, General Harney served as senior military member. Sherman despised newspapermen, and the correspondents found Harney much more affable. With nine reporters representing, either by direct employment or as freelance correspondents, some of the great metropolitan newspapers of the United States, the press corps was extensive for its time. Among the the reporters was Satanta's acquaintance of the previous year, Henry Stanley.[7]

The large entourage of bureaucrats, military escorts, news-

papermen and support personnel went into camp on the Arkansas River, six miles upstream from Fort Larned. Harney,
Tappan and the correspondents went to the post where Sanborn
and Agent Wynkoop waited to greet the correspondents at the
sutler's store. Taking them to a private room, Wynkoop offered
drinks from his personal liquor chest and conducted a briefing
on the efforts so far in assembling the Indians at the council site
and keeping them there until the commission arrived. The
reporters learned some of the Indians chiefs were on post and
would escort the commission to the council. Some of the chiefs
were even waiting outside, and Sanborn brought them in.[8]

The group of chiefs included Satanta, Stumbling Bear, the
Arapaho chief Little Raven, his son-in-law Yellow Bear, an
Arapaho named Wolf Slave, and the Crow, whom Stanley
described as "a tall, wiry fellow...cunning and unprincipled."[9]
Describing Satanta's entry into the room, Stanley wrote:

> Satanta, or White Bear, gave me a *bear's* hug as
> his greeting. He was introduced to the other mem-
> bers of the press, who looked upon him with some
> awe, having heard so much of his ferocity and bold-
> ness. By his defiant and independent bearing he
> attracted all eyes. He would certainly be a formida-
> ble enemy to encounter alone on the prairie. It is said
> that he has "killed more white men than any other
> Indian on the plains."[10]

Satanta repeated his embrace with the diminutive Milton
Reynolds, representing the Lawrence, Kansas, *State Journal* and
the Chicago *Times*, who wrote that the embrace "was more
prolonged than one cares to receive from lately hostile Indians
bedaubed with paint and covered with blankets, unless it be
strictly in the interest of God and Humanity."[11]

Satanta was about fifty, at the height of his powers, and his
imposing stature size contrasted not only with the smaller
whites, like Reynolds, but also with the fat, jovial Little Raven.
Correspondent William Fayel, of the St. Louis *Daily Republican*, observed that Satanta was

> a man of splendid physique, square, full face, and

sagacious looking eyes, which, when upturned, have a vindictive expression. His head is large and massive, measuring twenty-three inches around the cranium only one inch less than that of Daniel Webster.

Although Fayel was impressed by him, he remembered that Satanta's "name is a terror to the whites of the frontier....The Kansas people attribute many of the depredations committed to this Indian, and think that he richly deserves a hempen neck tie instead of any other more acceptable present."[12]

Satanta's views on one of the basic purposes of the council, free passage of a railroad through Kiowa territory, were already known, for earlier in the year army Captain John H. Page had visited his camp to discuss the railroad with him. At that time, Satanta told Page he not only expected all soldiers to be withdrawn from his country, but also that the Atchison, Topeka and Santa Fe Railroad was not to extend beyond Council Grove, except to bring goods for the Kiowas.[13]

Satanta was effusive and almost shouted his salutations to each man. Wrapped in a blanket, his face painted red and his bugle hanging from his waist, he dominated the room, and all the other Indians followed his lead in greeting the whites with embraces. Reynolds thought he was drunk.[14]

Satanta's bluster concealed his nervousness. Despite his commanding presence he realized that, unlike previous visits to the post, he was neither in control of the overall situation nor free to do as he pleased. No sooner were his loud, almost overbearing greetings finished than he abruptly announced that he wanted to leave because it "stink too much white man here." The government officials informed him he would have to remain and escort the commission to Medicine Lodge.[15]

The whites had continued drinking throughout their earlier briefing, and now the Indians were invited to join. After a few rounds Satanta mellowed and relaxed and, according to Stanley, "laughed gleefully like a child."[16]

The huge gathering of commissioners, soldiers, bureaucrats, news correspondents, Indians, and hangers-on spent less than a day at their camp near Fort Larned before heading south toward the council site. Altogether Stanley counted 600 people in 165 wagons and ambulances, with 1,250 animals including the 200 horses of the escorting battalion of Seventh Cavalry under the command of Major Joel Elliott.[17] Satanta rode in the lead wagon with General Harney.

Soon they were passing through buffalo country and found themselves in the midst of a herd which veteran buffalo hunters in the party estimated to contain one hundred thousand animals. Harney ordered a hunting party, composed of anyone who desired the sport, to bring back meat for the expedition. Both Stanley and young A.A. Taylor availed themselves of the opportunity, and they wrote that the camp dined on buffalo steaks and humps that night.[18]

The buffalo hunt initially drew no complaint from Satanta. As the expedition neared the Indian camps, Harney ordered that firearms not be discharged, but some of the hangers-on spotted another herd of buffalo and shot several animals, cutting out the tongues and leaving the carcasses for carrion. The act infuriated Satanta, who was already touchy about the growing slaughter of the buffalo.

"Has the white man become a child," he demanded, "that he should recklessly kill and not eat? When the red men slay game, they do so that they may live and not starve."

"This speech," Stanley reported, "produced the desired result. Two or three of the bummers were put under arrest, and the Major [Elliott] commanding the battalion was also arrested for not preventing the shooting. Satanta is a plain-speaking chief."[19]

Not everyone was impressed. "Why is this?" *Cincinnati Commercial* correspondent George Brown asked his readers. "Because we were in the hostile country, and because Satanta and the Indians with us found fault with the killing of their buffalo, since it was their country and their game, and since, also, the animals were some of them left to rot on the Plains to stench up the air that the noble red man was to breathe."[20]

On Monday, October 14, the expedition reached the Indian camps. Altogether there were about five thousand Indians scattered among five different camp circles, the largest of which was the Cheyennes with 250 lodges each housing an average of eight persons. Old tribal animosities lingered, and the commissioners found themselves walking a tightrope amid all the jealousies and factionalism. The Kiowas and Arapahos, who wanted to begin the council immediately, were already threatening to leave because they were suspicious of the Cheyennes, who had obtained a postponement. On Tuesday morning a preliminary council was held to conciliate both factions.

The commissioners lined up in front of the largest tent. The chiefs arranged themselves in a semi-circle around them, the most important Indians in the front row and the rest in the second and third rows in diminishing order of importance. In the forefront of the Kiowas were Satanta, Black Eagle and Kicking Bird, soon joined by Fishermore, senior counselor of the Kiowas. Poor Bear represented the Kiowa-Apaches, Ten Bears the Comanches, and Little Raven the Arapahos.

Commissioner Taylor opened the discussion by assuring the chiefs that no affront was intended toward their people, and that there had been no separate agreements with the Cheyennes. Replying for the Kiowas, Black Eagle said he was reassured but asked that the council be postponed only four days instead of the eight days requested by the Cheyennes. Several other chiefs expressed their views, but Satanta refused to become involved and remarked, "I don't want to say anything at this talk. I will say what I have to say in the grand council."[21]

Irritated by what he considered Satanta's vacillation, the Comanche Ten Bears remarked, "What I say is law for the Comanches, but it takes half-a-dozen to speak for the Kiowas."

Satanta lost his temper. A heated argument broke out between the Kiowa and Comanche leaders, and Satanta threatened to walk out. The commissioners were finally able to assure the chiefs that the council would be held and secured their agreement to wait.[22] Satanta sat down and listened to some of the other chiefs, who were not finished with their remarks even though the white commissioners were anxious to wind up the preliminaries.

The Apache Poor Bear expressed impatience at the postponement, indicating this was not the first delay he had encountered. "I have been here some time," he told the government officials, "I would like to get my annuity goods as soon as possible, as I understood they were here. I will wait four days for the talk. I have spoken."

With this, Satanta rose. Until now he had spoken Comanche, the universal language of the Southern Plains; now,

Medicine Lodge Treaty Conference. (Reproduced in Harper's Weekly, November 16, 1867)

however, he spoke Kiowa. What he said is unknown, because
a white interpreter did not understand, but his remarks drew an
enthusiastic response from the assembled chiefs.

After a few more speeches from other chiefs, the commissioners agreed to convene the main conference five days hence,
and the council adjourned.[23] Rations of sugar, coffee and flour
were then distributed separately to each tribe and gathered by
the Indian women. When the Kiowa women received their
portion, correspondent Fayel observed:

> Se-tan-ta, the noble looking chief of that tribe, rode
> about and gave directions with regard to the distri-
> bution with simply a move of the hand, and the
> gesture was understood by his subordinate chiefs
> and implicitly followed to the letter. Then there was
> a scramble and a hauling about of bags and boxes,
> and every thing was moved about till it got into its
> appropriated [sic] destination. Se-tan-ta had his bugle
> lashed under his arm. . . .[24]

Although Satanta's heavy-handedness is in character, one
wonders about the obedience of the "subordinate chiefs;" they
generally did not permit Satanta to take charge to such an
extent. Perhaps because he was to be their spokesman in the
great council, they allowed him to supervise the distribution to
lend him some authority in the eyes of the whites. It must be
remembered, however, that the whites already had a precon-
ceived notion of Satanta's importance, and newspaper accounts may have been tailored to fit this notion rather than his
actual authority in the Kiowa camp. Fayel, who only a few days
earlier had written that the people of Kansas "think that [Satanta]
richly deserves a hempen necktie,"[25] was beginning to fall
under Satanta's persuasive spell; the tone of his dispatches
became far more conciliatory.

While the Indians gathered their rations, the commissioners
were taking depositions from Agent Wynkoop concerning the
causes of the continual warfare on the plains. Wynkoop attributed the outbreak directly to Sand Creek, saying the initial
impact of that massacre had been subsequently aggravated by
Hancock's campaign. He attacked both the government's war

policy and its peace policy, accusing the Commissioner of Indian Affairs of providing shoddy material which was debited against the tribal allocations at an exorbitant rate. "They were not only killed, but the friendliest were cheated," he remarked.[26]

Wynkoop's statements were refuted by Major Douglass, the former commander of Fort Dodge who had negotiated the release of the Box women. He described his ransoming of the women and Satanta's cavalier attitude about the affair. He also testified that Satanta had demanded that troops and military posts be removed from the country, and that railroad construction and mail coach runs be stopped. "Satanta openly boasted that they had plenty of arms and ammunition, and were not afraid of the whites," Douglass testified.

"Do you not think that these Indians made that boast of cleaning out the whites as a joke?" Commissioner Sanborn asked.

Before Douglass could answer, General Harney interjected, "I never knew the Indians to jest. In their boasts there is always a meaning."

Douglass pointed out that he secured affidavits of depredations and made written reports of the Indians' boastings, all of which had been forwarded to General Hancock, who then organized his expedition shortly afterwards.[27] In light of Douglass' testimony and the subsequent report of the commissioners, it now appears Hancock had organized his force in response to reported Kiowa raids, but had ended up negotiating with the Kiowas while fighting Cheyennes and Oglalas in a classic example of the convoluted government policy toward plains Indians.

The correspondents used the five days before the primary council was to convene to explore the area, as much as they dared with so many Indians about. The valley and creek of Medicine Lodge had been named for a grove of cottonwood trees, about five miles from the council site, which the Kiowas considered sacred and in which they held religious ceremonies. According to A.A. Taylor, who visited the spot with the correspondents and an experienced guide, it consisted of

cottonwood trees, bushes and various undergrowth,

all planted in circular form, with open spaces in the center, more or less shaded. There were many circles of these trees and bushes—in fact the entire grove must have covered more than an acre of ground. There were all kinds of trinkets tied with rawhide strings to the bodies of the trees and limbs, and securely fastened and hanging all over the bushes.[28]

The correspondents also visited the Kiowa camp, where they found proof of Indian depredations—two white women captured when children and reared as Kiowas. One, about twenty-five years old, had been taken during a raid on one of the German settlements near San Antonio. Both her parents had been killed. "Her hair is light colored with the texture of a white person's," Fayel wrote, "but in all else, dress, dirt and bringing up, she is like the squaws with whom she has always associated. She would never consent to abandon the tribe to which she is attached, and probably that is the only sphere which she is now calculated to adorn. She talks some English, and she recollects the circumstances attending her capture."

The other was an Irish woman who had married a Kiowa and now had five children. "She was captured when quite a little girl, and from long habit, it would be next to impossible to wean her from the fascinations of her Indian home," Fayel observed.[29]

The great council opened at 10:00 a.m. on October 19 with four hundred chiefs representing virtually all the major plains tribes. As with the preliminary meeting, the principal chiefs sat in the front row of their half-circle facing the commissioners. The Kiowas were on the left of the half-circle, with Satanta sitting in front on an army camp stool wearing the military coat given to him by General Hancock.[30] Immediately behind him were old Satank, wearing a peace medal with a portrait of President James Buchanan, and Kicking Bird.[31]

Commissioner Taylor called the meeting to order, and he and Senator Henderson outlined the objectives of the council. As part of the government's plan to "civilize the Indian," the commissioners would set aside land for farms and would build churches and schools. The government would address Indian grievances, but nevertheless intended to have peace on the plains. Taylor's son noted, "The time had come when the red man and the 'pale face' could meet and exchange arguments instead of blows, and supplement argument with mutual concession,"[32] but the Indians were less impressed. The Arapaho Little Raven, whose appearance reminded the younger Taylor of President Johnson, delivered a blistering denunciation of the U.S. government's violations of the peace, specifically citing the Chivington Massacre and the white encroachments on land guaranteed by the Indians under treaty. Among other things, he demanded damages as well as the annuities for which the government was in arrears. He was eloquent, and his logic made the whites very uncomfortable.[33]

When the turn came for the Kiowas and Comanches, Satanta stood and replied for both. Ever the diplomat, he opened with miscellaneous pleasantries then got down to business.

> All the land south of the Arkansas belongs to the Kiowas and Comanches, and I don't want to give away any of it. I love the land and the buffalo, and will not part with it. I want you to understand well what I say....I want you to understand, also, that the Kiowas and Comanches don't want to fight, and have not been fighting since we made the [Little Arkansas] treaty. I hear a good deal of talk from these gentlemen [commissioners], but they never do what they say. I don't want any of these Medicine lodges [i.e., schools and churches] built in this country. I want the papooses brought up exactly as I am. When I make peace there is no end of it....
>
> I have heard that you intend to set apart a reservation near the mountains. I don't want to settle; I love to roam over the prairie; I feel free and happy; but when we settle down we get pale and die....I have told you the truth. I have no little lies about me; but I don't know how it is with the Commissioners. Are they as clear as I am? A long time ago this land belonged to our fathers; but when I go up to the [Arkansas] river I see camps of soldiers on its banks. These soldiers cut down my timber, they kill my

buffalo; and when I see that my heart feels like bursting; I feel sorry.[34]

Having spoken his mind, Satanta then sat down and wrapped a blanket around himself. His speech, once required reading in American literature classes,[35] has impressed later generations more than it did the peace commissioners who, according to Stanley, gave Satanta "a rather blank look." Despite his assurances, the Kiowas and Comanches had continued to raid after the Little Arkansas Treaty and everyone knew it.

As for being free "to roam over the prairies," the representatives for Kansas, Governor Crawford and Senator Ross, did not intend to allow him "to roam over the prairies" of *their* state. Satanta's adamant assertion that he had a right to go where he pleased was backed by Ten Bears and the Comanche delegation.[36]

It had become clear that the Kiowas and Comanches had no intention of accepting a treaty, and to persuade them the commissioners offered to continue their hunting rights below the Arkansas River and in the Texas Panhandle. Such an offer, however, was no more feasible than had been the reservation established under the Little Arkansas Treaty. The state of Texas had retained sovereign control over its land, and the lower reaches of the Panhandle were already being settled; to offer hunting rights to the Indians was to insure future conflicts with those settlers.[37] The commissioners may have believed that Texas, a former Confederate state undergoing Reconstruction, was in no position to object.

The Texans would have other ideas on the issue, but nevertheless the offer of hunting rights stood. By the end of the second day's negotiations, the Kiowas and Comanches had agreed in principle to a vast reservation in what is now southwestern Oklahoma. Ten Bears insisted that if the Comanches accepted the reservation, the Texans would have to be kept out of it. He echoed Satanta's objections to the establishment of schools and farms, but the notion was accepted grudgingly.

Satanta raised the point of annuities, which he said would have to be distributed on schedule. In a final jab at Leavenworth, he remarked:

> We need two agents—one [each] for the Kiowas and Comanches. There are so many hearts in the two tribes that it requires two. I have no objection to Colonel Leavenworth or anybody else in the Commission, but it requires two to distribute our goods properly. For myself and my band, we will take John Tappan [Samuel Tappan's cousin, a trader at Fort Dodge who had reasonably good relations with Satanta]; the other Kiowas may take Leavenworth if they will.

Senator Henderson's reply was courteous but coldly realistic.

> You say you do not like the medicine houses of the whites, but you prefer the buffalo and the chase, and express a wish to do as your fathers did.
>
> We say to you that the buffalo will not last for ever. They are now becoming few, and you must know it. When that day comes, the Indian must change the road his father trod, or he must suffer, and probably die. We tell you that to change will make you better. We wish you to live, and we will now offer the way. The whites are settling up all the good lands. They have come to the Arkansas River. When they come, they drive out the buffalo. If you oppose them, war must come. They are many, and you are few. You may kill some of them, but others will come and take their places. And finally, many of the red men will have been killed, and the rest will have no homes.

As an alternative, he said, the government was preparing to make them federal wards, to feed, clothe and educate them.

> We do not ask you to cease hunting the buffalo. You may roam over the broad plains south of the Arkansas River, and hunt the buffalo as you have done in years past, but you must have a place you can call your own.

They would learn to farm on this reserve, attend school and become productive members of society. With that, Henderson adjourned the council, saying he expected them to sign the treaty at 9 o'clock the following morning.[38]

As Henderson desired, the treaty was signed on October 21. The Kiowa signatories were Satanta, Satank, Kicking Bird, Black Eagle, Fishermore, Woman's Heart, Stumbling Bear, Lone Bear, Bear Lying Down and the Crow. Ten Comanches, headed by Ten Bears, also made their marks.[39] When the formalities were completed, annuity goods were distributed and the Kiowas quickly fell to fighting among themselves over brown sugar, coffee, bolts of calico and other items. Estimating the value of the goods at over $100,000, Stanley remarked, "Satanta cannot now have a shadow of a cause to justify his digging up the hatchet."[40]

Before the Kiowas left the correspondents and commissioners heard one last speech, soon to be regarded as one of the greatest ever made by a plains Indian. Incredibly it came from old Satank, who was not noted for oratory. The *New York Times* correspondent, or more probably an editor in New York, confused the names, so the *Times* attributed it to Satanta[41] and it has become known to history as "Chief Satanta's Speech." Stanley, however, knew both men, was incapable of confusing one with the other, and stated very definitely the speaker was Satank. So did Brown of the *Cincinnati Commercial*.

Until now, Satank had said nothing, sitting quietly throughout the proceedings and giving no indication of his presence other than silently exchanging hand signals with Agent Leavenworth while others talked.[42] Now he rode his pony up to the council tent, dismounted and faced the commissioners.

It has made me very glad to meet you, who are the commissioners sent by the Great Father to see us. You have heard much talk by our chiefs, and no doubt are tired of it. Many of them have put themselves forward and filled you with their sayings. I have kept back and said nothing—not that I did not consider myself the principal chief of the Kiowa Nation,[43] but others younger than I desired to talk, and I left it to them.

Before leaving, however, as I now intend to go, I come to say that the Kiowas and Camaches [sic] have made with you a peace, and they intend to keep it. If it brings prosperity to us, we of course will like it the better. If it brings prosperity or adversity, we will not abandon it. It is our contract, and it shall stand.

Referring to the secession of Texas and the Civil War, he said:

Our people once carried war against Texas. We thought the Great Father would not be offended for the Texans had gone out from among his people, and become his enemies. You now tell us that they have made peace and returned to the great family. The Kiowas and Camanches [sic] will seek no bloody trail in their land. they have pledged their word and that word shall last, unless the whites break their contract and invite the horrors of war. We do not break treaties. We make but few contracts, and them we remember well. The whites make so many that they are liable to forget them. The white chief seems not able to govern his braves. The Great Father seems powerless in the face of his children. He sometimes becomes angry when he sees the wrongs of his people committed on the red man, and his voice becomes loud as the roaring winds. But like the wind it soon dies away and leaves the sullen calm of unheeded oppression. We hope now that a better time has come. If all would talk and then do as you have done the sun of peace would shine forever. We have warred against the white man, but never because it gave us pleasure. Before the day of oppression came, no white man came to our villages and went away hungry. It gave us more joy to share with them than it gave him to partake of our hospitality. In the far-distant past there was no suspicion among us. The world seemed large enough for both the red and the white man. Its broad plains seem now to contract, and the white man grows jealous of his red brother.

The white man once came to trade; he now comes as a soldier. He once put his trust in our friendship and wanted no shield but our fidelity. But now he builds forts and plants big guns on their walls. He once gave us arms and powder and ball, and bade us to hunt the game. We then loved him for his confidence; he now suspects our plighted faith and drives us to be his enemies; he now covers his face with the cloud of jealousy and anger, and tells us to begone, as an offended master speaks to his dog.

Pointing to his Indian Peace Medal of an earlier decade, Satank continued:

Look at this medal I wear. By wearing this I have been made poor. Formerly, I was rich in horses and lodges—to-day I am the poorest of all. When you put this silver medal on my neck you made me poor.

We thank the Great Spirit that all these wrongs are now to cease and the old day of peace and friendship [is] to come again.

You came as friends. You talked as friend. You have partially heard our many complaints. To you they may have seemed trifling. To us they are everything.

You have not tried, as many have done, to make a new bargain merely to get the advantage.

You have not asked to make our annuities smaller, but unasked you have made them larger.

You have not withdrawn a single gift, but you have voluntarily provided more guarantees for our education and comfort.

When we saw these things done, we then said among ourselves, these are the men of the past. We at once gave you our hearts. You now have them. You know what is best for us. Do for us what is best. Teach us the road to travel, and we will not depart from it forever.

For your sakes the green grass shall no more be stained with the red blood of the pale-faces. Your people shall again be our people, and peace shall be between us forever. If wrong comes, we shall look to you for right and justice.

We know you will not forsake us, and tell your people also to act as you have done, to be as you have been.

I am old, but still am chief. I shall have soon to go the way of my fathers, but those who come after me will remember this day. It is now treasured up by the old, and will be carried by them to the grave, and then handed down to be kept as a sacred tradition by their children and their children's children. And now the time has come that I must go. Good-bye!

You may never see me more, but remember Satank as the white man's friend.[44]

The old man moved down the line of whites shaking hands with each. Then he mounted his pony and rode away.

Satank's speech left his white audience visibly moved. Stanley called it "a gem," adding, "There is a good deal of truth in it which strikes home."[45] Even Brown, who disliked Indians, was forced to admit, "Although Indian speeches are generally a bore—tedious and uninteresting—yet the [speech] of the old man Satank is well worthy of perusal...."[46]

Chapter 6
The Winter Campaign

The provisions of the Medicine Lodge Treaty were not implemented for months because congress, more concerned with the impeachment of President Johnson than the business of government, delayed approval and did not appropriate money to fulfill the government's pledges until the middle of 1868. By then even General Sherman, worried that the delays and resultant food shortages among the tribes might cause an outbreak, had taken up the Indian cause.[1]

In the meantime the Kiowas, Comanches and Apaches did not concern themselves with the treaty or its implementation and were soon raiding into Texas again. Men, women and children were murdered; women and children not killed were taken captive. Captivity was especially hard on the children, many of whom died en route to the Indian camps.[2] By March 1868, however, the Kiowas and Comanches had moved up to Kansas where Major General Philip H. Sheridan, who had replaced Hancock as commander of the Department of the Missouri, found them encamped at Fort Larned together with the Arapahos and Cheyennes. All were awaiting their annuity issue. Sheridan refused to meet with the chiefs and moved on to Fort Dodge, saying that he was on an inspection tour and not authorized to discuss the situation. When the chiefs followed him, he finally agreed to see them.

They told Sheridan that, because the reservations had not been established, they did not know where they were supposed to live, and their women and children were starving. Sheridan's advisers countered that the Indians could still hunt buffalo but,

General Philip H. Sheridan. (Courtesy National Archives)

to buy time, Sheridan issued them army rations. He also set up an intelligence system to monitor the Indians' movements.[3]

As tensions grew during the spring, old tribal grievances flared. Trouble initially broke out between the Cheyennes and the Kaws in central Kansas and soon spread to involve white settlers as the Cheyennes extended their raids north along the Solomon and Saline Rivers. Although only a few of the young Arapaho warriors joined the raiding parties, the Arapahos' traditional alliance with the Cheyennes led the government to consider itself at war with both nations.

At first the Kiowas remained neutral. Colonel William B.

Colonel William B. Hazen. (Courtesy National Archives).

Hazen, newly appointed commander of the Southern Indian Military District which included the Indian Territory, noted that the Kiowas, Apaches and Comanches were reasonably quiet except for the inevitable raids into Texas. As a pledge of good faith, in July the Kiowas surrendered two white captives, a four-year-old boy and a thirteen-old-girl, to John Tappan, the commissioner's cousin at Fort Dodge. The Kiowas and the Comanches were also allowing whites into their territory to trade.[4]

While the Kiowas and Comanches maintained their truce with the whites on the midwestern plains, they continued to raid both in Texas and among the tribes to the west as well. In late June or early July a Kiowa war party, heading west on an expedition against the Navajos, encountered a band of Utes hunting buffalo. The Utes fled, leading the Kiowas on a two or three-mile chase into the main Ute camp. Now outnumbered, the Kiowas turned to flee. After a fifteen-mile running fight the Utes finally abandoned the chase, leaving Satanta's associate, Heap of Bears, and five other Kiowa warriors dead. Returning to their camp on the Arkansas, some nine miles southwest of Fort Larned, the Kiowas slashed their arms, legs and torsos and wailed at their losses. Visiting the camp, Captain Albert Barnitz of the Seventh Cavalry, commented, "Satanta is in mourning...."[5]

* * *

Though reservations were not yet established according to the treaty, the Indian Bureau intended to reactivate Fort Cobb as a refuge for the Kiowas, Comanches and Apaches as well as for those Cheyennes and Arapahos who were friendly toward the government. Sheridan balked, however, insisting that the Cheyennes and Arapahos bore collective responsibility for the depredations in Kansas. He believed they should be crushed and reduced to poverty, and the ringleaders hanged.[6] Hazen's first duty, therefore, was to sort out the friendly Indians from the hostiles and to induce the friendly Indians to move in close to Fort Cobb.

Only a week short of his thirty-eighth birthday, Hazen was an 1855 graduate of West Point where he received more than 150 demerits in his senior year alone, primarily because of his forceful and outspoken character. After graduation he fought Indians in Oregon and Texas and received three citations for gallantry. He was teaching tactics at West Point when the Civil War broke out, then he served first in Tennessee and subsequently on Sherman's devastating march through Georgia and South Carolina. Finishing the war as a brevet major general, he was appointed colonel of the Thirty-eighth Infantry in 1866, serving primarily in administrative positions which led to his appointment to the Southern Indian Military District.[7]

Hazen knew Sheridan was ready, even eager, to deal with an Indian uprising. Phil Sheridan was a combative, rough-spoken Irishman who listed Albany, New York, as his birth-place for official purposes but who was probably born in Ireland before his parents emigrated. He struggled through West Point during a time when the odds were against his working class, Catholic background. Although his inclination to settle arguments with his fists nearly brought expulsion, he was graduated thirty-fourth in a class of fifty-two and sent west. His first Indian fight was against the Yakimas along the Columbia River in Washington in 1856. When the Civil War broke out he returned to the East.

Sheridan proved a daring and innovative soldier whose Shenandoah campaign hastened the collapse of the Confederacy and enhanced his reputation as a fighter. His Civil War experience imbued in him a sense of almost jingoistic nationalism. Sheridan viewed the nation as a single entity rather than a union of federated states; any threat to the nation—from Indians or whites—was to be crushed so completely that it could never again become a danger.

In 1868 the threat perceived by Sheridan was the Indians. Although it has never been established that he made the remark often attributed to him, that "The only good Indians I ever saw were dead," the comment nevertheless describes his attitude toward the Indians.[8] Despite Sheridan's flaws and prejudices, or perhaps because of them, his troops liked him. One private, who encountered Sheridan on the frontier, called him "a short, heavily built man, wears a dark blue suit, but not much gold out here....He is quite jovial and does not put on much style."[9]

Sheridan's intention to punish guilty Indians made perfect sense to Hazen, who was equally determined to put a stop to raiding once and for all. Hazen told Philip McCusker, the interpreter, that he intended to punish all Indians proven guilty of murder "or other crimes" committed since the Medicine Lodge Treaty. The same laws which applied to whites would apply to Indians, and there would be no statute of limitations. The difference between Sheridan and Hazen's intentions was that Sheridan meant to punish entire groups of people, while Hazen felt punishment should apply only to individuals convicted according to rules of evidence. McCusker, who was thoroughly familiar with the Indians, believed that if Hazen's policy had been implemented much of the bloodshed of the ensuing years could have been avoided.[10]

McCusker, however, was troubled by Hazen's attitude toward the Kiowas, who were as guilty as any but who were usually regarded as friendly because their raids against white settlements were confined largely to Texas. Despite General Hancock's insistence that the Kiowas leave Texas in peace, the federal government did not officially regard the depredations there as hostile acts. Although the Box family incident was well-known, the peace commissioners had excused it as "the only flagrant violation" of the Little Arkansas Treaty, stating the Kiowas

> supposed an attack on Texas people would be no violation of a treaty with the United States: that as we ourselves had been at war with the people of Texas, an act of hostility on their part would not be disagreeable to us.[11]

In fact, the federal government did not find the Box incident very disagreeable. Texas was, after all, an occupied former Confederate state and a recent enemy, and as such it did not possess the political influence of Kansas. McCusker considered this cavalier attitude toward Texas a mistake, but there was little he could do about it.[12]

On September 18 the Kiowas, Comanches and Plains Apaches met with Hazen and Sheridan at Fort Larned. The two soldiers told the Indians that hostilities were imminent and ordered them to report to Fort Cobb and stay out of the way. Satanta and Ten Bears were uneasy, but ultimately agreed to accompany Hazen to Cobb. Departure was delayed for a week, pending delivery of rations to Larned. Because the area immediately around the post was overgrazed, the Indians received permission to spend the waiting period hunting buffalo south of the Arkansas.

The following day, however, Sheridan advised Hazen that the presence of the Kiowas and Comanches in western Kansas was hindering his operations against hostiles. Sheridan would provide rations to the Kiowas and Comanches until October 31, contingent upon their immediately reporting to Fort Cobb. After October 31, Hazen was to provide for them out of fifty thousand dollars allocated for that purpose, plus clothing and stores.[13]

Hazen began the 225-mile trip southeast from Fort Larned to Cobb, but was forced by hostile war parties and lack of military escort to take a roundabout route. The Kiowa and Comanche chiefs, traveling on the more direct road, arrived first at Cobb, found no one to meet them, and resumed hunting.

Hazen's failure to arrive at Fort Cobb on schedule worried two influential whites for whom memories of Chivington's slaughter at Sand Creek were still fresh. Agent Wynkoop and John S. Smith, a government interpreter who had married into the Cheyennes, had trusted their superiors before the massacre at Sand Creek, and they did not intend to repeat the mistake. Wynkoop, who had initially persuaded Black Kettle's Cheyennes to place themselves under military protection prior to Sand Creek, resigned rather than advise any more Indians to comply with government edicts. Smith, also suspicious, warned the Kiowa and Comanche leaders to avoid both Fort Cobb and Fort Larned.[14] When Hazen finally arrived at Cobb on November 7, some Comanches and affiliated tribes were there, but the Kiowas and the main Comanche bands were still hunting buffalo. Hazen realized that this time the safety of the Indians depended on getting them back to the agency as soon as possible; he knew the army troops would attack any Indians found on the plains.[15]

Satanta's activities during this period are uncertain. On October 9 Indians attacked a wagon train bound from Colorado to Kansas and captured Mrs. Clara Blinn and her two-year-old son Willie before being driven off. Although the Indians were believed to be mostly Cheyennes, the wagon master claimed he saw Satanta among them.[16] By mid-November, however, Satanta was in the vicinity of Fort Cobb because Hazen stated that he was one of the first chiefs to report to him there. By November 20, Lone Wolf, Satank, and the main Kiowa and Comanche bands had all arrived. Hazen issued them ten days' rations and urged them to move in close to the fort to avoid trouble. Although he was convinced of their innocence in the recent raids, and also that the Kiowas and Comanches were not involved with the kidnapping of Mrs. Blinn, he was not so sure of the Cheyennes and Arapahos and turned them away with orders that they would have to make peace with Sheridan.[17]

The Kiowas were prompted to comply with Hazen's instructions and moved in close to the agency because of unsettling information they had received. As Hancock had warned more than eighteen months earlier, the grain-fed government horses possessed much greater range in winter than the grass-eating Indian ponies which were rendered virtually immobile by snow. Thus Sheridan had deliberately planned his campaign to catch the tribes off guard in their winter encampments along the Washita River some twenty miles northwest of Fort Cobb. On the night of November 26, some Kiowas returning from an expedition against the Utes saw a large trail of iron-shod military horses heading toward the Washita. Arriving at the Cheyenne winter camp, they passed on the information but were met with ridicule. Satanta, Satank and Lone Wolf, however, moved their bands to Cobb, leaving only Kicking Bird's band on the Washita River.

There were about six thousand Indians in a series of camps strung out more than ten miles along the river in the Washita Valley, a wide basin protected by bluffs and offering timber and grazing. It is generally believed that Black Kettle's Cheyennes were in the westernmost camp, followed by the camps of Little Raven's Arapahos, a larger band of Cheyennes under Medicine Arrow, another Cheyenne camp, Kicking Bird's Kiowas, and the Comanche and Apache camps.[18] Unknown to them, seven hundred men of the Seventh Cavalry under Lieutenant Colonel George Armstrong Custer were closing in from the north, and Governor Crawford's Nineteenth Kansas Volunteer Cavalry was marching southwest toward the Washita from Topeka. It was Custer's trail which had prompted the Kiowas to warn the camps. Unfortunately Custer, recrossing the trail of the Kiowas returning from their raid against the Utes, incorrectly assumed it had been made by a war party returning from raids against the white settlements.[19]

Less than ten days short of his twenty-ninth birthday, Custer had distinguished himself in the Union Army as a cavalry commander and had risen to the brevet rank of major general, but military cutbacks after the war had reduced him to the permanent rank of lieutenant colonel. Although nominally a subordinate officer in the Seventh, he was de facto commander

Lieutenant Colonel George Armstrong Custer with the winter clothing and beard he wore during the Washita Campaign. (Courtesy Little Bighorn Battlefield National Monument)

in the field because the regimental commanders—first Colonel Smith and later Colonel Samuel Sturgis—remained on detached duty. Custer's strategies of war had been shaped by the dashing, all-or-nothing cavalry charges against the Confederates, and he never modified his outlook. He failed to make the mental or emotional adjustment to the Indians' strategy of drawing small units of troops away from their support and annihilating them piecemeal.

When Sheridan began planning his Washita campaign, Custer was serving a one-year suspension under sentence of court martial. In the aftermath of Hancock's War, he had been tried and convicted of leaving his command without permission, using government transportation for personal business, ordering deserters shot without trial, and abusing men and animals. Desiring his services on the Washita, Sheridan arranged for his sentence to be lifted and ordered him to report for duty.

The lifting of Custer's suspension illustrates his psychological hold over Sheridan, an often ambivalent relationship that has never been completely investigated or understood. Despite his self-proclaimed expertise, Custer's knowledge of Indians remained rudimentary; Sheridan, who at this point probably knew as much as Custer about Indian fighting, nevertheless considered the young lieutenant colonel indispensable to his western campaigns. This was not the only time Sheridan would rescue Custer from oblivion to participate in an Indian war, and these interventions were ultimately to contribute to Custer's death at the Little Bighorn.[20]

Arriving near the Cheyenne camp on the Washita shortly after midnight November 27, Custer divided his men into four squadrons to surround the camp and ordered them to hold their positions until dawn. At daybreak the regimental band signaled the attack by striking up the old Irish drinking song "Garryowen," and the troops swooped down on the sleeping Indians. Ironically, the first camp they attacked belonged to old Black Kettle, totally unprepared for battle and still hoping for peace despite the bitter lesson of Sand Creek.

The startled warriors hurried their women and children away as they grabbed weapons and prepared to defend themselves. Many ran down to the river, standing waist-deep in the freezing water so they could use the bank for cover. Within minutes Custer had gained control of the camp but faced deadly fire from the Cheyennes. The soldiers dismounted and moved on foot against the Indian positions, and a vicious hand-to-hand fight ensued. Black Kettle and his wife managed to cross the narrow river before being shot. The old chief fell dead, face down in the stream, his wife's body in the water close by.

Seeing the Cheyenne women and children fleeing, Custer's Osage Indian scouts galloped to overtake them and broke off tree limbs for whips to lash them back into camp as prisoners.

Custer's attack on the Cheyenne Villages at the Washita. (From Custer, My Life on the Plains)

As the fighting tapered off the women, certain they would be killed, began chanting their death songs. The village and river-bank were littered with dead and dying. Major Joel H. Elliott, who had commanded the cavalry escort at Medicine Lodge, took seventeen men to round up the few warriors who were fleeing.

About 10:00 a.m., Custer began noticing groups of warriors on the surrounding hills. As the numbers grew, he summoned one of the captive women, Mah-wis-sa (also known as Meot-si), who claimed to be Black Kettle's sister and who told Custer that this was one of many villages in the vicinity, some of them larger.

Custer began to realize there were more Indians than he had at first anticipated. Pickets dashed into camp and reported they had been driven from their positions by Indians. A detachment under Lieutenant E.S. Godfrey went out on patrol, but was driven back after a fierce fight with a group of Arapahos. In the distance Godfrey heard gunfire but did not realize that Elliott's detachment of seventeen men was being annihilated.

About mid-afternoon Custer led his troops toward the villages upriver and the Indians withdrew ahead of him. About nightfall he turned around and returned to Black Kettle's village, a decision that probably postponed his death by over seven years. The next morning he reached his supply train and settled down to wait for Sheridan and for Crawford's Kansas cavalry. He did not bother to look for Elliott.

Not until December 11, when Sheridan and Custer returned to the area with a large escort, did they discover the bodies of Elliott and his men and learn their fate. Elliott's detachment had pursued and overtaken a group of women and children and were marching them back to camp when they were cut off and killed by Kiowas, Arapahos and Cheyennes.[21] There is little doubt these Kiowas were from Kicking Bird's band and may have included Kicking Bird himself. Despite his pacifism, Kicking Bird was capable and willing to defend his people in battle; Stumbling Bear later admitted he himself had killed and scalped five men during this campaign and that Kicking Bird had killed and scalped seven.[22]

Not long after the bodies of Elliott and his men were found, some members of the escort located the frozen bodies of a white woman and child. Back at the military camp it was later established that the woman was Clara Blinn, although the identity of the child has never been satisfactorily ascertained.[23]

Once the troops had settled in camp, Mah-wis-sa approached Sheridan to ask when they could expect to be killed. On being informed whites did not customarily kill women and children,[24] she began giving a detailed deposition about the fight. Rafael Romero, the interpreter, cautioned Custer not to trust her because she was telling them only what she believed the soldiers wanted to hear. To emphasize his point, Romero said Mah-wis-sa would kill Custer in a minute if given the opportunity.[25]

Custer ignored Romero's advice. Among Mah-wis-sa's pieces of information, which the soldiers found so attractive, was her declaration that

> The Kiowas and Arrapahoes [sic], our friends, run like dogs. They were worse cowards than women, Black Kettle was killed because they were afraid of the white man. They killed Black Kettle and our braves. If the white man fights the Kiowas and Arrappahoes [sic], I want a knife and will fight too, and kill all their papooses.

The other Cheyenne women all voiced their agreement and carried on about their hatred for Kiowas and Arapahos.[26]

The fact that the Kiowa camp belonged to Kicking Bird, already known as a peace chief, and that they may have fled simply to avoid fighting the whites, apparently occurred to no one. To the contrary, Mah-wis-sa stated that the village in which the bodies of Mrs. Blinn and the white child were found belonged to Satanta's Kiowas. She also left the impression, which the soldiers were quick to convert into a statement of fact, that Satanta had captured Mrs. Blinn and her child and held them prisoner in his camp up until the time he had them murdered before fleeing.[27] Accepting Mah-wis-sa's word at face value, Sheridan observed, "These captives had been taken by the Kiowas near Fort Lyon the previous summer [sic], and kept close prisoners...the poor woman being reserved to gratify the brutal lust of the chief, Satanta."[28]

Sheridan was determined to continue downriver toward Fort Cobb and attack any villages he found. Learning of his movements and fearing just that sort of action, Hazen sent a pair of couriers with a message addressed "To the Commanding Officer, Troops in the Field." It stated:

> Indians have just brought in word that our troops today reached the Washita some twenty miles above here. I send this to say that all the camps this side of the point reported to have been reached [by the troops], are friendly and have not been on the war path this season. If this reaches you it would be well to communicate at once with Satanta or Black Eagle, Chiefs of the Kiowas, near where you are now, who will readily inform you of the position of the Cheyennes and Arapahoes, also of my camp.[29]

The couriers were waylaid by the Kiowas, who took them into camp. One was given an escort of chiefs and leading warriors, while the other was detained in camp as a hostage for proper delivery of the message and the safe return of all concerned.

Early the next morning, December 17, as the Kiowas and Hazen's courier were en route to meet the troops, Sheridan's command started moving. The general understood there were villages nearby and he intended to attack them. The troops had marched four or five miles when they reached a ravine. As they prepared to cross, Hazen's courier was spotted ahead, signaling them. Custer and several other officers rode up to meet him and learned most of the Kiowas, including Satanta and Lone Wolf, were less than a mile behind under a flag of truce. He also informed them that his companion was hostage in the Kiowa camp. Sheridan was furious. With Mah-wis-sa's depositions on the so-called Blinn murders still fresh on his mind, he believed he now was about to face the murderer.

Yet Hazen had pronounced Satanta friendly. "Under such circumstances," Sheridan later wrote, "I was compelled to give up the intended attack, though I afterward regretted that I had paid any heed to the message...." He firmly believed Satanta and Lone Wolf "had deceived Hazen into writing the letter...."

Nevertheless, he ordered Custer to take a small party ahead to meet the Kiowas.[30]

As they drew closer, the Kiowas signalled a parley. Answering, the two interpreters rode forward, and Satanta and Lone Wolf came out to meet them. When they were within speaking distance, they asked to meet with the "Big White Chief." Custer, correspondent Keim, and Lieutenant Colonel J. Schuyler Crosby, Sheridan's adjutant, rode up while the general waited behind. All had their pistols ready. Custer, observing large numbers of warriors in ravines and on hilltops, believed the precaution was well-founded. The soldiers were convinced that an ambush had been planned and had been deterred only by the superior strength of the white forces.[31] Custer never considered the possibility that the Kiowas might be taking their own precautions against treachery.

Satanta greeted the soldiers with a "How!" and extended his hand to Crosby, who refused it. Irritated, Satanta slapped his chest and said in broken English, "Me Kiowa." After a pause, he offered his hand to Custer, who likewise refused, saying, "I never shake hands with any one unless I know him to be a friend."[32]

Some whites who knew Satanta later in life maintained he spoke and understood far more English than he was ever willing to admit. Whether he did or not, he realized these officers were not friends and went into a performance which may have been in earnest or may have been an elaborate charade. According to Indian accounts recorded by Colonel W.S. Nye, Satanta dispensed with the interpreter and shouted to some warriors who were hanging behind, "Where is that fellow who speaks English?"

A warrior named Walking Bird was ushered forward. He had picked up various expressions from the soldiers at Fort Dodge, and had convinced his comrades that he had total command of the language.

"Now, Walking Bird," Satanta ordered, "let us hear you use some of the white man's language. Go ahead, talk to them."

Inflated with his newfound importance, Walking Bird rode over to the officers and said, "Gimme blat."

When the soldiers indicated they had no idea what he was trying to say, he commented, "Por-dodge." Again no response.

Frustrated, Walking Bird now decided to flatter the officers. Remembering how the troopers had spoken to their horses in the stables at Dodge, he rode over to Custer, patted him on the arm and said, "Heap big nice sonabitch. Heap sonabitch!"[33]

Totally unimpressed and tired of what he considered, probably correctly, a delaying tactic, Custer demanded the Indians release the courier, and the chiefs agreed. They also dispatched a rider of their own to make sure their camps were close to Fort Cobb, and they agreed to accompany the column to the agency, which they expected to reach the next day. About twenty Indians, mostly Kiowas with some Comanches and Apaches, accompanied Custer back to the main column where Sheridan ordered rations for them. When the column resumed its march, the Indians rode along parallel and a short distance away.

That night the Indians received permission to send out another courier to give their people the location of the military camp. Custer ordered distribution of coffee, bread, beef and sugar, then visited with the Indians for awhile and, through Romero, received their assurances of friendly intentions. In turn, he suggested they remain close to camp to avoid being mistaken for hostiles by the sentries.

As the march continued the next day, more Indians were sent away until only Satanta, Lone Wolf, and a few lesser chiefs remained. Suspicious, Custer believed that Satanta and Lone Wolf, having sent their warriors off, would themselves bolt. He and Sheridan considered whether to hold the two chiefs hostage.

That afternoon a warrior was spotted up on a rise, waving to the column. Satanta said it was his son, Gray Goose, and asked permission to ride ahead and speak to him. Custer agreed but added that soldiers would escort him. Before they could do so, however, Satanta spurred his pony forward to the top of the rise and waved for the other chiefs to follow. This confirmed the soldiers' suspicions, and Sheridan sent some officers to bring in Satanta under arrest. When the officers caught up, Satanta reined in his horse and sat in the saddle with arms folded across his chest. Returning to the column, he and Lone Wolf were guarded by soldiers with drawn pistols and told they would be hostages for their peoples' fulfillment of military requirements. Gray Goose was not a hostage, but since the column would reach Fort Cobb in a few hours, Custer suggested he ride along. The remainder of the trip went without incident.[34]

The troops arrived at Cobb about dark on December 18. At 2:00 p.m. the next day, the Nineteenth Kansas was formed up for inspection on the parade ground in battalions of three companies each. Sheridan, Custer, Hazen and the Kansas officers sat on their horses in front. Fifty feet to their right were Satanta and Lone Wolf, joined by Gray Goose and the Comanche Chief Ten Bears. They were mounted and wore the bead and feather headresses denoting their rank.

Remarking on the Kiowa father and son, Private David L. Spotts of the Nineteenth called Gray Goose

> a fine looking boy, straight as an arrow and appears to be about 20 years old. Satanta is quite large and very strongly built, much more noble looking than the others who are darker and just ordinary looking Indians, only finely dressed.[35]

Soon, however, Satanta and Lone Wolf were placed in legirons and lodged in a Sibley tent. Sheridan, determined "to take some of the starch out of them before I get through with them," refused to talk with the Indians and instead sent Custer, who told them that "unless the entire tribe repaired to the vicinity of the agency...the war which had been inaugurated with such vigor and effect at the Washita would be renewed and continued until the terms of their treaty had been complied with."[36] Satanta and Lone Wolf begged for time. Some of the Kiowas suggested that the various bands would come in once Satanta and Lone Wolf were released.

Discussing the situation, Custer and Sheridan agreed the Kiowas were stalling in hopes of staying away from the agency until spring when the grass would be high enough to provide forage for their war ponies. Sheridan told Custer:

> We have given them every opportunity to come in and enjoy the protection of the Government if they so desired. They are among the worst Indians we have to deal with, and have been guilty of untold

murders and outrages, at the same time they were being fed and clothed by the Government. These two chiefs, Lone Wolf and Satanta, have forfeited their lives over and over again. They could now induce their people to come in and become friendly if they chose to exert their influence in that direction. This matter has gone on long enough and must be stopped, as we have to look after the other tribes before spring overtakes us. You can inform Lone Wolf and Satanta that we shall wait until sundown to-morrow for their tribe to come in; if by that time the village is not here, Lone Wolf and Satanta will be hung and the troops sent in pursuit of the village.[37]

The prospect of death by hanging was the worst possible threat that could be made, and as the impact sank in the prisoners became unnerved. Like most plains Indians, the Kiowas believed that the soul escaped the body through the mouth at the moment of death; any death which cut off the windpipe trapped the soul forever in the decaying body and condemned it to a hellish existence.[38] Gray Goose dashed out and returned with his pony. After a quick consultation the Kiowas asked for more time, saying their animals were worn out and would slow the packing and moving. Custer, however, was not authorized to grant an extension because Sheridan "was tired of their duplicity, and insisted on ... [his] ultimatum."[39] Satanta stepped aside while Lone Wolf, as paramount chief, issued orders to bring in the others. Gray Goose jumped on his pony and rode off as his father called after him to hurry.[40]

There was no question in Lone Wolf's mind that his orders would be obeyed. Raising his arm to a point in the sky comparable to the sun's position at 2:00 p.m., he told Custer, "Before that time Black Eagle and the other chiefs accompanying him will be here; and", indicating sunset, "by that time, the village will arrive."[41]

Satanta, however, was less certain. Lone Wolf was not Dohasen and did not command the instant obedience as had the late paramount chief. Observing Satanta as he waited, Lieutenant Colonel Horace Moore of the Nineteenth Kansas wrote:

He would wrap his blanket around himself and come out and sit down by the side of the tent, then swaying back and forth, chant the most doleful and monotonous death-song. Then stooping over he would scoop up sand and dirt and put it into his mouth. Then he would go around to the south and west side of the tent and, shading his eyes with his hand, would sweep the horizon to discover if possible the approach of his people.[42]

The impact of Sheridan's threat on the chiefs is clearly apparent, but the impact on the rest of the Kiowas is questionable. Satanta and Lone Wolf were not popular, and their prestige was diminishing with the split of the Kiowas into definite peace and war factions. In the 1930s when Colonel Nye compiled his monumental history of Fort Sill, surviving Kiowas told him Gray Goose did not mention a possible hanging but instead told them they would receive large quantities of free rations if they arrived at Fort Cobb by Sheridan's deadline. "They state that if they had known that Satanta and Lone Wolf would be hanged, they would not have come in at all," Nye wrote.[43]

Whatever their motive, on the following morning several Kiowa chiefs arrived with assurances that their bands were on the way. This mollified Sheridan to some extent, and two days later Black Eagle arrived with all of the main body except for Kicking Bird, who disliked Satanta and Lone Wolf and, at this stage of their relationship, wasn't particularly interested in what happened to them. Their arrival occurred later than Lone Wolf's prediction and was not within Sheridan's deadline, but it was soon enough to satisfy the military authorities. "There are at least three Indians here now to one white soldier," Private Spotts observed, and the Indians were ordered not to camp within a mile of the troops. In addition to the normal contingent of guards, the military camp was surrounded by a double line of pickets.

Satanta's family received permission to pass through the military lines and set up camp facing the prison tent. According to Custer's account, which is disputed by the modern Kiowa elders, Satanta had four wives who erected their respective lodges on a quadrilateral plan. Ever appreciative of Indian women, Custer described the wives as "all young and buxom, and each was sufficiently like the others in appearance to have enabled the lot to pass as sisters...." Each had a baby in a cradleboard on her back; the infants were approximately the same age. In single file the women approached the tent where Satanta waited seated on a buffalo robe. He reached out to each wife, who handed over her cradleboard so he could hold and kiss the baby while the mother stroked his face and shoulders, humming softly to herself. No one said a word the entire time. Custer was moved by the scene.[44]

During the weeks that followed, Gray Goose acted as courier between the two chiefs and the tribe and often hung around the military camp to be close to Satanta. He became friends with Custer, who learned Gray Goose was an excellent shot with a rifle and took him out beyond the boundaries of the camp for target practice, a sport which Custer felt was "a much more agreeable mode of testing our skill as marksmen than by using each other as a target."

Satanta considered Gray Goose the best shot in the Kiowa nation and was pleased, but he was disappointed to learn his son had come off second best against Custer and suggested possible reasons. Although Satanta was certain Gray Goose's shooting would improve as time passed, each target practice ended the same way and Satanta finally decided Custer had a better weapon. To even the handicap, Custer suggested that they trade weapons the next day.

When he handed his rifle to Gray Goose, Custer noticed that the Indian inspected the trigger, sights and action with the expertise of an experienced marksman and worried that this time the boy might beat him. It was a matter of prestige for both contestants, especially since Custer believed the way to keep Indians in line was to impress them with the U.S. military's superiority in marksmanship, horsemanship and the other skills of a warrior to which the Indians attached so much importance. The outcome was the same, however, and Satanta finally conceded that the soldier was a better shot.[45]

Chapter 7
"Peace on the Reservations; War Off of Them"

While the Indian tribes awaited the government's decision on their future, and while Satanta and Lone Wolf awaited Sheridan's decision on theirs, the general himself was pondering his base of operations. From a strategic standpoint Fort Cobb was ideally situated, centrally located in the favorite winter quarters of the Southern Plains tribes. Those tribes, however, had been largely defeated and were now waiting to be relocated among the reservations. The weather had deteriorated, and heavy rains had turned the military camp at Cobb into a bog; the soldiers were filthy. The Indian ponies had eaten the prairie grass for miles around, the forage contractor had not arrived, and the army horses were dying of starvation. Sheridan determined to relocate to a site more suitable geographically, if not strategically.

On December 27 an expedition consisting of Colonel Benjamin Grierson of the Tenth Cavalry, Hazen, Forsyth, Major Woodward, Captain J.W. Clous and correspondent Keim set out to reconnoiter the area, and after several days they reported a site to the west on a plateau near Medicine Bluff and Mount Scott. Sheridan was pleased with the choice, and on January 8, 1869, the first stake was driven for a new post which would replace both Fort Cobb and Fort Arbuckle. Located on the site of an old Wichita Indian encampment, the post was initially called Camp Wichita; within a year, it was to become Fort Sill.[1] The agency and tribes remained at Fort Cobb until the soldiers were settled in at the new post.

Meanwhile a large amount of annuity goods had accumulated at Fort Cobb under the terms of the Medicine Lodge Treaty, and December 30 had been designated for distribution. Early that morning the warriors and their families came in; the chiefs were in charge of distribution under the watchful eyes of the military officers. Despite the good intentions of the government commissioners at Medicine Lodge, it was obvious nothing had been done to wipe out the corruption of the system. Describing the scene, Keim wrote:

> The goods consisted of the following articles for males: a suit of black shoddy clothes, price paid by the government, thirteen dollars. Value nothing, labor excepted. Hats, red flannel shirts, case-knives[,] paint, red flannel in piece, looking-glasses, course and fine-toothed combs. For the women, calico, red flannel in piece, stockings, awls, fine combs and course needles. Tobacco for both sexes....A boy of six years was often the recipient of pantaloons large enough for a three hundred pounder. The contractor must have had a diabolical idea of the physical development of a red juvenile....The next day most of the articles found their way to the tent of the Indian trader, who gave sugar in exchange.[2]

There was absolutely nothing in the distribution that was of any practical use to the Indians and, as Keim noted, worthless goods had been sold to the government at extravagant prices.

* * *

Once the soldiers were settled in at the new camp to the west, the Indians were transferred. Satanta and Lone Wolf, who had been confined in the center of the Seventh Cavalry's camp, moved with the regiment, and Sheridan now had to decide what to do with the two chiefs. In December Sherman had suggested hanging them and Sheridan was willing to oblige, but if he hanged them he would have to hang every Indian whom he considered guilty of kidnapping and murder. As Nye later noted, this would have virtually exterminated the Kiowas. It was more practical to liberate the chiefs with a blunt warning that next time he would make good on his threats.

On February 15 Sheridan sent for Satanta and Lone Wolf and told them he knew all about their depredations, that there was no use denying them, and that he intended to put a stop to them. The chiefs were expected to use all their influence to persuade their warriors to cease raiding.

Satanta said little other than to assure Sheridan of his cooperation. Lone Wolf, more eloquent, gave a long oration that impressed Sheridan in spite of his dislike for the two Indians. That night he ordered the guard removed from their tent and, after a second conference with Satanta, Lone Wolf and the Comanche Chief Horseback, told them they were free to leave.[3] Sheridan was not at all certain he had done the right thing, and before the year ended, wrote Sherman, "I shall always regret...that I did not hang these Indians; they had deserved it many times; and I shall also regret that I did not punish the whole tribe when I first met them."[4]

A few days after Satanta's release, his son Gray Goose received a serious gunshot wound, the result of a romantic misadventure. Gray Goose (whom Keim called "Young Satanta") apparently had fallen in love with the wife of a leading warrior. Although the woman returned his feelings, she kept her distance for fear of a flogging by the husband. Finally Gray Goose decided to force the issue and began demanding the husband give her a divorce. During one of these confrontations an argument erupted. The frightened woman ran to take refuge with Satanta, Gray Goose right behind her with the husband close at his heels. Gray Goose's mother Zone-ty intervened, berating the boy in front of everyone and calling him a fool. Gray Goose drew his pistol and shot himself, although it is uncertain whether he did so accidentally or intentionally.

The badly wounded boy was taken to a medicine lodge where his father and the priests attended him. According to Keim:

> Satanta performed those usual acts of medicinal liberality, such as making a present of lodges and

ponies promiscuously, to invite the kind interposition of the Great Spirit as a response to his generosity.
Three medicine men were employed to exercise [*sic*]
the spirits of evil. Drumming and shouting and pow-
wowing were kept up without interruption for hours,
to drive out the bullet and keep away the spirits of
death.[5]

The next morning, Satanta visited the military headquarters
and told Sheridan what had happened. The general offered to
send a surgeon.

"No," Satanta replied. "The red man's medicine man must
try first; then the white man's. If white man first, then medicine
man say, if die, bad medicine. Our medicine man no good.
White man much good."

Privately, Satanta would have preferred the immediate
attention of an army surgeon over the chantings of the medicine
men, but the dignity of the Kiowa nation required that he give
his own people a chance. When they had practiced long
enough to satisfy Satanta of the futility of their rituals, he sent
for the surgeon, under whose treatment Gray Goose recovered.[6]

* * *

The inauguration of General U.S. Grant as president of the
United States in March 1869 was to affect Satanta and the other
Southern Plains Indians profoundly for the next several years,
for it heralded the controversial new "Peace Policy" toward the
Indian nations. This policy did not originate with Grant but was
rather the culmination of a complex, often independent series
of actions by the military, congress and religious groups. A
major concern was to insure the Indians received the full
measure allocated by treaty and to wipe out the corruption and
controversy which, as has been seen with the Fort Cobb
distribution, still permeated the Indian Bureau under the patronage system.

Even before Sheridan's expedition to the Washita, and
while congress was considering a bill to transfer the Indians

from the jurisdiction of the Department of the Interior to the War Department, the Orthodox Society of Friends—the Quakers—appointed a committee to discuss solutions to the problem. They believed that they, like William Penn whose honest dealings with the Pennsylvania tribes had maintained peace in the white settlements there, could inspire the plains tribes toward peace by example. In December 1868 this Friends Committee petitioned congress to allow it to assume jurisdiction of the agencies in the Indian Territory. The following spring, after his inauguration, Grant agreed to accept nominations for Indian agents.

Grant had an ulterior motive for working with the Quakers. On March 3, 1869, congress had approved the Army Reduction Act which cut the existing forty-five regiments of infantry to twenty-five. This created a surplus of officers and, on May 7, under an 1834 act of congress which allowed demobilized officers to replace civilian political appointees as Indian superintendents and agents, the army detached nine field grade officers and fifty-nine captains and lieutenants with orders to report to the Commissioner of Indian Affairs. According to General Sherman, who had been given his fourth star and who had succeeded Grant as commanding general of the army, it was "undoubtedly a change for the better, but most distasteful to members of Congress, who looked to these appointments as part of their proper patronage."[7]

Congress retaliated by approving a bill which cancelled the commission of any military officer who served in a civil capacity. Informed by some members of congress that this was deliberately intended to prevent the appointment of qualified military personnel to agency posts, President Grant replied, "Gentlemen, you have defeated my plan of Indian management; but you shall not succeed in *your* purpose, for I will divide these appointments up among the religious churches, with which you dare not contend."

Accordingly, army officers were relieved of agency posts, and the various superintendencies were divided among the Quakers, Methodists, Catholics, Episcopalians, Presbyterians and other denominations.[8] The Quakers were given the superintendency over the agencies of Kansas and the Indian Territory.

Grant was blunt in his reasons for removing management of the Indians from congressional patronage. Ever since the federal government was established, he said,

> the management of the original inhabitants of this continent—the Indians—has been a subject of embarrassment and expense, and has been attended with continuous robberies, murders, and wars....I do not hold either legislation or the conduct of the whites who come most in contact with the Indian blameless for these hostilities. The past, however, can not be undone, and the question must be met as we now find it. I have attempted a new policy toward these wards of the nation (they can not be regarded in any other light than as wards)...which I hope will be attended ultimately with great success.[9]

In implementing their part of the president's plan, the Quakers declared they would recommend as candidates for superintendent and agents only those who were "deeply imbued with the love of Christ, and who feel willing to accept the position from Christian and not from mere mercenary motives." The agents, especially, were to be "men of sound judgment and ready tact in managing such business as will necessarily claim their attention." A key requirement was a practical knowledge of agriculture and farm management, as the government hoped to convert the nomadic tribes into sedentary farmers. The agents were also expected to be competent in administering the government's money.[10]

Enoch Hoag of Muscatine, Iowa, was named superintendent of the Friends' agencies. Headquartered in Lawrence, Kansas, he was responsible for nine agencies in Kansas and the Territory serving a population of some seventeen thousand Indians. The various agents were to report quarterly to Hoag who, in turn, would answer to the Commissioner of Indian Affairs. One of the agents, who were all nominated by the Friends Committee and confirmed by the Senate, was Lawrie Tatum, an Iowa farmer who first learned of his appointment in a newspaper article. Assessing his new responsibilities, Tatum wrote:

My appointment was for the Kiowas and Comanches, who were wild, blanket Indians, and the
Wichita and affiliated bands, who were partially
civilized, some of them wearing citizens [*i.e.*, white]
clothes, all located in the southwestern part of the
Indian territory....Those in the southwestern part of
the territory were still addicted to raiding in Texas,
stealing horses and mules, and sometimes committing other depredations, and especially was this the
case with the Kiowas and Comanches. They were
probably the worst Indians east of the Rocky Mountains....

I knew little of the duties and responsibilities
devolving upon an Indian agent. But after considering the subject as best I could in the fear of God, and
wishing to be obedient to Him, it seemed right to
accept this appointment.[11]

Tatum was late middle aged. He was completely bald on
top with tufts of gray hair on either side, prompting the Indians
to call him "Bald Headed Agent." Although later in life he grew
a beard along the line of his cheek and chin, at this time he was
clean shaven. While deeply religious, he was not a fanatic and
did not feel bound to the Friends' Covenant if his conscience
and common sense dictated otherwise. His Quaker pacifism
did not contain the animosity toward the military which was
characteristic among Friends of this period, and he viewed the
army as a partner in his cause rather than an adversary. His
humble facade concealed an unbreakable will and iron nerves.

On July 1, 1869, Tatum formally assumed control of the
new agency, located about two miles from the military post of
Fort Sill and the headquarters for Colonel Grierson's Tenth
Cavalry. A few weeks later the agency was inspected by John
Butler and Achilles Pugh of Ohio, members of a subcommittee
of the Executive Committee of Friends on Indian Affairs who
had been sent to oversee the establishment of the agencies.
After visiting with Tatum and examining his progress, they
reported more correctly than they ever could have imagined
that, "we had the right man in the right place." They also
attended a council between the Indian chiefs and the members

of a presidential commission which was preparing to depart
after turning the agency over to the Quakers. In that council,
Butler and Pugh met Satanta who, they reported,

> made two speeches, which were said to be charac-
> teristic of the man, who is a daring and restless man.
> He said that "he took hold of that part of the white
> man's road that was represented by the breech-load-
> ing gun [which the government issued to the Indians
> for hunting], but did not like the ration of corn; it hurt
> his teeth." He also said, "The good Indian, he that
> listens to the white man, got nothing. The inde-
> pendent Indian was the only one that was re-
> warded." They wanted arms and ammunition.

Satanta was voicing a complaint often heard from agents
and Indians alike. As part of its Peace Policy, the government
had reversed Agent Leavenworth's practice of assisting peaceful Indians and withholding rations to those who were raiding.
Instead, the Indians who raided against each other or against
the white settlements received guns, ammunition, rations and
other goods in an effort to bribe them toward peace; but once
they accepted the reservations and settled down, they were
ignored, forgotten, and often allowed to starve.

The commissioners, however, refused Satanta's demand for
weapons and advised him that the Indians would be protected
as long as they remained on the reservation. If they left, they
were on their own. As Tatum noted, "It was peace on the
Reservations; it was war off of them. If they left the Reservations
without leave they would be punished." The commissioners
reminded Satanta that the buffalo passed through the reservation twice a year, so the Indians would have no trouble hunting
without leaving the reserve.[12]

* * *

The Indians were quieter than usual in 1869, although there
were some raids into frontier counties of north Texas such as
Jack, Parker and Palo Pinto. In his annual report to the committee, Tatum said he believed the chiefs were making an honest

*Lawrie Tatum, Kiowa-Comanche agent. (Courtesy Archives &
Manuscript Division of the Oklahoma Historical Society)*

effort to control the young warriors. But, he added, the chiefs
were no more able to control the warriors than established law
enforcement was able to prevent crime in white society.

One of the problems was the government's insistence on
buying peace with larger issues of annuity goods to hostile
bands than to those who remained friendly. As Tatum noted,
"They repeatedly told me that when they behaved well they
got but a small amount of goods, and the only way to get a large
amount was to go on the war path a while, kill a few white
people, steal a good many horses and mules, and then make a

Colonel Benjamin Grierson. (Courtesy National Archives.)

treaty, and they would get a large amount of presents and a liberal supply of goods for that fall." A perfect example was the annuity for 1869, a year of relative peace, which was only one-fourth of the amount for the previous year. The explanation for the shortage was that the balance had been charged against the tribes as reparations for raids prior to the Medicine Lodge Treaty. Coupled with the short annuity was the failure of the Indians as farmers. Not accustomed to produce, they ate corn, vegetables and melons before they were ripe and many became ill.[13]

The Fort Sill Agency in 1871. (Courtesy Fort Sill Museum, Oklahoma)

Perhaps because of the short rations, Colonel Grierson permitted the Kiowas, Comanches and Apaches to move up the Washita Valley to hunt buffalo at the beginning of September. About three weeks later the Comanche Chiefs Mow-Way and Ten Bears came in for rations and stopped by Fort Sill, where they told the military authorities "a considerable sickness" had broken out in the Indian camps. Some had already died, and Satanta and Fishermore, the Kiowa herald, were said to have been among them. [14]

Satanta, of course, was very much alive. Nevertheless, the quiet year of 1869 was not a good one for the Indians, and Tatum expected trouble in 1870. Consequently, he recommended a return to the policy of issuing a large amount of goods when the tribes behaved, and withholding them when they were hostile. In addition, he and Grierson agreed to shut down the market for stolen livestock by prohibiting traders or citizens from purchasing horses and mules from the Indians. "This prohibition makes it more difficult for the well disposed Indians to procure the necessaries of life," Tatum said, "but under the circumstances we think it best. While the Indians have an open market to sell horses, many of them will steal them to supply the market." [15]

Despite the prohibition, the Kiowas still wanted livestock. On January 11, 1870, Satanta attacked a herd of Texas cattle on the trail about forty miles south of Camp Supply, driving off the stock and stealing all the supplies from the trail boss and crew. Kicking Bird arrived in time to prevent the Texans from being massacred and then met with Major M.H. Kidd, who had taken four companies of cavalry from Camp Supply to hunt for Satanta. Kicking Bird assured the major that the Kiowas would settle down.

The raid caused consternation both among the soldiers at Fort Sill and the personnel at the Kiowa-Comanche Agency. [16] Carefully watching the tribes, Tatum noticed that by spring they had grown "restless and uneasy." Those who had raised crops the year before abandoned their plots. "They told me...that the next spring they would go to work at planting and cultivating their land. I believe they were aware that there was going to be trouble this summer." [17]

The Kiowas began raiding as soon as the grass was high

enough for their ponies, and the Sun Dance that May signalled the start of a particularly vicious summer. The new depredations began in the immediate vicinity of Fort Sill where two men were shot, one of them fatally, not two hundred yards from the agency office. The same morning another party killed and scalped a man six miles away. Horses were stolen from the agency and from the corrals of Fort Sill itself.

Reacting immediately, Tatum ordered rations withheld from the Indians until the stolen stock was returned. Then, realizing his situation had become dangerous, he called a meeting of the Quakers assigned to the agency and told them to decide for themselves whether they should remain. Everyone left except Tatum and Josiah and Lizzie Butler, teachers at the agency school.[18]

It wasn't long before the raids spilled over into Texas. In early June a Professor Roessler, geologist from the Interior Department, left Fort Richardson with an escort of Sixth Cavalry and several citizens of Jacksboro and Weatherford to investigate reported copper deposits about a hundred miles to the northwest. As the party neared its destination, it was attacked and a soldier and two civilians killed.

On June 2 a Kiowa raiding party killed the mail driver between Fort Richardson and Fort Griffin and carried off the mules and mail sacks. On July 12 this same band cornered a detachment of Sixth Cavalry along the Little Wichita River, pinning them down for four hours and sending them back to Fort Richardson badly mauled.

Surprisingly, the raid on the mail driver and against the soldiers on the Little Wichita was led by Kicking Bird. His growing pacifism had raised questions about his courage and his abilities as a warrior. If he was to maintain his prestige—if he was to remain a positive force for peace—he had to lead a raid to show that his conciliatory position was based on conviction rather than cowardice.[19]

The Indians at the Fort Sill Agency were now completely out of control. The Comanche chief White Horse, who had organized the raid on the Fort Sill corrals, led a foray into Montague County, Texas, where his warriors killed a settler named Gottleib Koozier and carried his wife and children into captivity. In the same foray, they kidnapped a boy named

Martin Kilgore.[20]

The Texas press howled, and laid the blame for frontier trouble on the federal government and the Quakers. The Austin *Weekly State Journal* fumed:

> The Indian Bureau reports that the gentle savages on the [Fort Sill] reserve, are making satisfactory strides in civilization, and all that is needed to make them unfledged cherubims [*sic*] are a few more grants and appropriations of money.
>
> Apropos to this, we learn that a number of these benign creatures who had been absent on a harmless (?) hunting trip to the frontiers of Texas, had returned to the agency *wounded*. Doubtless medicines, surgeons, and nurses will be hurried to them from Washington by express....
>
> The people of Jack, Parker and Montague counties, who have lost stock and horses, and can point to the new made graves of settlers, killed and scalped by these protoges of civilization, have a very keen and painful sense of these savage visits made by the Quaker pets on the government reservation, who are supplied by the United States with arms, clothing and rations, and who make war on the citizens of Texas, carrying back to their homes, on the reserve, scalps, prisoners and horses.[21]

Although it summed up the attitude in Washington reasonably well, the editorial was hardly fair to Tatum or Colonel Grierson at Fort Sill. They were doing the best they could to defuse an impossible situation, within the constraints imposed by the government and within the restrictions of their own consciences. Grierson could at least back his position with troops; Tatum, on the other hand, was prohibited by his religious beliefs from violence, either offensive or defensive. His only weapons were nerve and force of character.

The Indians began learning of the extent of his nerve and character on July 4 when two Kiowas came to the agency to see if the Comanches might draw rations. Tatum told them rations would be issued only if the animals stolen from the agency and from the corrals at Fort Sill were returned. Six days later he was told that several chiefs had joined the hostile Quahadi band of Comanches, but that the others wanted to come in. He repeated his demand for the livestock, and the Indians replied that Kicking Bird was assembling the animals and would return them. Tatum said rations would be issued at that time, but would not include ammunition. He also decided to withhold half the allotment of sugar and coffee, two items the Indians most prized, as additional incentive for good behavior.[22]

While dealing with the tribes on rations, Tatum was also making serious efforts to locate white captives. One effort involved Dorothy Field, who had been carried off in Satanta's raid to the Menard area in 1864. In a letter to her husband, Tatum admitted he had no word on her but hoped to acquire information from the Apaches who were due in soon. On the other hand, he said that in obtaining other captives,

> I had but a few words with the Indians on the subject. I told them that they must bring them and deliver them to me before they got any more rations, and I would make them such presents as I saw proper. After they were delivered, I gave them one hundred dollars for each capture, thinking they would be less likely to kill their captives if they got some presents for them.

Tatum's "few words" amounted to a showdown with the Indians. White Horse's group, which included Satanta and Lone Wolf, had arrived at the agency on August 7, bringing thirty-seven mules, the Koozier family and Martin Kilgore. Tatum demanded their release, saying rations would be withheld until the Kiowas complied. He pointed out that the people of Texas were among those whose taxes paid for the rations, that the Indians had no business raiding against them, and that to the best of his knowledge, the only Texans who did them any harm were those who slipped into the reservation to peddle illegal whiskey.

Satanta and Lone Wolf scoffed at the threat, boasting of their depredations and expressing contempt for the Indians who cooperated with the government. During the argument, one Indian kept loading and unloading his rifle, another snapped arrows in his bow and a third whetted his knife. This war of nerves brought yet another rule from the tough Quaker. Henceforth, all weapons would be left outside the agency buildings.

Although he was unable to report any news of Mrs. Field, whom he erroneously believed was carried off the previous year, Tatum did recover the Koozier family and Kilgore.[23] Having ransomed them, however, Tatum reconsidered his position and decided he would no longer pay for captives, thereby rendering kidnapping raids uneconomical. "No one knew whether it would work well or not," he wrote. "But I thought it was right, and therefore the thing to do. In practice it worked grandly. I procured many captives...afterwards without paying a dollar. That treatment made no inducement for them to obtain captives, while paying for them was an inducement."

To back his new regulations, Tatum went so far as to borrow troops from Grierson on days when rations were to be issued. While at the agency, the soldiers functioned as a civil police force. Strictly speaking, the practice was within Quaker beliefs and did much to quieten the Indians, although Tatum was roundly criticized for it by Friends in the east who had no idea of the problems he faced.[24]

As cold weather approached, the raiding season ended and the plains grew quiet. On the reservation the Indians settled in for the winter, while the people of Texas flooded the army with demands for military intervention.

Chapter 8
The Warren Massacre

The year 1871 brought a new figure to the forefront of Kiowa-white affairs. His name was Maman-ti or Sky-Walker, and his title was *Do-ha-te*, a medicine man and prophet who lived, the Kiowas said, "in the shadows of the past." His gift of prophecy came through the Owl Spirit. In his divinations he would retreat into his lodge and pray and chant, then his followers would hear the faint rustle of an owl's wings and Maman-ti would emerge to foretell the outcome of a proposed raid or some other enterprise.

Although not a chief as such, Maman-ti was nevertheless a warlord, a planner and leader of battles. Unlike Satanta and the other war leaders, however, Maman-ti sought no particular prestige and was content merely to plan and lead, letting others take the credit. His standing was due to his great and terrible magic; but it was magic strictly controlled, both by covenants with the spirits and self-imposed restrictions. The Kiowas who knew him remembered him as tall and erect, a kind figure who was beloved and admired.[1]

Despite his standing among his own people, Maman-ti preferred to remain in the background in Kiowa dealings with whites, and few had heard of him. Little is known of him prior to the 1870s, and even now he is a mystery. In the summer of 1871, as the government and settlers were still recovering from the worst of his depredations, one army officer who met him described him as "a Kiowa Chief of some note (I am informed)."[2] With Maman-ti's sudden and unexplained entry into the mainstream of events, the 1871 raiding season started extraordinarily early, less than a month into the new year.

On January 24 Maman-ti and the war chief Quitan led a raid along the Salt Creek Prairie of Texas between old Fort Belknap and Fort Richardson, overtaking and killing four black teamsters. One of these victims, Britt Johnson, had negotiated the ransom and return of the captives from the raid into Young County in 1864. Amused by the kinky hair of the blacks, the Kiowas tossed their scalps back and forth until, tiring of the game, they threw the hair away as being too short to have any value.[3]

Satanta appears to have remained in the background during most of the early raids of 1871, but as the summer raiding season approached he grew restless. Lieutenant Myers recorded one incident at Fort Sill that was a portent of things to come:

> One day in April 1871, Satanta came stalking into the office of the Post adjt. [adjutant] at Fort Sill, walked up and put his brawny hand upon the shoulder of the Adjutant who was busily writing at a desk, not having noticed his entrance, [and] accosted him with "Where big Chief?" (General Grierson).
>
> "No sabe" Sit down pointing to a chair—"how"?[4] continued the Adjutant[.]
>
> "No bueno!" [No good!] replied Satanta as he took the proffered chair where he sat for some time in silence watching the gliding pen of the Adjutant who betook himself to his writing again. "How long way, Big Chief?["]
>
> "Un poco tiempo"—mebby so—little while—be back. Take a cigar, Satanta.["]
>
> He mechanically extended his hand and took the cigar and the Adjutant again began his writing at which he continued a half hour or more having almost forgotten the presence of this great chief. Turning around to send an orderly to hunt the general, he [was] astonished to see that Satanta instead of smoking the cigar—of which he is very fond—had fallen into a reverie and was unconciously [sic] tearing it to pieces—his eyes fixed upon the floor.

Hello, Satanta! I'll send orderly—mebby so find "Big Chief." Hungry?

"No!" replied Satanta, "mebby so squaw—papoose, heap hungry—cold, heap agua [Spanish for water; Satanta meant rain]—

Want chuck-a-way (bread)[?]

"Ugh."

The Adjutant wrote him an order on the post baker for some few loaves of bread. The Adjutant saw that Satanta had something weighing heavily upon his mind, because his taciturn behavior [was] so unusual for him [,] and [the adjutant was] not feeling quite at ease at the desk unarmed with the terrible chief sitting as his back with quite a formidable magazine of weapons strapped around him and the orderly absent upon the errand he had just been sent[,] so he endeavored to engage the Indian in conversation But [*sic*] with little success, Satanta scarcely [speaking] any English and little Spanish—the Adjutant little Spanish, less Kiowa, and understood few signs so that [the] range of topics was not large, nor the conversation very animated. The Adjutant was so struck with the strange manner of Satanta, that when the General came in he called his attention to it—and suggested that the Indian might be meditating mischief.—After a while the Indian took his leave; and in the press of other important business the incident [was] slight.

That evening the probability of an Indian outbreak being discussed the circumstance recurred to the mind of the Adjutant and he mentioned it to a group of officers with the remark "I'll bet Satanta is going on a raid into Texas.["][5]

Although the Kiowas were already raiding into Texas, Satanta is not known to have become involved until mid-May when he joined a group of more than a hundred Kiowas, Kiowa-Apaches and Comanches who were camped on the North Fork of the Red River where, once again, the Do-ha-te Maman-ti prepared to lead them in a foray. Besides Maman-ti and Satanta, the group included old Satank, the chief Eagle Heart, and the teenaged subchief Big Tree.

Satank, who had pledged eternal friendship with the whites at Medicine Lodge, now burned with hatred for them. A year earlier his oldest son, also called Satank, had been killed on a raid into Texas, and the grief-stricken old man had almost committed suicide. As a constant reminder of his loss, he carried the bones of Young Satank wherever he went, carefully packed on a separate pony. The bones were with him now.[6]

Big Tree was about nineteen years old but, despite his youth, already had a record as an especially vicious war leader. In 1868 he had led a raid into Montague County, Texas, and created havoc for two days, killing several people and carrying women and children into captivity. Irritated by the crying baby of one of the women captives, Big Tree had pounded the infant's head with his pistol, then thrown the small body at the feet of its mother.[7]

Crossing the Red River between the sites of the modern towns of Vernon and Electra, the raiding party reached a place they called Skunk Headquarters because of the large number of skunks in the vicinity. Here they cached their blankets, saddles and all other non-essential supplies and left some young boys to guard them. This was to be a spectacular raid, one that the Texans would not soon forget, and they intended to travel lightly. Confident of capturing a large number of horses, they carried spare lariats and bridles and some of the men left their ponies at Skunk Headquarters, riding double or grasping the tails of other men's ponies and trotting behind.[8]

On May 17 they came to the Salt Creek Prairie in Young County, about half-way between Fort Belknap and Fort Richardson and a favorite spot for raiding because it was open country. Here the prairie's only features were a sandstone hill overlooking the Butterfield Trail, which ran between Belknap and Richardson, and another conical hill called Cox Mountain about three miles away. There was no cover except for a few trees at the base of the sandstone hill and a heavier stand of oak near the base of Cox Mountain. All the Indians had to do was wait for a potential victim to come along. There had already been many victims; an army officer had counted twenty-one graves a month earlier when the Fourth Cavalry passed along

Big Tree (Courtesy Archives & Manuscript Division of the Oklahoma Historical Society)

this road while transferring from Fort Concho to Fort Richardson.[9]

The Indians took a position along the sandstone hill, and that night Maman-ti went off alone and sat on the hillside to commune with the ancestor spirits. Soon the warriors heard the call of an owl and the rustle of its wings, indicating the ancestors had spoken.[10] The Do-ha-te returned to the others, raised his arms and announced:

> Tomorrow two parties of Tehannas [Texans, *i.e.*, whites] will pass this way. The first will be a small party. Perhaps we could overcome it easily. Many of you will be eager to do so. But it must not be attacked. The medicine forbids. Later in the day another party will come. This one may be attacked. The attack will be successful.[11]

At sunrise the Indians gathered to wait just behind the crest of the sandstone hill overlooking the trail. Shortly before noon, scouts positioned in the timber at the base of the hill saw some movement to the west and reported back to those on the hill. Presently a vehicle escorted by mounted outriders came into view. The warriors whispered excitedly among themselves. Some urged an attack but Maman-ti held fast; this was the first party of whites in his vision, and the vision had instructed him to allow it to pass. Perhaps the Do-ha-te was sincere in his vision, but he was also an experienced leader and no doubt observed that this party of whites was well organized and disciplined. Although it could probably be overwhelmed, the Indians would suffer severe losses.[12]

If Maman-ti guessed that this might be a military transport, he was correct; the vehicle was an ambulance and the passengers were General Sherman and Inspector General Randolph B. Marcy, two of the most senior officers of the army. They were en route to Fort Richardson as part of a general inspection tour to ascertain the accuracy of the constant reports coming into his office of Indian raids in Texas. So far Sherman was skeptical. Although he had heard reports of raiding during his trip, he personally had seen no evidence of any. Marcy was less sanguine; he had served on the frontier before the Civil War and was familiar with Indians from personal experience. He was impressed by what he saw as evidence of the devastation that had occurred in this part of the country since he had previously been in Texas.[13]

From their perch on the sandstone hill the Indians watched as Sherman passed, never realizing how close he had come to death that day. The rest of the day was without incident. The second party of whites failed to materialize, and Maman-ti began having trouble with some of the more impatient warriors who appeared ready to exercise the warriors' prerogative of striking out on their own. Eventually, however, he brought them under control and they continued to wait as May 18 dawned. Finally they saw a wagon train coming from the east, following the trail as it rounded Cox Mountain and entered the prairie. The ten wagons hauling corn to Fort Griffin were owned by Captain Henry Warren of Weatherford, Texas, who held a government freighting contract, and were led by wagonmaster Nathan S. Long.

The Indians watched excitedly as the train approached. Satanta had his bugle ready, waiting for Maman-ti to give him the word to signal the charge. When the train was in the middle of the prairie with no possible cover, Maman-ti motioned to Satanta who raised the bugle to his lips, but the Indians dashed down without waiting for the signal. Neither Big Tree nor the warrior Yellow Wolf remembered hearing the bugle but did recall the shriek of an eagle-bone whistle, also used by Indians to signal each other, and the tongue-rattling war chants of two women who accompanied the raiding party.[14] Each warrior was eager to prove his bravery by counting the first coup, to be the first to touch an enemy.

On the prairie the teamsters hurriedly pulled off the road and began to circle the wagons, but the Indians broke through the line before the circle was completed. Three or four teamsters were killed immediately and the rest jumped out of the wagons and hit the ground to open fire with their heavy rifles. Big Tree managed to count the first coup, Yellow Wolf the second. When Yellow Wolf turned to avoid the heavy gunfire, he saw the Comanche Or-dlee jump off his horse and charge the teamsters on foot, hoping to engage in hand-to-hand combat. One of the teamsters killed him, and another teamster was able to wound the Kiowa Chief Red Warbonnet in the thigh. The rifle fire was devastating, and the Indians pulled away and began riding in a circle around the wagons while the teamsters knelt under the wagons, firing through the spokes of the wheels.

The Apache Light-Haired Young Man, wounded in the knee, fell from his horse and bounced along the ground until two other warriors snatched him up and carried him away. Seven teamsters dashed from the circle of wagons, broke through the Indians and ran toward the timber at the base of

A fanciful woodcut purportedly by William Sidney Porter (later known as O. Henry) showing the death of Samuel Elliott during the Warren Wagon Train Massacre. Actually, Elliott was tied to a wagon tongue, rather than a wagon wheel, and roasted over a fire. (From Wilbarger, Indian Depredations in Texas.*)*

Cox Mountain. Several Indians gave chase and killed one of the teamsters only a short distance from the wagons and another just short of the timber. They let the other five go; the sky was growing dark, a storm was brewing, and they wanted to be in on the plunder back at the wagon train.

The remaining teamsters' gunfire began to decrease as the Indians continued to circle and fire into the wagons. Soon the train was quiet. The Indians continued to circle cautiously, fearing a trap but anxious to finish the work before the storm broke. The older warriors warned against moving in too soon.

Finally Hau-tau, a young warrior in his first fight, started toward the wagons, halting for a moment then starting forward again when nothing happened. Two Kiowa warriors, White Horse and Set-maunte, tried to hold him back but he dashed up to one of the wagons, touched it and shouted, "I claim this wagon, and all in it, as mine!"[15] Just then a wounded teamster, probably Samuel Elliott who was concealed in the wagon, threw off the cover and shot Hau-tau in the face. He fell backwards. The Indians who later told of the event declined to

General William Tecumseh Sherman
(Courtesy National Archives)

Colonel Ranald S. Mackenzie
(Courtesy Amon Carter Museum of
Western Art)

Post hospital at Fort Richardson, Texas, where General Sherman interviewed the
survivors of the Warren Massacre. (Author photo)

discuss the battle any further except to say they tore the train apart, but when the massacre site was discovered Elliott had been chained to a wagon tongue and roasted over a fire.

The Indians placed the body of the Comanche Or-dlee in a crevice in the side of the sandstone hill and piled rocks on top. The wounded men were tied to horses before the Indians started back north toward Skunk Headquarters and the Red River, driving more than forty mules captured from the train. As they moved out, the storm broke in full fury.[16]

At Fort Richardson General Sherman had received a delegation of the leading citizens of nearby Jacksboro, who presented him with a petition for relief. The petition pointed out that since January there had been twelve Indian-related deaths in Jack County, a county with a total population of less than six hundred. It also noted citizens "have been driven from their houses through fear and more than two thousand head of horses stolen from the citizens of the county." It concluded by asking Sherman's cooperation in protecting the area.[17] Although he listened politely, Sherman was still unconvinced.

About midnight two men, one badly wounded, appeared at the stables at Fort Richardson. They were two of the teamsters who had fled into the timber along Cox Mountain; the others were waiting at a nearby ranch where they had secured a horse to get the wounded man, Thomas Brazeal, to the fort.

Brazeal was carried to the post hospital and put to bed, but General Sherman was soon at his bedside listening to this first-hand account of an Indian massacre. Sherman ordered Colonel Ranald Mackenzie, whose Fourth Cavalry had recently relieved the Sixth Cavalry at Fort Richardson, to take a detail to the massacre scene and hunt down the Indians responsible.[18]

Only two months short of his thirty-first birthday, Mackenzie had already distinguished himself in his nine years as a soldier. After graduating first in his class at West Point in 1862, he had entered the Union Army and risen to the brevet rank of brigadier general before the war was over. He fought in the last action against General Robert E. Lee's Army of Northern Virginia, and General U.S. Grant later remarked, "I regarded Mackenzie as the most promising young officer in the army."[19] After the war he was assigned to the Texas frontier, where he commanded a black infantry regiment until the end of 1870 when he was named colonel of the Fourth Cavalry.[20]

The storm impeded Mackenzie's march to the massacre site. Streams were swollen and the mud so thick the soldiers often had to dismount and lead their horses.[21] They reached the scene about dark, and Mackenzie sent a brief note to Sherman saying, "statements concerning the wagon train are not exaggerated. Five mules lay dead around the wagon. The sergeant in charge of the detail, who was sent out in advance, found five men about the wagons with heads split open and badly mutilated."[22]

Examining the body of Samuel Elliott, Dr. Julius Patzki, the post surgeon, noted:

> One of the bodies was even more mutilated than the others, it having been found fastened with a chain to the pole of a wagon lying over a fire with the face to the ground, the tongue being cut out. Owing to the charred condition of the soft parts it was impossible to determine whether the man was burned before or after his death. The scalps of all but one [who was bald] were taken.[23]

A search of the area turned up the bodies of the two men killed while running toward Cox Mountain. Indian weapons scattered about were identified as Kiowa by Sergeant Miles Varily, a soldier with substantial frontier experience. Varily took charge of the burial detail. The earlier rain had been so heavy that the men digging the large burial pit had to stop and bail, but finally the bodies of the seven dead teamsters were placed in a wagon box and lowered into the ground. Several inches of water covered them as the soldiers filled in the grave. Only then did Mackenzie start after the Indians, but he had little to go by because the rain had obliterated the trail. Sherman had instructed him in such an event to continue on to Fort Sill, where the Indians might hopefully be located and the stolen livestock recovered. Acting on these instructions, Mackenzie turned north toward Sill.[24]

The massacre had completely altered Sherman's opinion of the Indian situation. "I do think the people of Texas have a right to complain," he wrote, "only their complaints are now against troops who are powerless, but should be against the Department [the Department of the Interior's Indian Bureau] that feeds and harbors these Indians when their hands are yet red with blood."[25] Because the tribes were under the jurisdiction of the Department of the Interior, he could not offer immediate military assistance; nevertheless, he accepted a petition charging that virtually all depredations in the vicinity were the work of reservation Indians from Fort Sill and forwarded it to the War Department. His inspection completed at Fort Richardson, Sherman departed for Sill where he hoped to be present when Mackenzie arrived and hoped even more that the Indians would be taken.[26]

The Indians, meanwhile, had reached the Big Wichita River where they constructed a crude boat for their wounded and plunder. The young Hau-tau was suffering terribly from screwworms which had infested the head wound inflicted by Elliott. The mules were swum across the river, and the able warriors also swam while pushing the boat.

Two Kiowas and two Mexican captives adopted into the tribe stayed behind to hunt a herd of buffalo which had come to the river. These four warriors had killed several of the animals and were skinning and butchering them when they were surprised by a scouting party from Fort Richardson. In the ensuing fight one of the Mexicans, whom the Kiowas called Tomasi, was killed and the others fled to join the main band. The soldiers took Tomasi's scalp and carried it back to Richardson, where they presented it to the adjutant, Lieutenant Robert Carter.[27]

Chapter 9
Arrest

At the Fort Sill Agency Lawrie Tatum was worried about the growing unrest on the reservation. Recently he had attended a council, between the Civilized Tribes and the Plains Indians at the Wichita Agency, at which the Cherokees and Creeks had urged the plains tribes to maintain the peace so long as the whites maintained it. The Cherokees and Creeks understood the true power of the federal government, which had uprooted and deported them from their eastern homelands a generation earlier, and they had emphasized that whatever affected one tribe affected Indians as a whole.

Responding for the Kiowas, Kicking Bird reiterated his preference for peace but added that his people would stand up to any white oppression. He suggested that the Civilized Tribes, which possessed more influence with the government, might persuade Washington to do more for the Kiowas.

Kicking Bird's interest in peace was not enough to offset the trouble brewing at Fort Sill, and Tatum saw a long and bloody summer ahead. On May 22 he wrote his committee:

> I think the Indians do not intend to commit depreda-
> tions here this summer, but from their actions and
> sayings they intend to continue their atrocities in
> Texas. I believe affairs will continue to get worse
> until there is a different course pursued with the
> Indians. I know of no reason why they should not be
> treated the same as white people for the same of-
> fence. It is not right to be feeding and clothing them,

and let them raid with impunity in Texas. Will the committee sustain me in having Indians arrested for murder, and turned over to the proper authorities of Texas for trial?[1]

Tatum's position was almost identical to General Hazen's in the days following Medicine Lodge, a position which Sheridan and Custer had nullified in blood on the Washita. Hazen had never been given the opportunity to put his belief into practice, but Tatum was to make such a decision on his own within twenty-four hours.

The following day, Tuesday May 23, General Sherman visited the agency, described the Warren massacre, and asked if Tatum knew of any Indians who might have been off the reservation. Tatum replied he was not surprised about the raid because the Kiowas and Comanches were completely out of control and "come and go as they please...." Likewise, there was no question in the minds of the Quakers as to who was responsible. As the agency teacher Josiah Butler noted in his diary, "It is believed that Satanta is leading the raid as he is absent from the reservation."

Based on the information he received at the agency, Sherman reported:

> I am certain that Satanta was with the party that attacked the wagon train near Fort Richardson, and I hope that Genl. McKenzie [sic] will track him to his camp. Meanwhile I advise that the Indian Agent here be instructed to issue supplies only to Indians present, that when there is proof of murder and robbery, the actual perpetrators be surrendered to the Governor of Texas for trial and punishment. A few examples will have a salutary effect.

To General John Pope, who had succeeded Sheridan as commander of the Department of the Missouri at Fort Leavenworth, Sherman wrote, "The Agent, Mr. Tatum, admits that according to information, Old Satanta with a large party of Indians is now off in Texas. I hope MacKenzie [sic] will catch and destroy the whole band."[2]

Unaware of the storm about to break, the Kiowas returned to their villages on the reservation. Hau-tau's death from the screwworm infestation of his head wound brought their death toll to three, the others being Or-dlee, killed during the Warren fight, and Tomasi killed in the fight with the scouts on the Big Wichita. These losses, however, were more than compensated by the plunder and prestige gained from the raid, and the Indians were pleased with themselves. Maman-ti, meanwhile, went his own way, apparently willing to let credit or blame for the raid fall where it would.[3]

On May 27 the Indians moved their camps close to the agency to draw rations; it was Saturday and they wanted to draw the entire issue at once because they knew Tatum would not work on Sunday. Most of the bands grouped together on the flats of Cache Creek below the agency, but Kicking Bird and Stumbling Bear were on bad terms with the other chiefs and situated their camps apart from the rest. About 4:00 p.m. Satanta, Satank, Big Tree, Eagle Heart, Lone Wolf, Kicking Bird and several others went to the agency and were told Tatum wanted to see them in his office with Matthew Leeper, his interpreter. Satanta took the initiative, saying he had a "Big Speech." But before he could begin, Tatum cut him off to describe the Warren massacre and ask if they knew who was involved.[4] Pointing to himself, Satanta replied,:

> Yes, I led that raid. I have heard that you have stolen a large portion of our annuity goods and given them to the Texans. I have repeatedly asked you for arms and ammunition, which you have not furnished, and made many other requests which have not been granted. You do not listen to my talk. The white people are preparing to build a railroad through our country, which will not be permitted. Some years ago, we were taken by the hair and pulled here close to the Texans where we have to fight. But we have cut loose now and are all going with the Cheyennes to the Antelope Hills. When Gen. Custer was here two or three years ago, he arrested me and kept me in confinement several days [It was actually several months]. But arresting Indians

"Santata's[sic] boastful harangue before the general," an imaginative 19th century drawing showing Satanta (center, arm raised) lecturing Sheridan. (From Wild Life on the Plains and the Horrors of Indian Warfare) .

is played out now and is never to be repeated. On account of these grievances, I took a short time ago about one hundred of my warriors, with the Chiefs Satank, Eagle Heart, Big Tree, Big Bow and Fast Bear, and went to Texas, where we captured a train not far from Fort Richardson, killed seven of the men, and drove off about forty-one mules.

At this point Satank interrupted, sharply ordering Satanta in Kiowa to stop mentioning names. Continuing, Satanta said:

Three of my men were killed, but we are willing to call it even. If any other Indian comes here and claims the honor of leading the party, he will be lying to you, for I did it myself.[5]

The comment that he had led the raid drew quick assent from Satank, Big Tree, Eagle Heart and the others, who apparently understood better than Satanta that there was more behind Tatum's interest than idle curiosity. Why then did Satanta prepare such a trap for himself and walk into it? Colonel Nye, who knew the last surviving Kiowas involved in the raid and who probably understood the classic mentality of the plains warrior as well as any man of the twentieth century, points out the key phrase was Satanta's claiming "the *honor* of leading" the raid. Nye writes:

He saw no disgrace in waging war against the Tehannas [Texans], or anyone else. It had been his life profession. On many occasions he and others had entered army posts with white captives for sale. These prisoners were prima facie evidence that murder had been committed. The whites knew this, and Satanta was aware that they knew it. Many times had he bragged to Hazen and others about his exploits. Yet he had received pay, in cash, for these captives— not punishment. Why should he think it would be otherwise on this particular occasion?[6]

The difference, which Satanta for the moment failed to grasp, was that *this* agent had made up his mind to put a stop to the raids and punish those responsible. The agent's resolve was backed by the commanding general of the United States Army, who was prepared to use the full power of the government.

To Tatum these chiefs were guilty of first degree murder; if he did nothing, he would become an accessory. Telling his staff to continue with the issue of rations, he went to the post at Fort Sill where he submitted a written request for Grierson to arrest Satanta, Eagle Heart, Big Tree, Big Bow and Fast Bear for murder.

Satanta had a valid point when he protested the shortage of rations, but he erred in accusing Tatum. It had been the Indian Bureau which had ordered the decrease in the already inadequate allowance of food, again charging the difference against the tribes as an indemnity for the raids prior to the Medicine Lodge Treaty. Sherman and Grierson, however, were not interested in moral positions; they saw the rations as a means of enticing the chiefs onto the post where they could be cornered and arrested. Tatum was sent back to the agency with the post interpreter, Horace Jones, to tell the Kiowas that the agent merely followed government orders in issuing short rations. If the Indians wanted to present their case, they could come to the post and meet personally with the commanding general of the army, who might then order Tatum to reinstate the full issue. Satanta, Satank and several other chiefs took the bait and followed Tatum and Jones back to the fort.[7]

Now one of the most important U.S. military installations, Fort Sill in 1871 was constructed around a quadrangle consisting of a rectangular parade ground with a row of officers' houses on one side, enlisted barracks on the opposite side, and administrative and utility buildings at either end. Radiating out from the quadrangle were various support structures such as stables, storage buildings, commissary and quarters for the laundresses. To the right of the officers' row, beyond the quadrangle, was a stone corral. The officer's houses, with Grierson's in the middle, all had open front porches. The modern post has preserved this part of the old post much as it appeared at the time, except for landscaping.

The officers waited on Grierson's front porch facing the parade ground, while the colonel positioned units of the Tenth

Cavalry, a black regiment which the unprejudiced Grierson was building into an elite combat unit. The blacks were unimpressed by the Indian mutilation of enemy corpses and the prolonged torture of prisoners which gave white soldiers an almost mystical terror and loathing of Indians. In the field the black regiment relentlessly hounded Indian raiding parties, and a vicious mutual hatred was already developing between the two races. The Indians' profound respect for black fighting ability gave Grierson a psychological advantage.

Several companies of the Tenth were told to saddle and mount but to remain in the stables where they would be concealed by the stone walls of the corral. Grierson positioned fifteen soldiers in line facing the porch, behind which was a second line of army officers and about twenty-five or thirty armed civilians. A squad of soldiers was placed behind closed shutters in the front room of the Grierson house. If a bugle sounded, a dismounted company standing off to the side was to send one platoon behind the bank of Cache Creek, covering the rear of the house, while a second platoon was to form an additional line in front to cover the porch. Two mounted companies would form lines to the left and right of the house so that the Indians would have to pass between them if they tried to escape. All women and children were confined to quarters with doors and windows shut.[8]

Sherman was pacing the front porch when Satanta dismounted and strutted up, accompanied by Jones, Tatum, Satank and about twenty other warriors. He said he had heard there was a Big Chief from Washington and indicated he had come to size him up. As Satanta went up the steps to the porch, Tatum excused himself and started to leave. His hasty departure drew Satanta's attention to the unusual number of officers, orderlies and soldiers present, and he started back toward his horse. Grierson's orderly drew his pistol, pointed it at him, and motioned for him to go back to the porch and sit. "From that moment, he was a prisoner," Sherman commented.[9]

As Satanta settled down on the porch, Kicking Bird and Stumbling Bear rode up. Satanta started down to meet them but was prodded back up the steps at bayonet point. The other chiefs went up on the porch and sat down, and without a break in his pacing Sherman told Kicking Bird to return to the camps and bring in the principal chiefs.

"Let me go," Satanta volunteered.

"No, Satanta will not leave!" Sherman replied.

As Kicking Bird rode off Satanta called after him, "Tell everybody to come."

Stumbling Bear later admitted he believed they were being assembled so the soldiers could conveniently massacre them. He kept these thoughts to himself, however, and remarked to Satanta, "I notice that when you stepped off the porch, the soldiers started to use their guns on you. What's the matter?"

"They aren't treating me right," Satanta complained.

When Kicking Bird returned, Sherman asked who had been responsible for the Warren massacre and who had thrown burning corn on the bodies of the victims. After Jones translated Sherman's questions, Satanta again described the raid, almost exactly as Brazeal, the wounded teamster, had recalled it to Sherman in the hospital at Fort Richardson. Satanta omitted only the burning of Samuel Elliott. According to the Indians present, Kicking Bird mumbled for quiet but Satanta looked at him contemptuously, pounded his own chest and said, "I'm the man." Sherman then advised Satanta that he, Satank, Big Tree and Eagle Heart (whom Sherman confused with Black Eagle) were under arrest and would be extradited to Texas for trial for murder.[10]

Satanta then changed his story and said he had not participated except to blow his bugle. Reporting the conversation in his journal, General Marcy wrote that Satanta said that his

> young men wanted to have a little fight and to go take a few white scalps, and he was prevailed upon to go with them merely to show them how to make war, but that he stood back during the engagement and merely gave directions. He added that some time ago the whites had killed three of his people and wounded four more, so that this little affair made the account square, and that he was now ready to commence anew—cry quits. General Sherman told him it was a very cowardly thing for one hundred warriors to attack twelve poor teamsters who did not pretend to know how to fight. That if he desired to have a

battle the soldiers would be ready to meet him at any time.

Sherman restated his position that the chiefs involved would be sent to Texas for trial. Unnerved at the thought of ropes around their necks, choking off their windpipes and trapping their souls inside their decaying bodies, the chiefs asked to be shot right then, but Sherman believed "that is too good a fate for them."[11]

At this Satanta flew into a rage, threw off his blanket and grabbed his revolver, saying he would rather die on the spot than be sent to Texas. Sherman gave a quick order and the shutters of the house flew open to reveal the soldiers of the Tenth, their carbines levelled at the Indians. This brought a quick change of heart and Satanta called, "Don't shoot! Don't shoot!"

To Kicking Bird the entire meeting was becoming an affront to the honor of the Kiowa nation. Badly as he hated Satanta, Kicking Bird was not going to stand by and see any fellow Kiowa warrior carried off in chains to die at the end of a Texas rope. Now he cited his own record as peace chief, which he said was well known to Grierson and Tatum. For these efforts he felt the government owed him, and now he was calling in the debt by demanding the release of Satanta, Satank and the others whom Sherman wanted. To even the score, Kicking Bird said he would personally return Henry Warren's captured mules or the equivalent value.

Sherman acknowledged Kicking Bird's role in Kiowa affairs, saying,

> The President has heard of you. He knows your name, and has written about you. We all appreciate what you have done. But today is my day, and what I say will have to go; I want those three [sic] men. I am going to take them with me as prisoners to the place where they killed those boys. There they will be hung and the crime will be paid for.

Losing his temper, Kicking Bird replied, "You have asked for those men to kill them. But they are my people, and I am

not going to let you have them. You and I are going to die right
here."

Sherman did not understand the remark because Horace
Jones, probably fearing a bloodbath, seems to have deliberately
mistranslated. Not grasping Kicking Bird's intent, the general
simply replied, "You and Stumbling Bear will not be killed, nor
harmed as long as you continue to do well."

Kicking Bird's threat went no further because shots were
heard in the distance, a bugle sounded, and the parade ground
was surrounded by armed cavalry. Some of the shots had been
fired at Big Tree, on the way to Grierson's house, who had
stopped off at the post trader's store where he was run down
when he tried to escape. Out of breath and covered with mud,
he was brought to the porch by a squad of soldiers. Elsewhere
a fight had broken out between Indians and troopers when old
Red Tipi, Satanta's father, and several others had ridden toward
the parade ground with concealed weapons for the chiefs on
the porch. When stopped by the soldiers they had opened fire,
and by the time the shooting stopped one Kiowa was dead and
one soldier had an arrow in his leg. Missing was the fourth
murder suspect, Eagle Heart, who had arrived late, noticed the
commotion, heard the shots and fled.[12]

Amid all the arguing, recriminations and gunfire, old Satank
said nothing but sat calmly on the floor, listening to the talk and
smoking his pipe. Finally, he looked up at the others and
remarked with undisguised contempt:

> If you men want to crawl out of this affair by telling
> pitiful stories, that is your affair. I am sitting here
> saying nothing. I am an old man, surrounded by
> soldiers. But if any soldier lays a hand on me I am
> going to die, here and now.

Satank would go down fighting like a Kiowa warrior if any
soldier touched him.

At this point Kicking Bird spotted Lone Wolf sitting on his
pony, hanging back from the crowd, and motioned him to
come forward. Carrying two carbines and a bow and a quiver
of arrows on his back, Lone Wolf galloped through the lines of
soldiers and dismounted. He tied his pony to the picket fence

fronting the parade ground, laid his weapons on the ground, adjusted his clothing, then picked up the weapons and started forward as if to shake hands with one of the officers. Suddenly he leaped through the inner circle of soldiers and landed in the middle of the group on the porch with a cocked carbine pointed at Sherman and Grierson. He handed his bow and arrows to Stumbling Bear, who strung the bow and fitted an arrow. Kicking Bird and Sherman were still talking when Stumbling Bear interrupted, "Do not say any more, Kicking Bird. I am not going to talk to the army people, only to my friends."

Turning to the crowd of Indians which had been rocking back and forth on the parade ground, wailing over the fate of the chiefs, Stumbling Bear told them Kicking Bird had done his best to keep the Kiowas out of trouble. Because they had failed to heed and had continued their wars against the whites, Kiowa honor was at stake. There would be bloodshed and he, Stumbling Bear, would be the first to die.

Sherman, who had never stopped pacing the porch throughout the discussion, continued up and down the floor and ignored the display. Some thirty or forty soldiers and civilians had cocked their weapons, however, pointing them at the Indians on the porch. As Sherman reached the end of the porch, turned and faced the chiefs, Stumbling Bear drew the bow. Tensions snapped and the Indians began shouting. One of the Indians leaped for Stumbling Bear, whose arrow went wild, and Grierson took advantage of the confusion to hit Lone Wolf with a flying tackle and they both crashed into Kicking Bird. The crowd started pushing angrily against the line of soldiers.

Sherman calmed the situation by ordering the soldiers to present arms against the crowd and then directing the immediate guards covering the chiefs on the porch to lower their carbines. He invited Stumbling Bear, Lone Wolf and Kicking Bird to sit down and assured them, as one soldier to another, that no harm would come to them.[13]

Night was drawing close, the mood of the crowd continued to be threatening, and Sherman was anxious to bring everything to a close. He told the chiefs that Satanta, Satank and Big Tree were prisoners, and he expected forty-one mules to be gathered and turned over to the troops to replace those stolen in the

Warren massacre. Kicking Bird obtained pledges for the animals from the other chiefs, and the Indians were told they could return to the camps, which they found abandoned; the women and children had fled to the hills when the shooting started. Satanta, Satank and Big Tree were ironed and placed in confinement.[14]

Sherman instructed Grierson to turn the three prisoners over to Mackenzie when the latter arrived at Fort Sill. Mackenzie, in turn, would convey them to Texas for trial. One way or another, Sherman intended that Satanta, Satank and Big Tree would pay for the massacre and that the Kiowas "will not again boast of their feats of murder at Fort Sill." Outlining the events leading to their arrest, Sherman wrote:

> In all these steps the Indian Agent has not only been consulted but his wishes have been the rule of conduct. These three Indians should never go forth again. If the Indian Department object to their being surrendered to a Texas jury, we had better try them by a Military Tribunal, for if from any reason in the world they go back to their tribes, no life will be safe from Kansas to the Rio Grande. Texas has Sheriff's Courts and all the machinery of a criminal code, and I believe it will have the best effect to follow the strictly legal course, which the Indians dread far more than the shorter verdict of a rifle ball.[15]

Although Tatum was the instigator of the arrest, it placed him in a quandary. On the one hand he was convinced he had done the right thing by instigating arrest and extradition to Texas for trial. As a Quaker, however, he could not condone Texas' death penalty, nor could he see any practical value in its application. He wrote a letter expressing his thoughts to Sherman and Grierson.

> Independent of my conscientiousness against capital punishment, as a matter of policy it would be best for the inhabitants of Texas, that they be not executed for some time and probably not at all; for the reason that if they are kept as prisoners, the Indians will hope

to have them released and thus [imprisonment will be] of a restraining influence on their actions. But if they are executed, the Kiowas will be very likely to seek revenge in the wholesale murder of white people.

Sherman gave the letter a courtesy endorsement, stipulating that it be turned over to Mackenzie with due consideration for Tatum's opinions.[16] Sherman, however, had his own ideas on handling the situation. In a letter to Sheridan, now a lieutenant general and commander of the entire Military Division of the Missouri, he wrote:

> Kicking Bird and Lone Wolf begged hard for Satanta, but I think it is time to end his career. The Kioways [sic] accuse him of acting the woman when you hold him prisoner, and he has been raiding in Texas to regain his influence as a great warrior. Old Satank ought to have been shot long ago....
>
> The impudence of Satanta in coming here to boast of his deed in Texas will satisfy you that the Kioways need pretty much the lesson you gave Black Kettle and Little Raven....
>
> Kicking Bird is about the only Kiowa that seems to understand their situation, but Lone Wolf ought to have been hung when you had him in hand [at Fort Cobb].[17]

Sherman did not mention Maman-ti, the true architect of the Warren massacre, simply because Sherman was not aware that he existed. Always a shadowy figure, Maman-ti was little known outside his own people and generally avoided both the agency and the fort. His prestige among the Kiowas was assured because of his position as a medicine man and prophet; he did not need a reputation as a war leader. During the brief time that the massacre had been considered an honorable enterprise, he had been perfectly willing for others to have the glory; now he saw no reason to share the blame.

Before departing Fort Sill, Sherman left Mackenzie instructions for conveying the prisoners back to Texas, adding that he felt things ought to be more quiet on the frontier with the execution of the three chiefs. The general's mind, however, still dwelt on Satanta, for he added:

> Satanta says many of the mules of the [Warren] train were killed and wounded; that in the attack he lost three of his warriors killed and three badly wounded, and that the warrior here killed [during the arrest] makes seven, so he says *"we are now even,"* and that he ought to be let off—but I don't see it.[18]

Soon after the chiefs were arrested, the Comanches Ten Bears, Horseback and Tosawi stopped by Fort Sill where they reported that they had encountered Kicking Bird, Lone Wolf and several other Kiowa chiefs who were trying to gather their people back to the camps. According to Grierson, "The latter party informed the Comanches that they did not care what became of Satanta and Satank and seemed to be very angry at them for causing so much trouble, and said that they would not, in any event, go to war on their account."

The arrests did not end the depredations, however, because on May 30 a party of Indians attacked a ranch on the Red River. They were driven off with a loss of three Indians and one white killed. Upon learning that a munitions train was heading toward Sill without a guard, Grierson sent a detachment to meet it and bring it in.[19]

Mackenzie arrived at Fort Sill on June 4 and rested his men for four days before returning to Fort Richardson with the chiefs. Satanta, Satank and Big Tree were brought out from their cell, blinking in the sunlight. Having misunderstood Sherman's demand for the mules, they thought he had moderated his insistence on extradition and trial and that they were being held hostage only until the indemnity was delivered. Not until they saw the transport wagons did they finally realize they were actually going to Texas. According to Grierson, they then asked "to be sent to some post on the Arkansas." When informed that this was impossible, Satanta said he had heard of "Washington to the East, North, and West, but never to the south." Then he went over and put his manacled hands on Grierson's shoulders, pitifully wailing, "My friend! My friend! My friend!"[20]

Satanta must have regained his composure quickly, because the school teacher Josiah Butler noted in his diary:

> Big Tree (twenty-two years old) is anxious to live; Santanta [sic] (fifty years old) is indifferent as to life and Satank (seventy years old) is determined to die in preference to going to Texas.[21]

Satank approached Grierson as though to shake hands, but he had a concealed knife and intended to stab the colonel; Satanta and Big Tree, less interested in dying warriors' deaths, grabbed him and pulled him back. When the two wagons drew up, partially loaded with corn, Satanta and Big Tree allowed themselves to be assisted into the rear one. Satank refused to be moved so the soldiers heaved him bodily into the forward wagon. As the wagons started to roll, Satank covered himself with a blanket and began to chant. Horace Jones did not like what he heard.

"Corporal," Jones called to Corporal John Charlton who was guarding Satanta and Big Tree, "you had better watch that Indian in the front wagon, for he intends to give you trouble."

When Charlton asked why, Jones replied, "He is chanting his death song now." The soldiers ignored the chanting, but the Indian scouts accompanying the column began moving out of the way. Satank spoke briefly to George Washington, a Caddo Indian scout, then resumed chanting.

George Washington dropped back to the rear where Satanta called out to him, "Tell the Kiowas to bring back the mules, and don't raid any more. Do as the agent tells them." Satanta then turned, pale and rigid, to face Corporal Charlton as Satank's chant filled the air. Suddenly a scuffle erupted in the front wagon as Satank slipped his handcuffs and slashed at one of the guards with his knife, grabbing his carbine. The two guards somersaulted backwards out of the wagon. In the rear wagon Charlton jumped to his feet, levelled his carbine at Satank's chest and fired. The heavy Spencer bullet slammed into the old chief and sent him spinning. Badly wounded, he pulled himself up and tried to lever a shell into the carbine. Charlton fired a second shot and the other soldiers began shooting; when the smoke cleared Satank was dying and a teamster had been wounded by a stray shot. Satanta and Big Tree sat with their arms in the air. They were immediately searched but had no concealed weapons. The soldiers pulled Satank's body out of the wagon and left it by the roadside, from where it was later recovered and buried in the post cemetery.[22]

The remainder of the trip back to Fort Richardson went without incident. Each night, Satanta and Big Tree were staked to the ground on their backs, their arms and legs extended, with a guard over them. As the column reached the swampy bottoms of the Wichita River, mosquitoes became so bad that the soldiers slept under makeshift mosquito netting with gauntlets on their hands. With no such protection the two Kiowas were covered with mosquitoes, and their moans could be heard by the soldiers. One night Corporal Charlton walked over to check on them and saw more than a hundred mosquitoes on Satanta. His muscles swelled and strained and the sweat poured off him as the insects bit into him and drew blood. No man deserved this, Charlton decided, and told the guards to fan the Indians with tree branches every night until they reached Fort Richardson.[23]

The column returned to Richardson on June 15. Although Lieutenant Robert Carter later wrote that Satanta and Big Tree were led in on horseback and attracted widespread attention, one Jacksboro resident of the period stated they arrived quietly, riding in the wagon as they had done the whole way from Fort Sill, and were already safely incarcerated in the guardhouse before local citizens were aware that the troops had come back.[24]

Chapter 10
The Trial

Satanta and Big Tree were indicted by a grand jury in Jacksboro on July 4, 1871. The indictment stated that the two Kiowas:

> with force and malice and not having the fear of God before their eyes, but being moved and seduced by the instigation of the devil...the said S. Long, James Elliott, N.J. Baxter, James Williams, Samuel Elliott, John Mullins and James Bowman willfully, unlawfully, feloniously and by their malice aforethought did kill and murder contrary to the form of the statute on such case made and provided, and against the peace and dignity of the State of Texas.[1]

The trial began on the following day in County of Jack, Cause No. 224, the State of Texas *vs*. Satanta and Big Tree. Twenty soldiers formed a screen around the chiefs for their own protection and marched them the quarter mile from the guardhouse at Fort Richardson to the courthouse.

The courthouse, completed earlier that year, was a two-story, sandstone structure about thirty feet square. The lower floor contained four rooms, including offices for the county judge (a primarily administrative position whose judicial powers do not include state felonies), county clerk, county treasurer, and jury. These offices were separated by two hallways running the length of the building, one north-south and the other east-west. The upper floor contained the court room where the two Kiowas were to be tried.[2]

Spectators and newspaper correspondents packed the courthouse and overflowed out onto the square. School was in session despite the season, but teacher Wesley Callway dismissed classes so the students could see the trial. Satanta and Big Tree, wrapped in blankets and manacled, were marched in accompanied by their attorneys, Thomas Ball and J.A. Woolfork, and by Horace Jones, the Fort Sill interpreter.[3] It is doubtful whether the two Indians had any grasp of what was happening to them. But if they did not understand the trial or their rights under Texas law, they did fully realize that their lives depended on the outcome.

The presiding judge was Charles Soward, a state circuit jurist from Weatherford, between Jacksboro and Fort Worth. In his first ruling on the case, he denied the defense's argument that the state had no right to try the prisoners who, Ball and Woolfork contended, were wards of the federal government. He did, however, grant a motion to sever Big Tree's trial from Satanta's. District Attorney S.W.T. Lanham, a young, South Carolina-born Confederate veteran who would ultimately become governor of Texas, announced the state was ready for trial. Twelve jurors were impanelled. It was a typically hot summer day in west Texas and the jurors sat in shirtsleeves; occasionally one would spit tobacco juice at a crack in the floor.[4]

In his opening statement Ball told how the Indians had been cheated of their lands and driven westward by white expansion until, like any cornered creature, they instinctively retaliated. Taking off his coat as the room grew warmer, he gave a history of Indian abuse by the whites beginning with the conquest of Mexico. Concluding, he reminded the jurors of the eagle as a symbol of American freedom and asked them to let Satanta and Big Tree "fly away as free and unhampered." The two chiefs nodded approval when this was translated, and the jurors listened closely.[5]

State witnesses included Jones, Mackenzie, the wounded teamster Brazeal, and the agency interpreter Matthew Leeper. Leeper's testimony was, in Mackenzie's words, "of the first importance to the ends of justice," since he had actually understood Satanta's boasting, while Tatum had heard it only in translation. The orderly sergeant, Miles Varily, also testified

Samuel W.T. Lanham, who prosecuted Satanta and Big Tree. This portrait shows him later as governor of Texas. (Courtesy Archives Division of the Texas State Library.)

that he had positively recognized weapons left at the massacre scene as being Kiowa. Testimony was brief and to the point; Ball and Woolfork "conducted their defense with excellent judgment and decided impressiveness," but soon it was time for the closing arguments.[6]

Summarizing for the state, Lanham pointed out the trial was unprecedented in American criminal justice. He noted:

The remarkable character of the prisoners, who are

leading representatives of their race; their crude and barbarous appearance; the gravity of the charge; the number of victims; the horrid brutality and inhuman butchery inflicted upon the bodies of the dead; the dreadful and terrific spectacle of seven men, who were husbands, fathers, brothers, sons and lovers, on the morning of the dark and bloody day of this atrocious deed, and rose from their rude tents bright with hope, in the prime and pride of manhood— found, at a later hour, beyond recognition in every condition of horrid disfiguration, unutterable mutilation and death....

Safe in the East, "where distance lends enchantment...where the story of Pocahontas and the speech of Logan, the Mingo, are read, and the dread sound of the war whoop is not heard," Indian appeasers saw nobility in the two chiefs, Lanham told the jury.

Satanta, the veteran council chief of the Kiowas—the orator, the diplomat, the counselor of his tribe—the pulse of his race:—Big Tree, the young war chief, who leads in the thickets of the fight, and follows no one in the chase—the mighty warrior athlete, with the speed of the deer and the eye of the eagle.

But Texans, who were forced to deal with the reality of regular Indian raids, knew differently.

We who see them to-day, disrobed of all their fancied graces, exposed in the light of reality...recognize in Satanta the arch fiend of treachery and blood—the cunning Cataline—the promoter of strife—the breaker of treaties signed by his own hand—the inciter of his fellows to rapine and murder—the artful dealer in bravado while in the pow-wow, and the most abject coward in the field, as well as the most canting and double-tongued hypocrite when detected and overcome! In Big Tree we perceive the tiger-demon, who has tasted blood and loves it as his

food—who stops at no crime, how black soever—
who is swift at every species of ferocity, and pities
not at any sight of agony or death—he can scalp,
burn, torture, mangle and deface his victims with all
the superlatives of cruelty, and have no feeling of
sympathy or remorse. They are both hideous and
loathsome in appearance, and we look in vain to see
in them anything to be admired, or even endured.

The government itself shared the blame for the depredations, Lanham said. The Indians took the policy of appeasement
as a sign of weakness, and this had led to robbery, murder,
kidnap and rape. This on-going Indian unrest meant a military
presence on the frontier, as well as annuity goods which the
government issued to the hostile tribes in a misguided effort to
buy peace. Both the annuities and the military contracts were
heavily padded, bringing fortunes to corrupt politicians. Because of this, Lanham said, "deaf ears have been turned to our
cries, and the story of our wrongs has been discredited."
Indeed, he pointed out, the only reason the chiefs were even
on trial was that Sherman himself had been present when the
Warren massacre occurred,

for it is a fact, well known in Texas, that stolen
property has been traced to the very doors of the
reservation, and there identified by our people, to no
purpose. We are greatly indebted to the military arm
of the government for kindly offices and co-operation
in procuring the arrest and transference of the defen-
dants. If the entire management of the Indian question were submitted to that gallant and distinguished
army officer, General Mackenzie, who graces this
occasion with his dignified presence, our frontier
would soon enjoy the immunity from these marauders.

In spite of it all, Lanham reminded the jury, Indians were
entitled to full legal rights according to the same rules of
evidence as any citizen. "You, gentlemen of the jury, have
sworn that you can and will render a fair and impartial verdict."

He then reviewed the following points of evidence:

——Satanta and Big Tree had been absent from the reservation during the time of the raid, and the length of that absence, thirty days, was sufficient for them to make the round trip to the scene of the crime.

—They had, in their possession, property belonging to the wagon train and to the individual victims.

—Satanta had boasted of leading a raid, killing the same number of people as had died in the Warren massacre, and returning with the property. He had implicated Satank and Big Tree, neither of whom denied it.

—Brazeal's description of the raid up until his escape matched Satanta's.

—Sergeant Varily, "an old Indian fighter," had recognized arrows recovered at the scene as Kiowa.

The same amount of evidence, Lanham said, would condemn any white man.

> All the elements of murder in the first degree are found in the case. The jurisdiction of the court is complete, and the State of Texas expects from you a verdict and judgment in accordance with the law and the evidence.[7]

Woolfork, once described by pioneer Texas cattle baron Charles Goodnight as a "peppery little lawyer,"[8] gave the defense's closing statements. Where Ball had sought compassion, Woolfork apparently tried to awe the jurors. According to Lieutenant Carter, Woolfork "took off coat, vest, collar, and necktie, rolled up his shirt sleeves, and advancing up to the foreman...shook his fingers at him and gesticulated in the most emphatic, even violent manner.[9]

The strategy failed, and after short deliberation, the jury returned a verdict of guilty. Judge Soward then pronounced sentence.

> It is therefore ordered and adjudged and decreed by the Court that the said Defendant, Big Tree be taken by the Sheriff and hanged until he (Big Tree) is dead, dead, dead! And may the Lord have mercy on his

Soul! And it is further ordered that the Sheriff [is] to take the said Defendant into close custody and hold him to await the sentence of this Court upon this Judgment herein.[10]

There is no indication Big Tree ever said anything during the trial. He was young and, following Kiowa custom, would have kept his peace, deferring to the older Satanta if there was any talking to be done.[11]

The following day, in his own trial, it was Satanta's turn to address the court. Speaking through Jones, in a mixture of Comanche and sign language, he began:

> Why should I lie, since I have been under the control of the white people since boy-hood. I started off with a party of my people for Texas, and stopped with a sick man on the Peasis [Pease] river.
>
> I have been abused by my tribe for being too friendly with the white man. I have always been an advocate for peace. I have always wished this to be made a country of white people.

Showing his handcuffs, he continued:

> I am wearing shackles because of the Kiowas and General Sherman. I am to suffer for what others did.
>
> This is the first time I have ever faced Texans. They know me not—neither do I know them. If you let me live, I feel my ability to control my people. If I die it will be like a match put to the prairie. No power can stop it. If I could see General Grierson and my people, I pledge myself that neither I nor my people will ever cross Red River again. That river shall be the long line. I am willing to pledge myself for the Kiowas, that if you grant my freedom, I will make permanent peace with the white man.—Whatever mischief has been done, has been done by the Kiowas [i.e., Kiowas other than Satanta]. This is the first time I have ever entered the war-path against the white man. If released, I will pledge myself in behalf

of the Kiowas for a lasting peace. I have but little knowledge of the Texas people now. I have never understood them as a people. Release me, and your people may go on undisturbed, with their farming and stock raising—all will go well.

When General Sherman [sic] and General Caster [sic] had me arrested [during the Washita Campaign] they did not put upon me the indignity of wearing these shackles. I could go about with my limbs untrammelled. I have seen these people—men, women and children in this council room for two days, and I have said in my heart, I am willing to make peace. Take off these shackles. I cannot treat now—I feel myself as a woman.

I expect to hear of mischief done by my people on this frontier. I think they are now awaiting my return or anticipating my death. Gen. Grierson and my father [i.e., agent] General [sic] Tatum, are now anxiously awaiting to hear from me.

Concluding, Satanta said:

Big Bow, Fast Bear, Eagle Heart and Parah [Parra-o-coom, a Comanche chief], have been committing depredations in Texas. I feel more enmity against them than I do against the Texans. I will kill them with my own hands if I am permitted to return to my home.[12]

Satanta, of course, was lying; he *had* made war in Texas many times. Part of his grudge with Kicking Bird was due to the latter chief's pacifism. Satanta *had* been an active participant in the Warren massacre, and both he and Lone Wolf *had* been shackled during their detention by Custer and Sheridan (who either Satanta or, more likely, the correspondent recording the speech apparently confused with Sherman). Satanta realized he had pushed his luck too far this time and was now running the bluff of his life.

As for his pledge that his release would secure "a lasting peace" and that neither he nor any of his people would ever cross the Red River into Texas again, the Austin *State Journal* commented:

> His execution will do more than anything else to convince these chronic and untameable robbers, that the policy of permitting open, incessant and bloody assaults on our line of settlements by these marauders, has been brought to a permanent close.[13]

The jurors agreed and condemned Satanta to join Big Tree on the gallows. Judge Soward denied defense motions for a new trial and, ignoring the exceptions Ball and Woolfork claimed, sentenced the two chiefs to die on September 1. For their own safety as well as that of the citizenry, they were confined in the most secure place available—the guardhouse at Fort Richardson.[14]

Throughout the proceedings Soward had followed the letter of the law. His home at Weatherford was in Parker County, often a target of Indian raids. He lived among frontiersmen, understood their sufferings, and realized he had virtually no option but to assess the maximum penalty for murder. Back in Weatherford, however, he could evaluate all the factors of the case free from the passions that inflamed Jacksboro. There were many reasons to execute the chiefs, particularly Satanta, yet there were also reasons—good reasons in Soward's mind—to keep them alive. Accordingly he sent a letter, to Governor Edmund Davis in Austin, in which he reiterated Lawrie Tatum's assertion that punishment by life imprisonment would make it easier for the agent to round up and extradite other reservation Indians who were guilty of depredations in Texas. Even though Tatum's desire for life sentences was based in part on his religious and moral objections to the death penalty, Soward told Davis that commuting the sentences to facilitate further extraditions and trials was a practical suggestion.

> I would have petitioned your excellency to commute their punishment to imprisonment for life, were it not that I know a great majority of the people on the frontier demand their execution. Your excellency,

however, acting for the weal of the State at large, and free from the passions of the masses, may see fit to commute their punishment. If so, I say amen![15]

In addition to the points raised by Soward, Governor Davis also questioned whether the state had jurisdiction in the case, since he believed "the killing for which these Indians were sentenced can hardly be considered...as coming within the technical crime of murder under the Statutes of the State, but rather as an act of Savage Warfare." This observation by the governor was contained in a proclamation he issued on August 2 commuting their sentences to life at hard labor. The proclamation also noted that the life sentences would "be more likely to operate as a restraint upon others of the tribe, to which these Indians belong...."[16]

The soldier responsible for containing these acts of "savage warfare" disagreed completely with the governor. Commenting on the proclamation, General Sherman wrote:

Satanta ought to have been hung and that would have ended the trouble, but his sentence has been commuted to life imprisonment, and I know these Kioways well enough to see that they will be everlastingly pleading for his release. He should never be released, and I hope the War Department will never consent to his return to his tribe....Kicking Bird can keep the Kiowas peaceable if Satanta is out of the way, and I don't believe him [Kicking Bird] sincere when he asks for his release, but that he is acting the part to maintain his influence with his own people.[17]

Because of public outrage over commutation of the sentences, Davis requested a military escort to make certain Satanta and Big Tree arrived alive at the state penitentiary in Huntsville. Departmental commander Colonel J.J. Reynolds ordered the commanding officer at Fort Richardson (Mackenzie was in the field) to deliver the prisoners under guard. The officer in charge was responsible for the custody and personal safety of the two Kiowas and was not to allow any contact between prisoners and civilians en route.[18]

Ruins of the guardhouse at Fort Richardson, where Satanta and Big Tree were held. The cellblock (finished stone structure center and left) was enclosed by a rough stone guardroom and office. (Author photo)

Huntsville was hundreds of miles away in the pine forests of east Texas, and preparations took weeks. The prisoners remained in the guardhouse at Richardson until October 16 when the military detail was ready. In good weather they were allowed to walk around the corrals and laundresses' quarters for exercise and fresh air. The ever-present leg irons and poor sanitary conditions of the guardhouse created a bad rash on Satanta's legs. The post surgeon prescribed a salve, and his handcuffs were removed so he could apply it and scratch his ankles.[19]

One company of Eleventh Infantry under Captain H.L. Chipman escorted the Kiowas to Huntsville where they arrived on November 2 after a seventeen-day trip. Satanta and Big Tree were received by prison authorities as Numbers 2107 and 2108 respectively. In accordance with Colonel Reynolds' orders, Chipman got a receipt from the warden which was forwarded to departmental headquarters in San Antonio.[20]

Chapter 11
Prison

With his usual sagacity Satanta realized that white idealists could be won over by telling them what they wanted to believe. From Huntsville he let it be known that he was not only principal chief of the Kiowas, "but of all the nations in the three agencies in the southwestern part of the Indian Territory, and if he were released he constantly declared he would keep all of them from raiding."[1]

This, of course, was exactly what Superintendent Hoag and the appeasers wanted to hear, and the Friends Committee began believing that Satanta's release would end the raiding in Texas. Their hopes were belittled by Tatum, who bluntly told them that Satanta was not the paramount chief and that the various tribes were headed by their own chiefs. He warned them Satanta had made similar promises before that had proven worthless. "My candid opinion of him was that he could not keep the other Indians from raiding if he wished to; and that he would not do it if he could," Tatum wrote. Rather than releasing Satanta and Big Tree, he said, "My judgment was to send some more of the leading raiders to the penitentiary, and in that way stop their unprovoked hostility." To Hoag he wrote, "The action of the Kiowas has been such that I think it would be very wrong to release them at this time."[2]

In actuality the arrest and imprisonment of the two chiefs seemed to have had the desired effect. The raw demonstration of federal power on the day of the arrest had, for the moment at least, given Kicking Bird's peace faction the upper hand. An attempt by Maman-ti and some of the other members of the war

Satanta and Big Tree in Prison. (Courtesy Archives Division of the Texas State Library)

faction to start a general uprising that summer had failed. True to his word, Kicking Bird had gathered enough horses and mules to indemnify Henry Warren for his losses the day of the raid. In a letter to the Friends' Committee, Tatum wrote:

> Colonel Grierson and Interpreter Jones, and many others who have been long known to Kiowas, say that they were never so effectively subdued before. I see much in the Kiowas and all of the other Indians to confirm me that it was right to have them arrested, and I see nothing to make me feel doubtful about it. It has probably saved the lives of many Texas citizens. He whom I endeavor to serve has, I believe, enlightened my understanding in times of need.[3]

For the time being Tatum was correct, but the Kiowas could remain quiet only so long. The arrest and imprisonment of two chiefs had damaged their prestige, but was not critical to their existence. Their economic and social structure dictated raiding, and soon the war faction returned to business as usual.

Its inspiration was the Quahadi band of Comanches, under the half-white war chief Quanah Parker, which had continued its depredations after the arrest of Satanta and Big Tree. Using Quanah as their example, Lone Wolf, White Horse and Big Bow began stirring the war faction. In 1872 Big Bow and White Horse led several raids into Texas, and in April they massacred a wagon train on the road between San Antonio and El Paso. In June White Horse's band killed a settler named Abel Lee and several members of a family near Fort Griffin, carrying his surviving children into captivity. They also attacked a military convoy between Camp Supply, Indian Territory, and Fort Hays, Kansas, carrying off 120 horses. By June 1872 the Kiowas had not drawn rations at the agency for five months, a sure sign of trouble, and Tatum estimated that at least one-fourth of their fighting men were off the reservation either raiding independently or with the Quahadis.[4]

Brigadier General Christopher C. Augur, newly appointed commander of the Department of Texas, sent the reports of these depredations to General Sheridan with the comment:

The Kiowas have always been regarded, and I believe justly, the meanest and the cruelest indians [sic] of the plains....the evil in them is not dormant—but extremely active and troublesome. They are in sympathy with the bad indians in all the adjacent tribes on the reservations, and keep them in a constant state of excitement.

My recommendation in their case is, that the whole Kiowa tribe be taken possession of and disarmed, and taken entirely out of the Indian Country, and distributed among the Military posts at the North—not breaking up families, and that the Kiowas as a tribe be no longer recognized....This example is richly deserved by them, will have a most wholesome effect upon the other tribes and may lead to quiet on the reservations, and a cessation of marauding on the adjacent frontiers of Texas, and probably avert a great indian war.[5]

Sheridan was already in a foul mood when he received this letter, for Colonel Hazen was now criticizing the government for its failure to attack and subdue the marauders. Endorsing Augur's letter, Sheridan told the adjutant general of the army:

Had it not been for Colonel Hazen, who represented that these Indians were friendly, when I followed their trail, without missing it for a moment from the Battle of the Washita until I overtook them, the Texas frontier would be on a better condition than now, and we would be free from embarrassment. He seemed to have forgotten...where he censures the Government for not chastising these Indians, that when I had my sabers drawn to do it, that he pronounced them in the name of the Peace Commission friendly.[6]

While Sheridan and Augur fumed, the Five Civilized Tribes held a council with the Kiowas at Fort Cobb on July 22, 1872. Tatum, believing a strong stand would accomplish more than negotiations, objected to the meeting. The Kiowas, he noted, "had been doing without rations a long time, and the women and children were becoming clamorous for coffee and sugar." If the government held fast for a little longer, he felt he could force them into submission and obtain the return of the Lee children.[7]

Unfortunately Cyrus Beede, Superintendent Hoag's clerk who represented the superintendent and shared Hoag's altruism, felt the council was an excellent idea and pressured Tatum into agreeing. The Indians met at Fort Cobb, where White Horse announced he had no intention of ceasing his raids. When the subject of Texas captives was raised, Lone Wolf said he would not discuss their captives until Satanta and Big Tree were freed, until all military posts in the Indian Territory were closed, and until the reservation was extended to include all the area between the Rio Grande and the Missouri River.

The Civilized Tribes knew Lone Wolf was demanding the impossible. Forty years earlier thousands of them had been uprooted from their homes in the East and transported under military escort to the Trans-Mississippi West; more than any other Indians they understood the power of the federal government and realized Washington's present attitude was based on lack of resolve rather than lack of strength. Their leaders told the Kiowas they had no choice but to surrender the Lee children and keep the peace. If they didn't, the federal government "would surely inflict on them severe retribution." In deference to Tatum, who had been summoned back to Fort Sill where his wife was ill, the government officials advised Lone Wolf all rations would continue to be withheld until the children were returned.

Withholding rations had the desired effect. Pressured by the Civilized Tribes, by Beede and the government, and by Kicking Bird, the Kiowa war chiefs agreed to free the Lee children and remain quiet on the reservation. The exuberant government officials, without considering the fact that Satanta and Big Tree were state prisoners and that the federal government had no authority to release them, promised that the two chiefs would be released no later than March 1873.[8]

Two of the three Lee children were delivered to the Wichita Agency the following month, and on September 30 the third was brought to the Fort Sill Agency. They were turned over to an adult brother who took them back to Texas.[9]

* * *

Oblivious to these events, Satanta and Big Tree settled into prison life. The state correctional system of the period kept few records, so there is little official information about the two chiefs and much of what is known must be gleaned from second-hand accounts.[10]

According to Clarence Wharton, Satanta and Big Tree were working in a chain gang of one hundred convicts leased to Albert Denson, construction contractor for the Houston and Texas Central Railroad. By coincidence Johnnie Jenkins, the wagon guard during Satanta's attack on the train on the Fredericksburg Road, was the gang's foreman and timekeeper. Jenkins decided to get to know Satanta better. At first Satanta pretended not to understand Jenkins; finally, being lonely, he would talk. As Jenkins later related to Wharton:

> He understood English and could make himself understood, though all his life he had pretended otherwise. A plug of tobacco and an extra ration of sugar and coffee would guarantee a long talk.[11]

They discussed the fight on the Fredericksburg Road, and Satanta told Jenkins about the Indians' movements after the fight. He described the attack on the Box family "with as little feeling as if he were telling of a hunt or a horse race." He seemed to gain respect for Jenkins on learning he had killed the Yellow Chief, who Satanta said was his nephew. He also told Jenkins that he had advised against attacking the train but had been overruled by his warriors, a story which was highly unlikely. More realistically Satanta finally said that "the Indians' day was about over, that there was no hope for his people and that they might as well die fighting."[12]

After Satanta and Big Tree had been on the chain gang about a month, the sergeant of the guard ordered them separated from the others, chained together and carried off. Although no immediate explanation was given, they were bound for St. Louis to meet with a delegation of leading Kiowa, Apache and Comanche chiefs who were en route to Washington.[13]

The trip had originated in a council, held about six weeks after the meeting between the Kiowas and the Civilized Tribes, organized by Captain H.E. Alvord, a member of the Indian service who actually had frontier experience. The purpose of the council was to review the obligations of the Medicine Lodge Treaty, on both sides, and to advise the Kiowas that if their raids did not cease, military operations would commence, all reservation Indians found in Texas would be attacked without question and, if necessary, followed into their camps by armed troops. The chiefs were also to be invited to Washington to impress upon them the extent of power of the government.[14]

The Kiowas initially resisted the idea, but Alvord convinced them by promising they could see Satanta and Big Tree en route. With that assurance they formed a Kiowa delegation consisting of Lone Wolf, Sun Boy, Wolf Lying Down and one other whose name is not recorded. The rest of the group was primarily Apaches and Comanches.[15]

The trip raised suspicions in Texas that the federal government was up to no good. The *Galveston News* remarked:

> It is certainly something strange that two of the most notorious murderers should be thus taken from their place of confinement and treated as the representatives of a power.
>
> That the object of the Indians in making this request is to obtain the freedom of their great chiefs, no man can doubt. They may even return in quiet to Huntsville, but, if they do it will be because they hope to accomplish that by duplicity which they fear to attempt by force.
>
> Once...these two Indians are freed from confinement, there will be no certainty of their return, and there will be a certainty of their taking the war-path, and wounding and slaughtering the inhabitants of the frontier.[16]

The Texans needn't have worried; Alvord was even more cold-blooded than Tatum about the Kiowas. His own report fully supported Tatum's position, something Tatum's own superiors had failed (or refused) to do. Alvord bluntly stated that the present cessation of hostilities meant nothing because it was now autumn and the raiding season was over; the Kiowas habitually preferred going into winter camp and drawing government rations this time of year. As for the commutation of Satanta and Big Tree's sentence from death to life imprisonment, he said that the continued existence of the two chiefs did not guarantee good behavior, and that instead the Kiowas used the two chiefs as an excuse to continue raiding, claiming they would not cease until the Satanta and Big Tree were freed.

Alvord recommended that, when the delegation reached Washington, the government should dictate and enforce the following terms:

—That the entire Kiowa nation be given until November 30 to move close to Fort Sill where their movements could be conveniently monitored by troops;

—That all horses and mules taken from the government or private parties be surrendered;

—That the three chiefs responsible for the raids of the past year (i.e., Lone Wolf, White Horse and Big Bow) be surrendered for trial in federal courts;

—That no annuities be issued for the remainder of the year;

—That Kiowa hunting parties be required to have military escorts.

Finally Alvord recommended the Kiowas be told "that the recent conduct of the tribe prevents all present hope of the release of their two prisoner chiefs, and that the liberty of those and the others to be given up will depend entirely upon future good behavior."[17]

Alvord's recommendations flew directly in the face of Superintendent Hoag. As far as Alvord was concerned, Satanta and Big Tree were hostages as, hopefully, Lone Wolf, White Horse and Big Bow would soon be. The Kiowas should be put under military rule and allowed to move about in their daily lives only at the will and pleasure of the army. Hoag, who often let his perception of Christian charity outweigh good sense, preferred to release Satanta and Big Tree as an act of faith, trusting in the word of the Indians that they would justify the faith by abandoning their ancient culture and warrior heritage.

Strangely enough no one appears to have consulted Governor Edmund Davis of Texas, the only man who could legally decide the fate of Satanta and Big Tree, and whose name would increasingly be bandied about by both Indian and white.

* * *

With no direct rail connections between Huntsville and St. Louis in 1872, Satanta and Big Tree were taken by train to Dallas where a company of cavalry took them to the Missouri, Kansas & Texas railhead at Atoka, Oklahoma. According to Lieutenant Robert Carter who commanded the detachment, their route was intended to go through Fort Sill, although this is hard to understand because Atoka and Fort Sill are in opposite directions from Dallas. Carter claimed, however, that Fort Sill was ultimately bypassed because Major G.W. Schofield, commanding the post in Colonel Grierson's absence, advised him that a large body of well-armed Indians had gathered near the post and were ready to make trouble.

Whatever the case, Satanta and Big Tree and their accompaniment of United States marshals arrived at the railroad station in Dallas at 8 a.m. on September 9 and were turned over to the military. During the ride north, Carter noted that the country was familiar to Satanta.

> Often as we rode along the trail, between Denton [Texas] and the Red River, especially near Gainesville, we saw the old red scoundrel point with his hand to some distant peak, prominent butte or lone tree, and with the sign language and gutteral tongue call Big Tree's attention to them as he recognized these landmarks so long identified with and so familiar to them along this dangerous Indian passway.[18]

Satanta and Big Tree arrived in St. Louis on the morning of September 19 and were taken to the Everett House, one of the city's hotels. At 11:00 a.m. Alvord and Hoag took the delegates from the various Indian nations into the dining room and seated them in chairs around the walls.

Then Satanta and Big Tree were brought in. Moving to the center of the room Satanta addressed the crowd, his remarks punctuated with grunts of approval by the Indians.

"I come as one risen from the dead, to meet my friends again," he began. "I recognize you, and I call you by name." He began naming the various chiefs present, then he continued:

Comanches, take pity on me. Work for me. Quit raiding on the Texans: it don't pay; it don't pan out well; it's a fraud, a delusion and a snare. I, Satanta, say so, for I am in a position to know. Abandon the war-path; give it up and listen to your white teachers. My father in Texas[19] has told me big talk, and told me to say to you that the Comanches must keep their young men at home. He said I was a big chief, to whom the Indians would listen, and he told me to urge you to quit warring on Texas, knowing that you would listen to me.

You have heard that I was dead, but it is a lie; I am yet alive and have a strong heart. I have been told that if I can keep your young men out of Texas I shall be liberated, and they have asked me to use my influence with the braves of the Kiowas. Washington and the Governor of Texas will protect you. I think they have told me the truth.

General Grierson told the Governor to cut my throat. But he would not do it; may his shadow be long. The Governor said he would use me for making friends with the Indians on the prairie. He told me that I was a big chief, but that Washington is bigger.

I have been well used. They never whipped me nor abused me. I am a Texan, and I want the Texans let alone.

This is the good talk the Governor told me. Look to Washington and the Governor of Texas. To-day we have met under the eye of the Great Spirit. I have thrown aside my bad ways and ask you to do the same. I am a man whom you all know. No chief on the prairie has a better record than Satanta. You all know him. I want you to listen to my words and make friends with the Texans.[20]

Satanta then strode around the room greeting friends and embracing relatives, followed by Big Tree who acted with more restraint until he met a boyhood friend and the two fell crying on each other's shoulders. Many of the Indians sobbed and wailed in grief. Several spoke, endorsing peace. Finally the Comanche Milky Way commented:

> We believe that Capt. Alvord is a friend of ours, and we will help him bring about a peace with the Indians. I indorse Satanta's views. He is my brother-in-law. We want a broad road, wide enough for the Indians and whites to travel together.[21]

It all sounded very promising, but those who lived in the paths of the Indian raids had little faith in promises given in the dining room of a St. Louis hotel. Voicing the feelings of the Texans, the *McKinney Enquirer* editorialized:

> Santanta [sic] and Big Tree, the Indian Chiefs, are being feted and feasted on the route to Washington, after which, we presume, they will be furnished with guns and ammunition, and turned loose on the Texas frontier.[22]

While the fears of the frontiersmen about government-Indian relations in general were well-founded, their specific worries about Satanta and Big Tree were not. The two chiefs were returned to the prison at Huntsville, while the rest of the delegation continued on to Washington where they met with Commissioner of Indian Affairs Francis Amasa Walker and Assistant Secretary of the Interior B.R. Cowen.

Walker bluntly stated the government's position. The Kiowas and Comanches were to move all their people, including every chief, warrior, and their families, to within ten miles of Fort Sill and the agency by December 15. They were to remain there quietly until spring and would not be allowed to leave without permission from the agent. Prior to the December 15 deadline they were to deliver all stolen livestock to their agent or, if stolen livestock could not be returned, they would make restitution from their own herds. Anyone who was not at Fort Sill by the deadline would be considered hostile; they would receive no benefits from the government and would be killed by troops wherever found. Those who complied with the ultimatum would be cared for by the government.[23]

The government officials, however, contrary to Alvord's recommendation, then told the Indians that the government was considering a pardon for Satanta and Big Tree conditional on the Kiowas' good behavior.[24] Although Hoag and the members of the Friends' Committee were pleased at this turn of events, Tatum and Grierson were absolutely opposed to the release of the chiefs. Grierson believed imprisonment of the most notorious raiders was the only long-term guarantee for good behavior.[25] Tatum advised the committee that releasing Satanta and Big Tree would be "very wrong." He complained that it was obvious his opinions meant nothing, and that he was being accused of involving himself with the military in contradiction to Quaker principles. He believed a major outbreak was brewing at the agency, and he stated he would be unable to contain it. He had done his best, and his best was extraordinary, but undermined and betrayed from above he could do no more. He resigned effective March 31, 1873, and James M. Haworth, a man who shared Hoag's appeasement philosophy, was appointed to succeed him.[26]

* * *

While the soldiers, Quakers and bureaucrats argued about Satanta, prison officials were trying to incorporate him into prison life. Upon their return from St. Louis, he and Big Tree had been assigned to the prison shops where Big Tree rapidly settled into the routine and soon became known for the speed and quality of his workmanship. Satanta, however, viewed the system as demeaning and refused to cooperate. After trying various means to coerce him including (the story goes) putting him in a vat of water so that he at least would have to pump in order to keep his head above water, the prison authorities gave up and left him alone.[27]

As time passed Satanta became an object of curiosity and rose to the occasion, receiving visitors in prison with his usual aplomb and holding court, as it were, in the shops. One such scene in 1873 was described by Edward King, who visited Satanta while doing a series of articles on Texas and the South for *Scribner's Monthly*, a New York magazine.

> In the corridor of the penitentiary I saw a tall, finely-formed man, with bronzed complexion, and long. flowing, brown hair, a man princely in carriage, on whom even the prison garb seemed elegant, and was told that it was Satanta, the chief of the Kiowas, who with his brother chief, Big-tree, is held to account for murder. I was presently introduced to a venerable bigamist who was Satanta's chosen boon companion, on account of his smattering of Spanish, and through this anxious prisoner was presented at court. Satanta had come into the workroom, where he was popularly supposed to labor, but where he never performed a stroke of work, and had seated himself on a pile of oakum, with his hands folded across his massive chest. His fellow prisoner explained to Satanta, in Spanish, that we desired to converse with him, whereupon he rose and suddenly stretching out his hand gave mine a ponderous grasp, saying: "How!" He then responded, always through the aged wife-deceiver, to the few trivial questions I asked, and sat down, motioning to me to be seated with as much dignity and grace as though he were a monarch receiving a foreign ambassador. His face was good; there was a delicate curve of pain at the lips, which contrasted oddly with the strong Indian cast of his other features. Although he is much more than 60 years old, he hardly seemed 40, so erect, elastic and vigorous was he.[28] When asked if he ever expected liberation, and what he would do if it should come, he responded, "Quien sabe?" [Who knows?] with the most stoical indifference. Big-tree was briskly at work plaiting a chair seat in another apartment and chewing tobacco vigorously. His face

was clear cut and handsome, his coal black hair swept his shoulders, and he only paused to brush it back and give us a swift glance as we entered, then briskly plaited as before.[29]

Chapter 12
Parole

The plains did grow quiet, but not through the charitable policies of Enoch Hoag. Instead, the determining factor was a military one. Even as the delegation of chiefs, less Satanta and Big Tree, were meeting with government officials in Washington, Ranald Mackenzie attacked and destroyed a Comanche camp in the Texas Panhandle, taking over 120 prisoners who were interned at Fort Concho in what is now San Angelo, Texas.

The prisoners were mostly women and children, the families of the warriors. Their captivity and the destruction of the camp with its provisions were a bitter blow to the Comanche war effort. Hoping to negotiate for the release of their people, the Comanches moved close to the Fort Sill agency for the winter and began delivering stolen livestock to the military authorities in compliance with the government ultimatum. The situation further calmed when the chiefs returned from Washington awed and shaken by their first encounter with the full might of white civilization. The Kiowas and Comanches needed time to think about these developments and ponder their next move.[1]

Incredibly, the federal officials failed to understand the true reasons for the Indians' behavior and assumed the peace policy was finally showing some success. On March 22, 1873, Secretary of the Interior Columbus Delano wrote Governor Davis:

> During the negotiations with the Kiowa & Comanche Indians, held in this city last summer, the subject of the conviction & imprisonment of Satanta

& Big Tree in Texas was discussed & the prospective pardon of these prisoners was intimated to them upon the condition that the continued good behaviour of the tribe to which they belong, would justify the Department in recommending them for Executive clemency.

The Kiowas having conducted themselves in a manner to meet the approbation of the Department, it is believed that the time has arrived when their expectations in relation to the release of the prisoners may be properly realized.

I have therefore the honor to inform you that, in view of all the facts of the case, the President assents to the release of Satanta & Big tree [sic], & I respectfully request that you take the necessary action for the pardon of said prisoners, to take effect on or about the 15th April 1873, provided your judgment in all respects approves the pardon.[2]

The "facts" cited by Delano were no more than wishful thinking. The Kiowas still had not recovered from the impact of the trip to Washington, and the Comanches were quiet because their families were hostages at Fort Concho. Furthermore, it was not the prerogative of the president of the United States to "assent to the release" of state prisoners. Nevertheless, on April 9 Hoag went so far as to suggest to Davis an appropriate itinerary and timetable for the transfer of Satanta and Big Tree to Fort Sill for their release.[3]

The efforts of the Quakers and Interior Department received a profound setback, however, from events over a thousand miles to the northwest. On November 29, 1872, U.S. troops had tried to force the Modoc Indians of California into a reservation, but the Modocs resisted and fled into the virtually impenetrable lava fields of northern California. As word spread throughout the United States of their valiant stand and the injustices they had suffered, public support rallied behind them. Finally the departmental commander, Brigadier General Edward Canby, himself sympathetic to the Modoc cause, asked for a parley in an effort to redress grievances and reach a peaceful solution. On March 10, 1873, the unarmed Canby met with the Modoc chiefs, who murdered him during the peace talks.[4] Support for the Modocs turned to outrage against all hostile Indians, and the American public was in no mood to condone the release of Satanta and Big Tree. Delano withdrew his request.[5]

Despite the outcry against the Indians, Hoag, Agent Haworth at Fort Sill, and members of the Friends Committee continued pushing for the release of the two chiefs. On June 3 Hoag was able to write Haworth, "It now appears the pressure bro[ough]t to bear on the Pres[iden]t & Secy. [of the Interior] by the public, growing out of the Modoc War—and opposition from Genl. Sherman—has been overcome by better councils— and I hope the Governor will yield to the request and that thou wilt manage with all possible prudence for the maintenance of peace."[6]

Meanwhile Edward P. Smith, the latest in the long line of commissioners of Indian affairs, sent Secretary Delano a perfunctory recommendation that Satanta and Big Tree be released, although the tone of his letter indicated he was more interested in the release of the Comanche prisoners at Fort Concho. They had been interned for more than nine months while the government provided not only rations for the people but forage for their horses, and Smith wanted to be relieved of the expense.[7]

If Smith was lukewarm to the release of the chiefs, it was because he realized that the federal government had no jurisdiction in the case, a point he raised to Agent Haworth.[8] This reminder from the Indian commissioner caused Hoag and Delano to consider ways to convince Governor Davis to release Satanta and Big Tree. The situation was becoming even more acute because it was now well into the raiding season and the Kiowas, whose families were not hostages at Fort Concho, were becoming restless. Haworth and Agent Jonathan Richards at nearby Anadarko were instructed by their superiors to do everything in their power to keep their charges under control and encourage them to believe the release was near.[9]

Hoag himself was encouraged by the long-awaited release of the Fort Concho prisoners, who arrived at Fort Sill on June 10. This, he believed, would demonstrate to the Kiowas that Comanche good behavior had hastened the release of their families; Kiowa good behavior might also do the same for Satanta and Big Tree. The more realistic Smith, meanwhile, had written to Davis proposing a council with the Indians, to be attended by Delano, the governor and other Texas officials. Hoag took this to mean "the Indians may be encouraged to *hope* for the release of their captive chiefs." Writing in the third person, he told Haworth:

> While the bad behavior of other Indians [*i.e.*, the Modocs] has caused some delay, we have confidence in the Kiowas, that no breach of conduct on their part will now be allowed to cause an indefinite postponment [*sic*]. Thou wilt impress upon Lone Wolf and other chiefs the responsibility of their present position. If they fail at this time to control their young men, and to maintain friendly relations with the Government and people of the United States including Texas *all will be* lost and their friends who are working continually for the restoration of their chiefs will have little to hope for in the future....The Supt. asks the Kiowas to have patience until they can see the Secretary and Commissioner face to face, in their own country, with Governor Davis, and Satanta present.[10]

Davis, meanwhile, was in Washington where he agreed to a council at Fort Sill in October and, upon his return home, was prepared to send Satanta and Big Tree under guard to Sill to attend the council. His decision was just in time, for the Kiowas were becoming more and more restless and conducting sporadic raids. When a government surveyor was killed near the Red River, the commander at Fort Sill, Lieutenant Colonel John W. Davidson, became convinced that the reservation was once again providing sanctuary for marauders.[11] The raids were another complication Hoag would face with the governor.

* * *

Edmund J. Davis is sometimes described as "the governor

Governor Edmund J. Davis commuted Satanta and Big Tree's sentences, and later paroled them. (Courtesy Archives Division of the Texas State Library)

Texans love to hate." His Radical Reconstruction administration so stygmatized the Republican Party in Texas that, following his ouster in 1874, it would be eighty-eight years before a Republican would again win a state-wide election, and 104 years before Texans would elect another Republican governor. Nevertheless, Davis was not a carpetbagger as he has often been portrayed. He had moved to Texas in 1838, when it was still an independent republic, and after annexation had served as a state district judge. Opting for the Union in the Civil War, he had served as an officer in a loyal regiment of Texas cavalry operating on the Mexican border and had helped reestablish federal control when the war ended. With his long background in the state, he understood the frustrations of the citizens on the frontier and was prepared to defy his federal patrons over the release of Satanta and Big Tree.

First, he intended to make Hoag understand that he, and not the federal government, was in charge, for he advised the superintendent:

> The Indian Chiefs await an escort to take them to Fort Sill when they will be under the controll [sic] of the military to await our proposed conference. It is expecially [sic] to be understood that [neither] you nor your subagents are to make any promises to the Indians in regard to any action to be had about these chiefs.[12]

Lest there be any mistake about the military's role, Davis telegraphed Colonel Davidson:

> Because the Tribes to which these Chiefs belong, have, as I am informed, unwarrantably been led to misunderstand the conditions under which I have concluded to pardon and release them, I will be obliged to you to give the Chiefs as well as their Tribes, to understand distinctly, that they are to accept no promises touching such release, as binding on me, which they do not have from me in person or in writing.

Noting the new rounds of raids, Davis continued:

> I am...forced to conclude that the Kiowas and Comanches, especially the former, even while their Agents are asserting their entire peacefullness, are engaged in raiding on the Frontier, and that more or less this has continually been the case. It is asserted by those Agents that if I do not abate my conditions of release of the chiefs, a general war must prevail along the Frontier, for which I will be responsible. I do not think even that in that event it could be much worse than it is now. At any rate it is not advisable to yield to threats.
>
> I know the Indian character well enough to be aware that this will but open the door to endless demands. It is better to have this matter settled at once.[13]

In late August, prison officials in Huntsville turned Satanta and Big Tree over to a military detachment which conveyed them to Fort Sill. They arrived on September 4 and were placed in the guardhouse under orders from General Augur that they "should be held securely guarded to await the final action of the Governor of Texas and the Secretary of the Interior." Big Tree's brother Dangerous Eagle was at the agency when the chiefs arrived, and Haworth took him to the post where he was allowed to visit "after which he started for his Camp at full gallop," Haworth added, "I presume his horse will not know what rest is till he reaches the Camp."[14]

* * *

If the Quakers expected that the chiefs' transfer to Fort Sill would automatically guarantee their release, they were mistaken. Davis was now under too much public pressure against it. Despite Hoag's hopes and the efforts of his agents, the frontier was once again suffering from full scale raids. Long-suffering Jack County was particularly hard hit, with attacks sometimes reported less than a mile from Fort Richardson. On September 13 Indians attacked three deer hunters a few miles from Jacksboro and, after a brief fight, two of the hunters were killed. The bodies were recovered, and the coroner's jury noted the evidence of the spent cartridge cases revealed that the Indians were using government-issue weapons from the Fort Sill reservation. In the wake of this attack, one citizen sent a prophetic letter to Davis saying, "If Satanta and Big Tree are given up, *without adequate Security* for the protection of the frontier, the Republican Party is *defeated*—and *you* will be *unjustly censured.*"[15]

When Governor Davis arrived at Fort Sill to attend the conference he had agreed to in Washington, he brought not only complaints of the latest Kiowa raids but also important information and advice from Captain H.E. Alvord, the man who had accompanied the Kiowa and Comanche chiefs to Washington and who was probably as knowledgeable of the overall situation as anyone. Alvord, who was now living in New England, had declined Commissioner Smith's invitation to attend the council but had written the governor outlining what Alvord saw as a Quaker conspiracy.

Although Hoag affected dismay and injured innocence when Davis first suggested that unauthorized guarantees had been made concerning the release of Satanta and Big Tree, Alvord confirmed that these guarantees had been given in a plan, originated by Hoag, to hand Davis an agreement already reached with the Indians in an attempt to force the governor to accede to the release. Davis, Alvord said, should place the

entire blame, for any of the Indians' false hopes, on Hoag and
the officials of the Interior Department. Alvord also told the
governor to insist on Horace Jones and Philip McCusker as
interpreters. Although the Quakers disliked the two men,
Alvord said they were "the *only safe* interpreters in the country," and the Indians trusted them.[16]

* * *

The council convened October 6 under an awning in front of
the headquarters building at Fort Sill. The chiefs of the Kiowas,
Comanches and Kiowa-Apaches were present as negotiators,
with Wichita and Caddo chiefs as observers. The federal representatives included Hoag, Haworth, Richards, Agent John D.
Miles of the Cheyennes and Arapahos at Darlington, and
Commissioner Smith. Colonel Davidson had restricted the
entire garrison to the post, and one company of cavalry were
saddled in the stables to put down any disturbance which might
arise.[17]

A day earlier Davis had stated his position to the Indians
and the federal government. He reminded them that the decision on freeing Satanta and Big Tree was his alone, and that no
one else had the authority to commit the State of Texas. He also
warned the Indians that if the raids did not desist, the people of
Texas were ready "to have open war and settle this matter at
once."[18] Now that the chiefs were assembled, Davis addressed
them.

> People of the Comanche and Kiowa, I have
> brought back Satanta and Big Tree. They are here and
> we all see them. They were prisoners to the Texans,
> and they could have taken their lives, but did not. I
> have come here because the people of Texas have
> been suffering a long time. I want to have peace if
> possible. We are at peace with all others [*i.e.*, tribes]
> of the Territory, and want peace with the Kiowa if
> we can. I have come here to make my talk as to what
> the Texans want. I will hear your talk and then tell
> them [the chiefs] what the Texans want them to do,

so that they can consider whether they want peace or war with Texas. Satanta and Big Tree can tell them what they have seen in Texas and how they were treated. They will make their talk, and then we will hear what the Kiowa have to say. I will then make my talk.[19]

At that point, the ancient Red Tipi addressed Davis as a father pleading for his son. The old man placed his hands on the governor's head and intoned a blessing then said, "I am an old and poor man, and I ask that you take pity on me and give me my son. You have your squaws and your children. I love my children as well as you love yours, and I want my son."

To his father's pleadings, Satanta indicated his striped convict clothing and added in Comanche, "Strip these things off of me that I have worn in prison. Turn me over to the Kiowa, and I will live on the white man's road forever. Turn me over to my people, and they will do as the white man wants them." Satanta told the assembled chiefs that he had been treated kindly in prison and never beaten or abused. Then he began speaking in Kiowa which the interpreters could not understand. Ordered to speak Comanche again, he instead stopped and sat down.

The practical Lone Wolf had heard enough preliminaries and asked for the governor's terms. Davis began with a veiled threat—that Texas was capable of invading the Indian Territory and cleaning up the reservations without federal help. He added, however, that the Texans felt bound by treaties made by the federal government, but he pointed out the Indians were also bound to them. As for his terms:

—The Indians were to settle permanently and convert to farming, with agents placed in their camps. No more than three day's rations would be drawn, with each man drawing them personally at roll call.

—The Comanches responsible for recent raids were to be arrested and extradited to Texas for trial. The Indians would assist federal troops in hunting down the raiders. All horses stolen from Texas were to be returned and all captives freed.

—Satanta and Big Tree would remain in the guardhouse at Fort Sill until the post commander was satisfied that the Indians

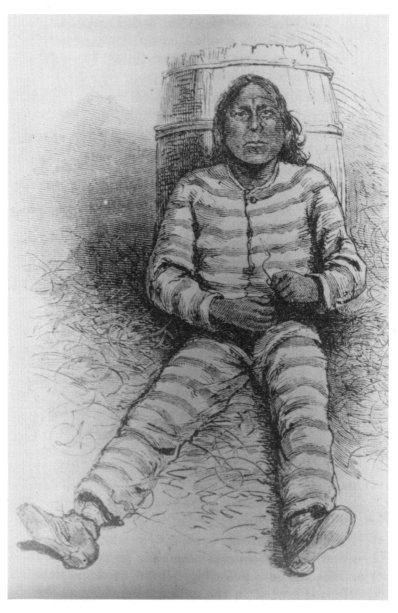

An 1874 illustration of Satanta, in prison stripes, sitting on the pile of oakum where he held court for news correspondents. (Scribner's Monthly, February 1874)

were making a good faith effort to comply with Davis' conditions, after which they would be freed.

"But it must be understood by them that they are not to be
pardoned, but will be subject to re-arrest and return to the
Penitentiary of Texas to suffer for their old crime, if at any time
the Kiowa violate this arrangement," Davis said. He concluded
by saying the Indians could comply with the terms if they
wanted to; if not, Texas was ready to go to war.[20]

Commissioner Smith was appalled at the governor's blunt-
ness, but Lone Wolf was impressed. Where the Kiowas treated
the federal bribes and entreaties with contempt, they could
respect Davis and his implied use of force. He said the governor's conditions sounded reasonable, and he was prepared to
agree, but Quirts Quip, a Yamparika Comanche, objected:

> The governor is too particular to want all the young
> men delivered up who have raided; they canot [sic]
> be changed in a day & [I] don't see why Satanta and
> Big Tree should still be held, when today was looked
> for, and today they were to be released. You blame
> us for not getting on your road, but you have broken
> your promises to us...and you cannot blame us for
> breaking some of our promises....We must have
> time. Give us Satanta and Big Tree and [I] will feel
> glad and try to do right.

After more arguments and allegations from some of the
other chiefs, Davis remarked:

> I will not change the conditions. If they love Satanta
> and Big Tree and want them to go to their camps
> soon, they must comply with my conditions. And the
> sooner they comply, the sooner these chiefs will be
> released.

Hoag's plan to corner Davis was falling to pieces. In a
desperate attempt to salvage some prestige, Hoag reminded the
governor that the Indians did not understand the principal of
state sovereignty and presumed that the federal government
had the authority to promise delivery of the chiefs. Throwing

the blame back on the Interior Department, Hoag said he had been instructed by the department to promise the release, and his agents had repeated those promises to the Indians in good faith.

"Texas has control of this matter entirely," Davis retorted, "and as to the conditions on which these chiefs should be released, in the conditions I exact, I am governed by a desire to have peace and protect the people of Texas. I think my terms are moderate, and if they desire to comply with them they could do so before many suns." To the Indians, he said, "Your agents, Mr. Hoag and Mr. Hayworth [sic], want me to comply with their promises, but I do not agree to their request and will not do so."

Asking the interpreters to stop translating, Hoag advised Davis that the Indians might rise up if Satanta and Big Tree were not released.

The governor was not impressed. "If they are so warlike as that, then we had better settle this matter at once!" he replied, again indicating that Texas was ready to fight.

By now, Commissioner Smith was beginning to realize the full extent of Hoag's duplicity, and decided to put an end to the day's proceedings until he could sort things out. Turning to the chiefs, he demanded they bring in the warriors responsible for the current raids by 3:00 p.m. the next day, in accordance with Davis' terms. "And when those men are here, you will get your captives and the governor and I will be agreed. Now go home and talk of this, and talk of nothing else."[21]

Smith's deadline came and went without any response from the Indians, and Davis' ground became even more solid. Uneasy about what the governor's refusal might bring, Smith made one last effort with Davis. Detailing the situation in writing, Smith acknowledged the state's "full control of these prisoners," but added that the distinction between state and federal jurisdictions "cannot be satisfactorily explained" to the Indians. However wrongly, they had been promised the release of Satanta and Big Tree and had accepted the promise in good faith. The federal government was now prepared to agree and enforce all of Davis' terms in exchange for an immediate parole for Satanta and Big Tree. If the parole was violated, they or chiefs of comparable rank would be turned over to Texas authorities to carry out the sentence. The most a parole would do would be to provide two more fighting men for the Kiowa ranks, although Smith personally doubted that either Satanta or Big Tree had much interest in continuing to fight. A refusal to release the two chiefs, however, might provoke a general war.[22]

While Smith worked on Davis, the Kiowas pondered their next move. Believing they had been deceived, they and the Comanches decided to take the prisoners by force. Arriving at Fort Sill on October 8, warriors with concealed weapons took positions in the crowd. They planned to kill Davis, the military guard, Smith and the agents, then hurry Satanta and Big Tree to fast horses placed nearby.[23]

When Davis arrived, however, he ordered Smith's letter read to the crowd. He then read his reply acknowledging the government's acceptance of his terms and paroling Satanta and Big Tree. Ordering them to stand, he told them they were free and obligated to make certain all raiding ceased. Otherwise, he said their paroles would be revoked and they would return to prison. Satanta and Big Tree embraced Davis then mounted horses and rode with the Quakers to the agency office.[24]

* * *

The citizens of Texas were outraged, particularly when the raids continued in the west Texas counties. Texas newspapers called for Davis' impeachment, and in Washington an angry Sherman told a congressional committee on military affairs that Satanta should have been executed and that Davis had been negligent in commuting his sentence.

Learning of Sherman's comments, Davis responded that the Warren Massacre was an act of war and therefore came under military jurisdiction. Sherman, he said, should have taken punitive action, but instead had avoided the responsibility of executing Satanta and Big Tree by placing the burden on the state.

This was too much for Sherman, who castigated Davis in a venomous letter:

I had the authority to do exactly what I did, viz: with the assent and approval of the Agent, Tatum on the spot, to send them to the jurisdiction of the Court having authority to try and punish. Once there they passed under a Texas Court, and under your authority as Governor of the State. Without the interposition of your authority, these murderers could have been hung on the spot as a matter of course, but you remitted them to the Penitentiary, and then afterwards set them free.

I believe in making the tour of your frontier with a small escort, I ran the risk of my life, and I said to the [congressional] Military Committee what I now say to you, that I will not again voluntarily assume that risk in the interest of your Frontier, that I believe that Satanta and Big Tree will have their revenge, if they have not already had it, and that if they are to have scalps that yours is the first to be taken.

I can make all allowances to the kind gentlemen of Philadelphia, who were so busy in accomplishing the release of these two murderers but I was amazed that you, who felt the constant inflictions of these Texas Raids should have yielded.[25]

Chapter 13
The Red River War

Despite Sherman's dire predictions, prison had mellowed Satanta and much of the old fire was gone. He now understood the full extent of the power behind white society. Soon after his release, and standing just outside the boundaries of Fort Sill watching off-duty soldiers lounging about, he picked up a handful of sand and let it fall through his fingers. "The white men are as numerous as the sands in these hills," he said. "We may kill these, but others will come. The Indians' days are over."[1]

Regardless of his intentions, however, trouble followed him. On the night of May 7, 1874, Satanta, Kicking Bird and several other Indians were at the Fort Sill trader's outside the boundaries of the post proper. About the hour of tattoo when the fort was secured for the night, Satanta followed a black soldier from the trader's toward the stables. He was stopped and arrested by a sentry in obedience to an order prohibiting Indians from entering the post.

According to Captain C.H. Carlton, commanding the post in the absence of Colonel Davidson:

> When arrested he backed away from the sentinel, yelling 'Kicking Bird', then turned and ran. It seems he immediately went to the Indian Camps, shouting that 'The soldiers were coming to attack them' and making them pack and start [to flee] at once.

Fortunately, Kicking Bird was asleep in the trader's store,

In this undated photograph Satanta appears older, leaner and more subdued than in other photographs. It may have been taken after his release from prison. (Courtesy Kansas State Historical Society)

and some of the young warriors came to tell him what was happening. Kicking Bird, whose influence was now greater than Satanta's, sent word to the camps for the people to quiet down then presumably went back to sleep.

The incident seemed innocent enough; but the fact that Satanta was involved was enough to make Captain Carlton suspicious.

> I understand that it is not an unusual thing for Satanta to pursue the Negro[es] comin[g] in the Post. In this case I think he considered himself liable to arrest and thought if he could induce his people to run away from the Post and make them afraid to return he might regain his influence and give us trouble. He gives a variety of reasons of the affair this morning.[2]

Satanta soon left the immediate area of Fort Sill on a buffalo hunt, and it wasn't long before the Texas newspapers began reporting that he was once again raiding on the Texas frontier.[3] The accusations brought a vehement denial from Thomas Battey, the agency school superintendent, who threw the charges back against the Texans.

> It is a well-known fact that there is a gang of desperadoes, having their headquarters about Red River Station, Jacksboro, and Waco, in Texas, who make a regular business of horse-stealing and other desperate deeds. These are furnished, as I have been informed from reliable sources [i.e., law enforcement], with false hair, masks, and other Indian disguises, so as to pass readily for Indians when it suits their convenience to do so; and I have no doubt, while it must be admitted that Indians have done, and are still doing, more or less raiding in that state, that a large amount of the so-called Indian depredations and barbarities, even of the darkest dye, are committed by these savages with white skins....
>
> This has lately been the case with Satanta and Big Tree, whose doings in Texas since their release have furnished hundreds of paragraphs for the news-

papers, while to my certain knowledge the latter was
at home, sick in his lodge, and the former enjoying—
after two years' confinement in prison—the pleas-
ures of the buffalo chase, on territory assigned for the
purpose.[4]

While whites disguised as Indians raided among their own
people in Texas, whites from Kansas were entering the Territory
and stealing large numbers of ponies from the Indians. In May
1874, horse thieves stole forty-three ponies from the herd of the
Cheyenne chief Little Robe. Little Robe's son organized a party
and chased the whites back to Kansas but failed to recover the
animals. In retaliation, the Indians ran off a herd of Kansas cattle
but were caught and pursued by soldiers; Little Robe's son was
badly wounded.

For the Cheyennes, the incident amounted to a declaration
of war. Raiding parties were sent out and several whites were
killed in Kansas and the Indian Territory. Agent Miles wrote
Haworth that he was losing control.[5]

The raids on the pony herds were an affront to Cheyenne
honor, but what truly frightened all of the tribes was the
unprecedented slaughter of buffalo. The extermination of the
huge beasts threatened the Indians with economic and cultural
disaster as well as starvation; government rations were designed
only to supplement, rather than to substitute completely, the
buffalo meat acquired by hunting. The massive, commercial-
ized buffalo hunts had begun early in the decade when it was
discovered that buffalo hide made the best grade of industrial
leather. By 1874 the buffalo had been hunted almost to extinction in Kansas, and the hunters moved south and established a
depot near the ruins of Adobe Walls from where they fanned
out into north Texas and the Indian Territory.

Faced with the destruction of their way of life and unable
to find any hope, many Indians turned to drink. Abetted by
white whiskey traders, alcoholism among the Indians became
rampant.[6] Conditions on the reservations were so deplorable
for the normally secular and pragmatic Comanches that something new and unprecedented occurred—a prophet arose. His
name was Isa-tai and it was said that he could cure the sick and
raise the dead. He could vomit an unlimited number of bullets

for the Indians and charm the guns of the whites to render them harmless. Under Isa-tai's influence, the Comanches held a Sun Dance for the first time in their known history. When Haworth inquired about their intentions, the Comanches notified him to mind his own business if he valued his life. Throughout the ceremony, Isa-tai harangued the warriors, stirring them to action.[7]

The ensuing conflict, known to history as the Red River War, began at dawn on June 27, 1874, when Isa-tai led over seven hundred Comanches, Kiowas, Cheyennes and Arapahos in an assault on the buffalo-hide depot near Adobe Walls. In the day-long fight, the well-armed hunters drove off the Indians with heavy losses, but during the battle the defenders heard a bugler playing military calls. Many people incorrectly believed the bugler was Satanta, but the musician was actually a deserter, from one of the black regiments stationed in the Indian Territory, who was killed later in the fight.[8]

Despite the allegations against him, Satanta may actually have been trying to keep his people under control. Always shrewd, he probably realized that his parole depended on the good behavior of the Kiowas as a whole. On July 18, Commissioner Smith wrote Secretary Delano:

> Late information from the Indian Territory leads me to believe that there is now progressing at Fort Sill and the Cheyenne and Arapahoe Agency an open withdrawal of the loyal and friendly Indians from the hostile; and that among the most prominent of the friendly Indians who insist upon peace is Satanta, who was released from the Texas penitentiary on his parole.

Smith felt the government shared a large portion of responsibility for the outbreak, and listed the causes as:

> (1) The failure to punish the Comanches according to promise for their repeated and persistent raids and murders in Texas; (2) the failure of the Government to protect the reservation Indians from the white buffalo hunters and horse thieves and whisky traders,

who have swarmed over this Indian country during
the past winter, slaughtering the buffalo by the thousands, for their hides, and driving off large numbers
of Indian ponies at Kansas.[9]

Two days later, Smith advised Hoag that the military had
been ordered to attack hostile Indians in the Territory, but that
friendly Indians would be protected. Agents were instructed to
cooperate with military authorities in protecting the innocent
and punishing the guilty. All friendly Indians were required to
report immediately to the agencies, and all those capable of
bearing arms would be subject to daily roll call. Once the rolls
were prepared, no additional Indians would be received into
the friendly bands without permission from the government.[10]

The majority of the Kiowas had not yet taken a position on
the conflict, and as they prepared for their Sun Dance the Indian
nation's peace and war factions prepared for their final confrontation. Kicking Bird argued for peace while Lone Wolf, who
had lost both his favorite son and his nephew during a raid into
Texas the preceding December, demanded war and revenge.
When the time came for Satanta to state his position, he
ceremoniously gave away his medicine lance and shield, thus
resigning his position as a paramount war chief. Officially, at
least, he would never again lead warriors in battle.[11]

The debate between the war and peace factions ended
when the paramount medicine man Nap-a-wat declared for
peace with Kicking Bird, who then led three-fourths of the
Kiowa nation to Fort Sill to enroll as neutrals in accordance with
Commissioner Smith's directive. Satanta himself enrolled on
August 5. He was told to remain in his camp, and he was
specifically forbidden to go to the Wichita Agency at Anadarko
where a friendly band of Comanches was camped. The Do-ha-
te Maman-ti, reemerging as a planner and leader of battles,
joined Lone Wolf to gather the remnants of the war faction for
new raids into Texas.[12]

Back at Fort Sill, Satanta was absent from the August 13 roll
call. Some of the other chiefs said he was sick, and Captain B.G.
Sanderson of the Eleventh Infantry, who was in charge of the
enrollment, sent a message to Satanta's camp ordering him to
report as soon as he was able. Sanderson then learned that

Satanta had accompanied several other Kiowa chiefs to the Wichita Agency in direct violation of his enrollment terms. On August 16, Sanderson sent a letter to Agent Richards at Anadarko, ordering the Kiowas to return to Fort Sill immediately.[13]

Satanta's decision to go to the Cheyenne Agency was incredibly bad judgment. On August 22, Colonel Davidson arrived at the Wichita Agency to deal with hostile bands that were reportedly filtering in. The Indians opened fire from behind the buildings, inaugurating two days of sniping in which four soldiers were wounded before the Indians broke off and departed. In his report Davidson wrote, "We positively know [the attackers] to have been the bands of Satanta, Red Otter, Woman's Heart, Poor Buffalo, [and] Double Vision, of the *presumed* friendly Kiowas who had been enrolled at Ft. Sill, absent from their camps without permission with their enrollment papers in their pockets and headed by the outlawed Lone Wolf."[14]

Satanta himself later admitted that he was present during the fight but denied any involvement. It didn't matter. To the soldiers, the fact that he was present automatically made him guilty.

Less than two weeks later, on September 9, the Kiowas attacked a government supply train commanded by Major Wyllys Lyman and were driven off after a thirty-six-hour running fight. Lyman's commanding officer, Colonel Nelson Miles, noted that the Indians "are believed to have been led by Satanta and Big Tree." In reality, the attackers were led by Lone Wolf and Maman-ti, but Satanta and Big Tree are thought to have been present when the fight occurred.[15]

* * *

The government's overall strategy during the Red River War was for a series of converging columns—Mackenzie coming north from Texas, Lieutenant Colonel William R. Price east from New Mexico, Miles south from Kansas, and Davidson west from Fort Sill—which could batter the Indians back and forth until they were worn out. These massive military movements frightened the Indians. Their initial war fever had cooled and now they began to think of refuge. Lone Wolf and Maman-ti decided to take their people far out onto the plains. Eventually Maman-ti joined several other hostile chiefs in a winter camp in the recesses of Palo Duro Canyon about twenty-five miles southeast of what is now Amarillo, Texas.

Kiowa oral tradition states that Satanta also took refuge in Palo Duro and was there on September 28 when Mackenzie descended into the canyon and won a decisive victory.[16] His presence there, however, is virtually impossible because on September 30, when Big Tree surrendered at the Cheyenne Agency at Darlington, Satanta is known to have been nearby with twenty-four lodges; the distance is simply too great for a defeated band burdened with women and children to have traveled in two days. More likely, according to Nye, Satanta, Big Tree and Woman's Heart decided to turn themselves in to the military authorities soon after the Lyman fight.[17]

After notifying departmental headquarters in Fort Leaven-worth that Big Tree was in custody, Lieutenant Colonel Thomas H. Neill, military commander of the Cheyenne Agency, was ordered "to endeaver [sic] by all means in his power to get possession of Satanta and party and to hold Big Tree and parties and all other Indians he may capture securely and at all hazards as prisoners until he receives further instructions relative to them, and, under no circumstances permit any of them to escape."[18]

Satanta was camped in the Red Hills about thirty or forty miles west of the Cheyenne Agency, waiting the outcome of Big Tree's surrender to Colonel Neill. He wanted to surrender at the Cheyenne Agency too, rather than Fort Sill because, he said, "Things were so mixed up there."

Neill sent a Kiowa woman and a friendly Apache chief to Satanta with his terms for surrender. Satanta's band was to stop outside the agency and camp at a designated spot two miles to the west where he and his followers were to surrender their arms. They were to remain in camp as prisoners until Neill received orders on their final disposition from Brigadier General John Pope, commander of the Department of the Missouri, in whose jurisdiction the agency lay.[19]

Satanta surrendered to Neill on October 3, 1874.[20] He was

accompanied by thirty-seven warriors, forty women, sixty-six children and two old men. Neill confiscated thirteen rifles, three pistols, eighteen bows and four lances which, he noted were "all the arms they had." He also found a letter of recommendation issued to Satanta by Agent Haworth on January 29, 1874.

Even in defeat, Satanta was able to rise to the occasion with a speech:

> I am tired of fighting and do not want to fight any more. I came in here to give myself up and do as the white chief wishes. I want to cultivate a farm at the Cheyenne Agency here. I do not like the Agency at Fort Sill. I am half Arapahoe, half Kiowa, and I want to live near the Arapahoes. At Fort Sill the Comanches would go on the war path, and raid in Texas whilst the Kiowas would be blamed for their bad acts. I have done no fighting against the whites, have killed no white men and committed no depredations since I left Fort Sill.
>
> When the fight commenced at Wichita Agency, all were excited; I packed up and left, and took no part in the fight. Soon after, I left the Kiowas and Comanches, who have gone to the Staked Plains, and I remained at the headwaters of Washita with the party now with me.

Neill replied that Satanta and Big Tree would be held under close guard as hostages and prisoners, while the other Kiowas were to remain in camp and attend roll call. Satanta objected, but Neill informed him the matter was not up for discussion.[21]

To the question of what to do with Satanta and other hostile or supposedly hostile chiefs who were now prisoners, General Sheridan suggested a military tribunal to try all those who might have committed depredations in the past two years and confining those who might, for some reason, be exempt from trial to Fort Snelling, Minnesota. Presumably he meant Satanta as well, although he did not mention him by name. After consulting with Assistant Secretary of the Interior B.R. Cowen, Secretary of War William W. Belknap forwarded Sheridan's recommendation to President Grant but suggested that Satanta be turned over to the governor of Texas. Grant agreed.[22]

Satanta was transferred from the Cheyenne Agency to the guardhouse at Fort Sill. On October 30, Captain Carlton was ordered to return him to Huntsville because he "has violated the conditions on which he was released...," and a few days later Satanta was en route back to Texas where Davis' successor, Governor Richard Coke, instructed the inspector of the penitentiary to "receive and return him to imprisonment in accordance with the terms of the original sentence."[23]

Not everyone agreed that Satanta belonged in prison. Upon learning that Satanta was on his way to Huntsville under military escort, Commissioner Smith expressed his objections in a letter to Secretary Delano. Smith indicated there was no conclusive evidence that Satanta was actively engaged in hostilities, and that his leaving the Wichita Agency during Davidson's fight "may possibly be attributed more to panic, or the stampede among his people, than to any hostile intent on his part...." Despite indications that Satanta was probably present during the Lyman fight, Smith believed he and his band had largely kept to themselves until they voluntarily surrendered at the Cheyenne Agency. On the other hand, Smith wrote,

> There are other Kiowa Chiefs and head men, who became responsible on release of Satanta for the future good behavior of the tribe, who would have been guilty of raiding in Texas, and who would be fit subject for the Texas Penitentiary, "Lone Wolf" who is the head chief of the Kiowas, is known to be a bad man, and his [is?] charged with having committed robbery and murder in Texas since Satanta's release.
>
> The condition of Satanta's parole provided that if there be any further raiding in Texas the raiders themselves should be returned or Satanta given up. It is probably that the military now hold as prisoners raiding Kiowas and Comanches, and if not already captured, Lone Wolf is quite likely to be a prisoner within a short time.

That being the case, Smith said Satanta should not be imprisoned until his involvement in the uprising could be thoroughly
investigated.[24]

Delano sent Smith's letter to Secretary Belknap with a cover
letter of his own stating that he concurred with Smith and asking
Belknap to consider the problem. Because Satanta was already
en route to Texas, Belknap preferred to regard the matter as
closed but, after discussing the case with Grant, suggested the
final disposition of Satanta be put on hold pending further
investigation.

"There is no doubt about Satanta's guilt," Sheridan replied,
"but it would be best to get all the particulars, which I will do."
Sheridan turned the matter over to General Augur, who in turn
referred it to Captain Sanderson noting that he "is familiar with
the Satanta case...."[25]

Sanderson reviewed the entire case all the way back to the
Warren massacre and Davis' terms of parole. He pointed out
that, upon enrollment the previous August, Satanta had been
specifically instructed to stay away from the Wichita Agency
but had gone there anyway and been present when the fight
occurred.

> The Com[issione]r of Ind[ian] Affairs is certainly
> and positively misinformed as to the idea that Satanta
> was frightened off by the Wichita Agency Affair." It
> was the going away of Satanta and party [to the
> Wichita Agency] that brought about the Wichita
> Agency affair. It was this same party who fired on the
> troops, and that were in company with Lone Wolf,
> and under his control and direction, this after they
> had been expressly told that they must not hold any
> communication with the hostiles.

Sanderson also pointed out that while it could not be
positively proven that Satanta was present at the Lyman fight,
"he was unquestionably with the same party for five weeks, and
it would be more difficult to prove that he was not engaged in
it."[26]

Even in a modern legal case, a report such as Sanderson's
would be damning to the accused. In Texas the burden of proof

is entirely on the state during the initial trial, but the state subsequently has a much easier time revoking parole. Whether in 1874 or 1997, it is enough for a parolee to be present when an offense is committed, such as the fight at the Wichita Agency; it is enough to violate the orders of a parole officer such as Sanderson, and it is enough to associate with people whom the state considers known criminals, such as Lone Wolf. The generals readily acquiesced to Texas' judicial philosophy; Satanta would spend the rest of his life in prison.

If Satanta was to be returned to prison, why wasn't Big Tree? Sheridan's attempt to explain away this discrepancy, "I did not send Big-Tree back, because I never supposed him guilty—not only that, but I took off his shackles and held him prisoner *only because he was out with the hostile Indians this summer* [italics added]"[27] was a complete contradiction. Satanta went back to prison in part because he also "was out with the hostile Indians" as established in Sanderson's report, and Nelson Miles believed both Satanta and Big Tree shared at least some of the responsibility for the Lyman fight. Big Tree had been paroled under the same conditions as Satanta, and justice would seem to have decreed that Big Tree join Satanta in Huntsville.

Sheridan, however, was not interested in justice. To him, Big Tree was peripheral; Satanta was a symbol, and Sheridan intended to remove that symbol.

Chapter 14
Death and Immortality

In a serious moment, humorist Jack Douglas once equated a life sentence for an Indian to six years because, he said, six years was about as long as an Indian could last in prison. In Huntsville Satanta seemed to bear out Douglas' observation. Most of the time he could be found once again sitting on a pile of oakum, no longer holding court but seemingly indifferent to life. Occasionally he would stare north toward the Red River.[1]

As Satanta's life dwindled to mere existence, the world he knew came to an end. Lone Wolf, Maman-ti and the other leading chiefs surrendered. Instead of being tried before a military tribunal, they were exiled to Fort Marion at St. Augustine, Florida, where Maman-ti died of consumption on July 29, 1875. Lone Wolf would remain in Florida four years and die of malaria shortly after being allowed to return to his home country. Kicking Bird, who had assisted the government in selecting those to be transported to Fort Marion, was assassinated by poison, probably slipped into his coffee by an adherent of Maman-ti, on May 4, 1875. Conquered, disarmed and dismounted, the Kiowas and Comanches prepared to endure their new role as government wards on the plains they had once ruled as supreme warlords.

As Satanta entered his sixties his health began to fail. With the Indian wars on the southern plains essentially ended, prison officials began to consider his continued incarceration as pointless. On August 10, 1878, Thomas J. Goree, superintendent of the penitentiary, sent a letter to Agent P.B. Hunt at Fort Sill, describing Satanta as "very feeble. If he remains here [he] can not live long. [I] will heartily second any effort made for his release."[2]

The government, however, intended that he remain in prison. On October 10, when Satanta inquired if there was any chance of his release, he was told there was none. "I cannot wither and die like a dog in chains," he remarked.[3]

The next day, Satanta slashed several arteries. An attendant stopped the bleeding and took him to the prison infirmary where he was lodged on the second floor. When the attendant left him alone, Satanta jumped from the landing. The prison record states he died "from effects of a fall received by voluntarily jumping from a second story landing of the prison hospital."[4]

Satanta's body was placed in a simple pine coffin and carried to a brush-covered rise, known as Peckerwood Hill, where the prison system maintained squatter's rights for use as a potter's field. A clearing was hacked out of the thicket and the body was buried. In December a headstone arrived from Houston marble cutter Thomas E. Byrne with the inscription

SATANTA, CHIEF OF THE KIOWAS.

Byrne stated a woman had ordered the stone anonymously, paying $127 in cash. The stone was placed on the grave but later disappeared.[5]

The Kiowas have always disputed that Satanta committed suicide, saying that suicide was not in his nature. Some have even advanced the theory that he was drugged and thrown from the landing,[6] but this theory, while interesting, does not correspond to the known facts. By 1878 Satanta had become a figure of sympathy around the prison, as shown by Superintendent Goree's very pointed suggestion that he be released. When it became obvious that he would remain in prison with his every move always controlled by the whites, Satanta rose to the occasion as he had so often done throughout his life; he denied them their victory by killing himself. The whites had his corpse, but they did not have his obedience.

With Satanta dead, Big Tree was the last surviving chief of those arrested for the Warren massacre. Just as he had earlier adjusted to life in prison, so he now adjusted to the new world forming on the plains. In his forties he converted to Christianity and became a deacon and Sunday School teacher in the Baptist Church. To the church he gave witness of his early depredations as examples of sin and redemption. When he died on November 13, 1929, he was a leading citizen of the Anadarko area where his death was mourned by both Indians and whites.[7]

Gray Goose, who inherited the warrior name Satanta, enlisted as an army scout and became a warrior for the government. Unlike the British Army, which used native troops as regular soldiers, the United States considered them auxiliaries until 1892 when the government decided to integrate them into the service. A largely Kiowa detachment, Troop L of the Seventh United States Cavalry, was formed at Fort Sill under the command of Captain Hugh L. Scott. The officers and two senior sergeants were white, but the other noncoms and the troopers were Kiowas including Mark Auchiah, one of Satanta's younger sons.[8]

The experiment at integrating the Indians into the service lasted only briefly, and in 1897 the War Department disbanded the native contingents. Scott, blaming the army for the failure, wrote in his memoirs:

> Innumerable obstacles were thrown in my way by unthinking officers, and support in Washington was withheld by a change of the secretary of war. The men of that troop nevertheless are men of power and influence now in the Kiowa reservation and dictate its policies, and I have been told by a number of agents that the marked difference between this agency and those surrounding it was caused by the discipline, instruction, and general improvement brought about by service in that troop....[9]

Apart from his military duties Scott was genuinely interested in Indian history and culture. He transcribed the Kiowa stories of Satanta and his medicine shield, and eventually came into possession of the shield itself, claiming it had been left to him in Gray Goose's will.[10] The Kiowas dispute this, saying contemporary Kiowa legal tradition did not provide for a will in the white sense, and that the shield had in fact been confiscated as military equipment.

The shield is in the Phoebe Hearst Museum of Anthropology of the University of California at Berkeley, which acquired Scott's collection of Indian relics. The Kiowas' several efforts to regain possession of the shield are based both on the fact that it is the last sun shield in existence and is an important part of their heritage, and on their contention that it was not properly acquired by Scott. They believe they would be better served if the shield were turned over to the museum at Fort Sill where it would be preserved on their behalf. In response to an inquiry by Senator David Boren of Oklahoma, Burton Benedict, director of the Hearst Museum wrote:

> It is our responsibility to preserve our collections for future generations and to make them available for research and teaching, as well as to show them to the public. The shield is important in these respects.
>
> As I wrote previously to Mr. Towana Spivey, Director of the Fort Sill Museum, we have considered his request [to transfer the shield to Fort Sill] and obtained the opinion of the University's legal counsel. Documentation reveals that the University obtained possession of the shield through voluntary transfer of title by the lawful owner [Hugh Scott] and that the University accordingly has right of possession.
>
> Therefore, we decline his request.[11]

Benedict offered to loan the shield to Fort Sill "for a specific exhibition and under our usual terms for loans," a proposition that Spivey did not consider appropriate. In a letter to Betty Washburn, Satanta's great-great-granddaughter, Spivey noted that although the Hearst Museum "may have a clear title to the shield when it was donated, it is still a sacred object covered under the law and subject to return to the proper organization." At present the Kiowas are considering legal action under the Native American Repatriation Act.[12]

Although the Kiowas have been unable to retrieve Satanta's shield, they were able to obtain Satanta himself. The movement to reinter Satanta's remains was started by Mark Auchiah's son, James, Satanta's grandson, who initiated an effort to repatriate

Satanta to Oklahoma for burial in the Fort Sill Cemetery. In 1963 a joint resolution was introduced into the Texas Legislature directing the Department of Corrections "to accede to the wishes of the Kiowa Indians of Oklahoma, and to take whatever steps are necessary to allow for the removal of the bones of Setainte and for their return to his people."[13]

Despite the good intentions, the resolution sparked a minor controversy. In the House of Representatives, Representative James Cotten of Weatherford fought the bill, saying, "Satanta led numerous raids on the white settlements in Texas, including some in my district. Satanta was a murdering, thieving Indian. He killed a lot of white people in my area."[14]

James Auchiah himself was infuriated by a paragraph in the resolution which stated that

> [Satanta's] descendants, the Kiowa Indians of Oklahoma, have offered precious relics to a Texas museum in exchange for the remains of Setainte. The request has come from James Auchiah, a grandson of the great red man.[15]

"I would not consider bargaining like this in such a sacred matter," Auchiah countered. "Never, at any time, have I promised I would procure Kiowa relics in exchange for moving the grave of my grandfather."[16]

The issue became further complicated when the city of Satanta, Kansas, submitted a claim for the body. Russell Witner, president of the Satanta Chamber of Commerce, pointed out this was the only city in the nation named for Satanta and therefore Satanta's remains should be "placed here on the high plains of western Kansas where history indicates most of his activities, however nefarious, were carried out."[17]

When the furor subsided, the resolution surrendering Satanta's remains to the Kiowas was approved by both of Texas' legislative houses and signed by Governor John Connally on May 17, 1963.

Peckerwood Hill is no longer a potter's field. The land was donated to the prison system in 1885, and by the time the Kiowas came for the body in June 1963, teams of convicts under Captain Joe Byrd had cleaned and landscaped it. The area is well-tended and could be mistaken for a city park except for row after row of white stone markers. Satanta had been buried on top of a rise, separate from the others, in a grave marked by a simple white stone and a solitary pine tree.

Byrd, noting the grave was shallow, and the sandy loam of the soil damp and porous, personally did not expect the delegation of Kiowas, news reporters and other interested parties to find anything. The grave was nevertheless opened after James Auchiah performed the necessary purification rituals, and a few bones, a hand-made nail, and some pottery were recovered. Gillette Griswold, then-director of the Fort Sill Museum, identified the bones as human. They were placed in a plastic bag and returned to Fort Sill for burial with honors.[18]

Today, Satanta's grave at Fort Sill is marked by the standard military headstone, although the Kiowas hope to raise money for a more imposing monument. The former grave site at Huntsville is surrounded by an iron pipe fence erected by Byrd, with a marker noting that this was once Satanta's resting place. The prison grave is still well tended and covered with flowers because, according to Dr. Robert Pierce, director of the Texas Prison Museum, the Kiowas still consider it sacred as the grave of a chief. The Kiowas themselves have traveled to Huntsville to visit the grave and perform their rituals for the dead, as well as to display their culture at local folklife festivals.

* * *

The story of Satanta does not end with his death or even with his reinterment in Oklahoma. It is a living story, carried on by living people. In November 1989, his heirs formally organized themselves as the Chief Satanta (White Bear) Descendants, with headquarters in Apache, Oklahoma. Their emblem is a red and yellow vest similar to that worn by Satanta. When they gather at pow-wows, they erect their heraldic red tipi to remind everyone who they are.

Nor has the name Satanta died; it has been carried on from Gray Goose through the female line. Gray Goose's daughter At-me-ponyah gave the name to her son, Clarence Sankadota, who was Betty Washburn's father. In July 1992, shortly before he died, Clarence Sankadota passed it on to Mrs. Washburn's 21-year-old son Kendall, who is now the fourth Satanta.

In ancient times it was believed that a person was immortal so long as his name was remembered and spoken. If such is the case, then Satanta has achieved immortality.

Chapter Notes

Abbreviations

AG	Adjutant General
AAG	Assistant Adjutant General
AAAG	Acting Assistant Adjutant General
AGO	Office of the Adjutant General
DptMo	Department of the Missouri
DT	Department of Texas
MilDivMo	Military Division of the Missouri
USA	United States Army

Introduction

[1] New York *Times*, October 30, 1867.

[2] Kiowa informant: Betty J. Washburn [At-me-ponyah Sankadota], Satanta's great-great-granddaughter, in consultation with Kiowa elders, letter to the author, January 18, 1993.

[3] C.L. Douglas, *Cattle Kings of Texas*, 194-96, 198-200.

[4] C.F. Doan, "Reminiscences of the Old Trails," 775. Doan, who recalled the incident fifty years later, said it was prior to the Warren massacre. Since the massacre occurred in 1871, and Doan did not arrive in the Indian Territory until 1874, he was most likely referring to the Red River War which broke out in June of that year.

[5] Nye, *Carbine and Lance*, 40-41.

[6] Brown, *Bury My Heart at Wounded Knee*, 243.

Chapter 1
—Satanta and the Kiowas—

[1] Kiowa informant: Betty Washburn, letter to the author, December 23, 1992.

[2] In an article on Satanta for the *Handbook of American Indians North of Mexico* (2:469), James Mooney placed Satanta's birth about 1830, and that date has been accepted in most subsequent works. This, however, is in total contradiction to the available contemporary evidence. DeB. Randolph Keim (*Sheridan's Troopers*, 185), who knew him in 1868, estimated his age then at about fifty. Josiah Butler ("Pioneer School Teaching," 505) figured it at about fifty in 1871. Wharton (*Satanta*, 61) believed Satanta, the paramount chief Dohasen, and Lone Wolf, Satanta's

associate and sometime political rival, "were born technically Spanish subjects," which is to say prior to 1821 when Spain was expelled from the North American mainland. In researching the family genealogy for Satanta's descendants in the 1980s, Parker Paul McKenzie of Mountain View, Oklahoma, placed his birth in 1815.

[3] Mooney, *Calendar History*, 168.

[4] Kiowa informant: Betty Washburn, letter to the author, December 23, 1992.; Colonel Thomas H. Neill to AAG DptMo, October 4, 1874, in Wallace, ed., "Official Correspondence," *Museum Journal* 10:125 (hereinafter cited as "Official Correspondence"); Wharton, *Satanta*, 15. Satanta told Colonel Neill that he was half Arapaho. The story of the Mexicans at Fort Chadbourne was recorded by Wharton.

[5] Mooney, *Calendar History*, 210, 231; Battey, *Life and Adventures*. 196. Battey gives the Kiowa spelling as "See-ti-toh." "Set-t'ainte" is the version used by Mooney throughout and is generally considered more correct.

[6] Mooney, *Calendar History*, 233-35.

[7] Myers, Papers, Folder 10.

[8] Mooney, "Kiowa," 1:699-700, and *Calendar History*, 153-55.

[9] Mooney, *Calendar History*, 228-29; Myers, Papers, Folder 10.

[10] Mayhall, *The Kiowas*, 16, 142; Mooney, *Calendar History*, 233.

[11] Catlin, *Letters and Notes*, 2:74.

[12] "to take the white man by the hand...." Kicking Bird to General W.S. Hancock, Record of Council at Fort Larned, Kansas, May 1, 1867, Special File, Military Division of the Missouri—Hancock's War. Hereinafter referred to as Special File—Hancock.

[13] Kicking Bird's Kiowa name *Tene-a-gopte* actually translates as "Eagle Who Strikes with Talons." The more familiar form is used throughout.

[14] Mayhall, *The Kiowas*, 142; Mooney, *Calendar History*, 230, 233.

[15] Nye, *Carbine and Lance*, 127.

[16] Mayhall, *The Kiowas*, 143; Battey, *Life and Adventures*, 329-30.

[17] No connection with the great Oglala chief, Crazy Horse. The name of this society probably refers to the actions of a horse after eating skunkberries.

[18] Mooney, *Calendar History*, 230. The modern Kiowas mention an additional society, the Gourd Clan, and say that Satanta was a member of that group as well as the Black Legs and Koiet-senko. (*Chief Satanta Descendants Newsletter* 8:2, February 8, 1995.)

[19] Mooney, *Calendar History*, 284-85.

[20] *Chief Satanta (White Bear) Descendants Newsletter*, 8:2, February 8, 1995.

[21] Mooney, *Calendar History*, 329. Like Satanta, the date of Satank's birth is disputed, with some sources giving it as about 1818. This is

unlikely, however, because Satank was a powerful war chief as early as 1837. From contemporary accounts, one must conclude he was in his early seventies when he died in 1871, which would put his birth near the close of the eighteenth century.

[22] Ibid., 284.

[23] Lowe, *Five Years a Dragoon*, 131.

[24] Jacob, "Military Reminiscences," 28.

[25] Keim, *Sheridan's Troopers*, 185; Stanley, *My Early Travels*, 62; Mooney, *Calendar History*, 206.

[26] Kiowa informant: Betty Washburn, letter to the author, December 23, 1992; Custer, *My Life*, 464-65.

[27] Mooney, *Calendar History*, 233; Mayhall, *The Kiowas*, 140, 143.

[28] Hancock, *Reports*, 73.

[29] Myers, Papers, Folder 10.

Chapter 2
—The Making of a Raider—

[1] Myers, Papers, Folder 10.

[2] Betty Washburn in *Chief Satanta (White Bear) Newsletter*, 8:2, February 8, 1995.

[3] Kiowa informant: Betty Washburn, letter to the author, January 18, 1993; Mooney, *Calendar History*, 242. The spelling *"Skaw-tow"* is used by Mrs. Washburn, who spoke Kiowa as a child and heard stories of the old traditions from elderly relatives who knew Satanta. Mooney spells the Kiowa word for Sun Dance *"k'ado."* When pronounced, the two forms sound similar.

[4] Mooney, *Calendar History*, 242-43.

[5] Kiowa informant: Betty Washburn, letter to the author, January 18, 1993.

[6] Day and Winfrey, *Texas Indian Papers, 1825-43*, 18-19.

[7] Ibid., *Texas Indian Papers, 1844-45*, 45.

[8] Mooney, *Calendar History*, 271-72; Lavender, *Bent's Fort*, 186, 418; Grinnell, *Fighting Cheyennes*, 47-48. Any reference by Lavender to Satanta must be approached with caution.

[9] Mooney, *Calendar History*, 274-76; Lavender, *Bent's Fort*, 188; Grinnell, *Fighting Cheyennes*, 65-66.

[10] Worcester, *"Satanta,"* 108.

[11] Grinnell, *Fighting Cheyennes*, 84-91. Mooney (*Calendar History*, 174-75) says the alien Indians in the Pawnee camp were Sauk and Fox. Grinnell acknowledges that some Sauk and Fox were probably present, and suggests the visitors may not have been the Shawnee proper, because plains Indians used the term *"Savane'"* (Shawnee) for all recently arrived Eastern tribes.

[12] Grinnell, *Fighting Cheyennes*, 93-94; Mooney, *Calendar History*, 174-75.

[13] Lowe, *Five Years a Dragoon*, 108.

[14] Myers, Papers, Folder 10.

[15] Lowe, *Five Years a Dragoon*, 131-33.

[16] Ibid., 133-34.

[17] Ibid., 135-36; Mooney, *Calendar History*, 173-74.

[18] Mooney, *Calendar History*, 174.

[19] Ibid.

[20] "Tsait-ante's Shield"; Kiowa informant: Betty Washburn, letter to the author, January 18, 1993; Mooney, *Calendar History*, 210.

[21] Wharton, *Satanta*, 15, 71.

[22] "Tsait-ante's Shield."

[23] Mooney, *Calendar History*, 327.

[24] Betty Washburn, "Chief Satanta," 1; Mooney, *Calendar History*, 306.

[25] Washburn, "Chief Satanta," 1.

[26] J.E.B. Stuart to Lt. John A. Thompson, AG, Kiowa Expedition, July 12, 1860; John Sedgwick to Capt. R.D. Jones, AAG, Department of the West, July 24, 1860; William Steele to Thompson, July 14, 1860, all in Russell, "Jeb Stuart's Other Indian Fight," 12-16.

[27] Russell, ibid., 14.

[28] Pike to unspecified officer (probably General Earl Van Dorn, commanding the District of the Trans-Mississippi which included the Indian Territory), May 4, 1862, *War of the Rebellion: Official Records of the Union and Confederate Armies*, Series 1, 13:822. Hereinafter cited as OR.

[29] Pike to Davis, July 31, 1862, ibid., 868.

[30] Mooney, *Calendar History*, 181.

[31] Ibid., 177.

[32] Lowe, *Five Years a Dragoon*, 364.

[33] Ibid., 381-82.

[34] Ibid., 384-85.

[35] Ibid., 385.

Chapter 3
—"This Fiend Satanta"—

1 Mooney, *Calendar History*, 311.

[2] Quoted ibid., 177. The doctor's reference to a "French horn" does not necessarily mean the instrument as is presently understood, since

Richard Wagner had only recently developed the modern orchestral French horn. More likely he meant a circular type of bugle still used in the British Army where it is called the post horn. The post horn was also known to the U.S. Army, which used a representation of it as the badge of the infantry until the 1870s.

[3] Ibid.

[4] Nye, *Carbine and Lance*, 35. Mrs. Field was never recovered, although Lawrie Tatum, appointed Kiowa-Comanche agent in 1868, made a determined effort to find her. Tatum, who was under the impression that Mrs. Field was a recent captive, described his efforts in a letter to her husband, Patrick Field, which was printed in the Austin, Texas, *Weekly State Journal*, November 3, 1870.

[5] Mooney, *Calendar History*, 312-13; Nye, *Carbine and Lance*, 35; Major General S.R. Curtis to Major General James G. Blunt, September 22, 1864, OR, Series 1, Vol. 41, Part 3:314. Like so many others, Worcester ("Satanta," 109) confuses names and says it was Satanta who was challenged and shot the sentry. Every other source, including Satanta himself, maintains it was Satank. Satanta commented on the incident during a council with General W.S. Hancock, recorded in RG 393, Special File, Military Division of the Missouri—Hancock's War, hereinafter cited as "Special File—Hancock".

[6] Colley to Governor John Evans, July 26, 1864, quoted in Mooney, *Calendar History*, 314.

[7] S.R. Curtis to John Evans, July 30, 1864, OR Series 1, Vol. 41, Part 2:483.

[8] William Bent to S.G. Colley, August 7, 1864, ibid., 732; Major Edward Wynkoop to Lieutenant J.S. Maynard, AAAG, District of Colorado August 9, 1864., ibid., Part 1:231. Bent referred to Dohasen as "Little Mountain," the English translation of his name.

[9] Colley to Evans, August 7, 1864, ibid., Part 2:483.

[10] Wynkoop to Maynard, August 9, 1864, ibid., Part 1:231-32.

[11] Curtis to Blunt, September 22, 1864, ibid., Part 3:314.

[12] Nye, *Carbine and Lance*, 37.

[13] Lieutenant N. Carson to Colonel James Bourland, October 16, 1864, OR, Series 1, Vol. 41, Part 1:885-86.

[14] Ledbetter, *Fort Belknap*, 118.

[15] Robinson, "Kit Carson's Last Fight," 27-28.

[16] Mooney, *Calendar History*, 314-15; Nye, *Carbine and Lance*, 36.

[17] Mooney, ibid.; Nye, ibid.; Christopher Carson to Captain Benjamin Cutler, AAG NM, December 4, 1864, OR, Series 1, Vol. 41, Part 1:840-41.

[18] Carson to Cutler, December 4, 1864, OR, Series 1, Vol. 41, Part 1:340-42; Nye, *Carbine and Lance*, 36-37.

[19] Quoted in Mooney, *Calendar History*, 317.

[20] Ibid.

[21] Carson to Cutler, December 4, 1864, OR, Series 1, Vol. 41, Part 1:842; Mooney, *Calendar History*, 315-16.

[22] Mooney, ibid., 315, 317.

[23] Guild and Carter, *Kit Carson*, 255.

[24] Agent Leavenworth was the only son of General Henry Leavenworth, founder of Fort Leavenworth, Kansas. An 1830 graduate of West Point, he served in the infantry for six years until resigning to go into civil engineering. In 1862 he organized a cavalry regiment, known as the Rocky Mountain Rangers, which protected the frontier during the Civil War. When the war ended, he became the Indian agent.

[25] "Diary of Samuel A. Kingman," 443; Mooney, *Calendar History*, 180.

[26] Mooney, *Calendar History*, 179.

[27] Stanley, *Travels and Adventures*, 14-17.

[28] Ibid., 63.

[29] Quoted in Mooney, *Calendar History*, 179.

[30] Ibid., 180.

[31] Ibid.

[32] Kicking Bird's life is covered in Robinson, "Kicking Bird: Kiowa Martyr for Peace."

Chapter 4
—Bloodshed and Politics—

[1] Mooney, *Calendar History*, 180, 318; Nye, *Carbine and Lance*, 40. The Kiowas say Stumbling Bear was Satanta's cousin as well as Kicking Bird's.

[2] Wharton, *Satanta*, 1-3, 5-7, 201. Wharton heard the story from his father, who was a driver on the train, and from Johnnie Jenkins, one of the wagon guards.

[3] Ibid., 7.

[4] Ibid., 8.

[5] Ibid., 9-11. The Kiowa calendars mention a raid in southwestern Texas during this period in which one warrior was killed. The details, however, and the locale do not correspond to the events recounted by Wharton. Mooney (*Calendar History*, 319) notes that the white records generally refer to continual raiding without going into detail.

[6] Wharton, *Satanta* 11-13.

[7] Ibid., 14, 81-82. Satanta later related this episode to Johnnie Jenkins, the wagon guard who was supervising the convict gang to which Satanta was assigned. The murder of the settler's daughter is unusual, however, because Kiowas generally took white females as captives, as subsequent events on this same raid would show. (See ibid., 199-200)

[8] Ibid., 82-84, 200.

[9] Ibid., 84-85; Nye, *Carbine and Lance*, 41; Mooney, *Calendar History*, 181. Wharton says Satanta, irritated by the crying of Mrs. Box's baby during the trip north, took it away from her and dashed out its brains against a tree. Other sources, however, state Mrs. Box and all four children who survived the initial attack were ransomed at Fort Dodge. The story of brains dashed out is an old one, repeated many times on many occasions about many Indians, and appears to have been a relatively common practice.

[10] Stanley, *Travels and Adventures*, 24. Hancock's War is described in Robinson, "Blundering on the Plains," 28-34.

[11] Stanley, *Travels and Adventures*, 61.

[12] Headquarters, DptMo, in field, Camp No. 17, near Fort Dodge, Kansas, April 23, 1867, in RG 393, Special File—Hancock. This report is also reprinted in Hancock, *Reports*, 57-61.

[13] Stanley, *Travels and Adventures*, 61.

[14] Ibid., 63.

[15] The council was recorded verbatim, with a transcript's appearing in Special File—Hancock, and Stanley, *Travels and Adventures* 63-82. It is also reprinted in Hancock, *Reports*, 67-78.

[16] Hancock, *Reports*, 78.

[17] Stanley, *Travels and Adventures*, 82; Hancock, *Reports*, 33.

Chapter 5
—Medicine Lodge: "My Heart Feels Like Bursting."—

[1] Taylor, "Medicine Lodge," 98.

[2] Ibid.; Andrew Johnson, Third Annual Message, December 3, 1867, in Richardson, *Messages and Papers*, 5:3774; Sherman, *Memoirs*, 924-25.

[3] Sherman, *Memoirs*, 925-26.

[4] Taylor, "Medicine Lodge," 98-99; Johnson, Third Annual Message, in Richardson, *Messages and Papers*, 5:3774; Jones, *Treaty of Medicine Lodge*, 17.

[5] Taylor, "Medicine Lodge," 99-100.

[6] *Cincinnati Commercial*, October 19, 1867.

[7] Stanley, *Travels and Adventures*, 222; Jones, *Medicine Lodge*, 30-31.

[8] Jones, *Medicine Lodge*, 48-50.

[9] William Fayel, St. Louis *Daily Republican*, October 18, 1867; Stanley, *Travels and Adventures*, 223-24. Stanley called the Crow an Apache chief, but Mooney (*Calendar History*, 186) said he was Kiowa.

[10] Stanley, *Travels and Adventures*, 222-23.

[11] Quoted in Jones, *Medicine Lodge*, 51.

[12] Fayel, St. Louis *Daily Republican*, October 18, 1867. Correspondent George C. Brown of the *Cincinnati Commercial* (October 21, 1867) wrote of the same meeting that Satanta's head "measures twenty-four inches just above the eyes. Webster's, it will be remembered, measured the same." One wonders if the correspondents actually sat Satanta down and measured him, a scenario not unlikely considering their curiosity, the nineteenth-century fascination with physiognomy, and Satanta's vanity.

[13] Worcester, "Satanta," 112.

[14] Jones, *Medicine Lodge*, 51-52; Stanley, *Travels and Adventures*, 223.

[15] Fayel, St. Louis *Daily Republican*, October 18, 1867.

[16] Stanley, *Travels and Adventures*, 224.

[17] Stanley, *Travels and Adventures*, 225. Stanley (ibid., 218) called the commander Major Allen, but no such person appears on the rolls of the Seventh Cavalry during that period. Taylor ("Medicine Lodge," 100) correctly identifies Major Elliott.

[18] Stanley, *Travels and Adventures*, 225-26; Taylor, "Medicine Lodge," 101-102.

[19] Stanley, *Travels and Adventures*, 228-29.

[20] Brown, *Cincinnati Commercial*, October 21, 1867.

[21] St. Louis *Daily Republican*, October 24, 1867; Stanley, *Travels and Adventures*, 229-33.

[22] St. Louis *Daily Republican*, October 24, 1867; Stanley, *Travels and Adventures*, 233; Jones, *Medicine Lodge*, 124-25.

[23] Stanley, *Travels and Adventures*, 231-32; Mooney, *Calendar History*, 321.

[24] Fayel, St. Louis *Daily Republican*, October 24, 1867.

[25] Fayel, St. Louis *Daily Republican*, October 18, 1867.

[26] Stanley, *Travels and Adventures*, 236-41.

[27] Ibid., 242-43; Indian Peace Commission, *Report*, 17-18.

[28] Taylor, "Medicine Lodge," 100, 106.

[29] Fayel, St. Louis *Daily Republican*, October 25, 1867.

[30] *New York Times*, October 30, 1867, says the coat was given to Satanta by General Harney, but the circumstances indicate it was the one presented by Hancock.

[31] Fayel, St. Louis *Daily Republican*, October 25, 1867; Jones, *Medicine Lodge*, 11.

[32] Taylor, "Medicine Lodge," 112-13; *New York Times*, Octrober 30, 1867.

[33] Taylor, "Medicine Lodge," 113-14.

[34] *New York Times*, October 30, 1867; Brown, *Cincinnati Commercial*, October 28, 1867.

[35] Miller, et. all. *America Reads*, 343-44.

[36] *New York Times*, October 30, 1867; Stanley, *Travels and Adventures*, 249.

[37] Hoig, *Tribal Wars*, 239.

[38] Stanley, *Travels and Adventures*, 253-56; *New York Times*, October 30, 1867.

[39] Mooney, *Calendar History*, 187.

[40] *New York Times*, October 30, 1867; Stanley, *Travels and Adventures*, 258, and St. Louis *Missouri Democrat*, November 2, 1867.

[41] *New York Times*, November 4, 1867.

[42] Stanley, *Travels and Adventures*, 235.

[43] Lone Wolf was, in fact, the paramount chief now that Dohasen was dead. Satank may have meant that, as leader of the Koiet-senko, he was the principal war chief.

[44] Stanley, St. Louis *Missouri Democrat*, November 2, 1867; Brown, *Cincinnati Commercial*, November 4, 1867; *New York Times*, November 4, 1867; Jones, *Medicine Lodge*, 155-57.

[45] Stanley, St. Louis *Missouri Democrat*, November 2, 1867; *New York Times*, November 4, 1867; Jones, *Medicine Lodge*, 157.

[46] Brown, *Cincinnati Commercial*, November 4, 1867.

Chapter 6
—The Winter Campaign—

[1] Hoig, *Washita*, 41.

[2] Philip McCusker to William B. Hazen, July 19, 1874, in Hazen, "Some Corrections," 317.

[3] Hutton, *Phil Sheridan*, 34-35.

[4] Hoig, *Washita*, 52.

[5] Utley, *Custer's Cavalry*, 174.

[6] Hoig, *Washita*, 53.

[7] O'Neal, *Fighting Men*, 142-43. Hazen's story is told in Kroeker, *Great Plains Command*.

[8] Sheridan's career is described in Hutton, *Phil Sheridan and His Army*.

[9] Spotts, *Campaigning With Custer*, 104.

[10] McCusker to Hazen, July 19, 1874, in Hazen, "Some Corrections," 317.

[11] Peace Commission, *Report*, 8-9.

[12] Hazen, "Some Corrections," 313, 318. Hazen initially claimed to be concerned about the raids into Texas (313), but later contradicted himself (318). The bulk of the evidence indicates that neither he nor most other federal officers cared what happened to Texas at this juncture.

[13] Hazen, "Some Corrections," 300-301.

[14] Ibid., 301-302, 304-305; Keim, Sheridan's Troopers, 161-62; Hoig, Washita, 87-88.

[15] Hutton, Phil Sheridan, 56-57.

[16] Keim, Sheridan's Troopers, 150; Hoig, Washita, 67-68.

[17] Hazen, "Some Corrections," 302; Hutton, Phil Sheridan, 57.

[18] Hoig, Washita, 93-95. This assumption notwithstanding, the actual layout of the camps will unfortunately never be precisely known; this knowledge would have done much to locate the camp in which the bodies of Clara Blinn and the child presumed to be her son were found. The Blinn murders were a key factor in the campaign, since Sheridan used them to justify his subsequent actions. Yet no two military sources agree even on the physical conditions of the bodies much less their locations, so the assignment of guilt is based on unfounded suspicion and further muddles any agreement on the arrangement of the camps. The layout is also complicated by subsequent statements from Cheyenne prisoners, who tailored their depositions according to what the soldiers wanted to hear. Based on Cheyenne statements, Custer reported Black Kettle's camp was uppermost, then Little Raven and the Arapahos, followed by the Kiowas under Satanta and Lone Wolf, and finally "remaining bands of Cheyennes, Comanches and Apaches." (Custer to Lt.Col. J. Schuyler Crosby, AAAG, Department of the Missouri, December 22, 1868, RG 94 AGO R 1870, Letters Received, Main Series, 1861-1870). Keim (Sheridan's Troopers, 151) likewise claims the Kiowa villages belonged to Satanta and Lone Wolf. Despite these allegations, Hazen ("Some Corrections," 306) states that Satanta, Lone Wolf and Satank were all with him at Fort Cobb at the time of the Washita fight and did not leave for their own camps until several hours after the fight ended.

[19] Custer, My Life, 434-35.

[20] Custer is the subject of one of the largest bodies of literature in the English language. Among the classics are Edgar I. Stewart's Custer's Luck, and Frederic F. Van de Water's Glory Hunter. More recent are Robert Utley's Cavalier in Buckskin, and Charles M. Robinson III, A Good Year to Die.

[21] The Washita fight is described in Hoig, The Battle of the Washita, and by Sheridan (letter to Sherman, November 1, 1869) and by Custer (to Crosby, December 22, 1868), both in Letters Received, 1861-1870.

[22] Robinson, "Kicking Bird," 15.

[23] Spotts, Campaigning With Custer, 75-76, 169n. In editing and arranging Spotts' diary for publication, historian E.A. Brininstool investigated the Blinn kidnapping and murders and contended it was exclusively a Cheyenne affair. Among his sources was T.P. Lyon of Los Angeles, Calif.,

a trooper with the Seventh Cavalry on the expedition, who claimed to have witnessed the death of the child presumed to be Willie Blinn and to have shot the Indian woman responsible. All indications are that the death of the child took place in Black Kettle's Cheyenne camp, which was separate and distinct from the Kiowa camp.

[24] Sheridan meant, of course, regular soldiers, because territorial volunteers such as Chivington's often did kill women and children.

[25] Hutton, *Phil Sheridan*, 73-74.

[26] Keim, *Sheridan's Troopers*, 154.

[27] Custer to Crosby, December 22, 1868, Letters Received, 1861-1870; Custer, *My Life*, 435; Keim, *Sheridan's Troopers*, 150. Hazen ("Some Corrections," 305) claims to have interviewed many Indian participants in the fight who uniformly stated that the two white victims were held by Arapahos, and that the Kiowas were not involved in any way.

[28] Sheridan, *Personal Memoirs*, 2:330-31.

[29] Quoted in Custer to Crosby, December 22, 1868, Letters Received, 1861-1870; and Hazen, "Some Corrections," 299.

[30] Sheridan, *Personal Memoirs*, 2:334; Custer, *My Life*, 431-32; Keim, *Sheridan's Troopers*, 154-55.

[31] Custer, *My Life*, 432-33; Keim, *Sheridan's Troopers*, 156-57.

[32] Keim, *Sheridan's Troopers*, 156.

[33] Nye, *Carbine and Lance*, 73-74.

[34] Keim, *Sheridan's Troopers*, 156-57; Custer, *My Life*, 444-47; Hoig, *Washita*, 166; Sheridan, *Personal Memoirs*, 2:324-35.

[35] Spotts, *Campaigning With Custer*, 81.

[36] Custer, *My Life*, 449-50.

[37] Custer, *My Life*, 452-53; Sheridan, *Personal Memoirs*, 2:335; Sheridan to Sherman, November 1, 1869, Letters Received, 1861-1870. The quote is from Custer, as he recorded the conversation soon after it occurred. Sheridan gave essentially the same version, except he says the Kiowas were given two days. In his initial report to Colonel Crosby on December 22, Custer said two head chiefs of the Apaches were also held, although he did not give their names. (Custer to Crosby, December 22, 1868, Letters Received, 1861-1870).

[38] Dodge, *Our Wild Indians*, 103; Keim, *Sheridan's Troopers*, 163.

[39] Sheridan, *Personal Memoirs*, 2:335.

[40] Custer, *My Life*, 456-57.

[41] Ibid., 458.

[42] Moore, "Nineteenth Kansas," 360-61. The practice of eating dirt for various mystical reasons was common to primitive societies throughout the world. It appears to have been familiar to the whites in the nineteenth century, which may explain why Moore did not bother to elaborate. (See Bourke, *Apache Medicine-Men*, 87-90).

[43] Nye, *Carbine and Lance*, 75.

[44] Spotts, *Campaigning With Custer*, 83; Custer, *My Life*, 464-66; Kiowa informant: Betty Washburn. Custer is hardly an unimpeachable source, and *My Life on the Plains* is generally acknowledged as an effort at self-aggrandizement, pretending to an expertise on Indians which Custer did not have. His Seventh Cavalry subordinate, Captain Frederick Benteen, openly referred to the book as "My Lies on the Plains." Fortunately, much of his writing can be cross-checked with other contemporary sources. It is in those areas which cannnot be cross-checked, such as routine camp life with his prisoners, personal conversations with Satanta, and observations on the chief's family, that Custer rings most true. While the truth of these segments will never be known, he had no reason to misrepresent them.

[45] Continental, *Wild Life on the Plains*, 265-66. This compilation of writings about the Indian wars contains portions of Custer's *My Life on the Plains*, including the marksmanship contest between Custer and Grey Goose which was edited out of the University of Nebraska Press edition of Custer's work.

Chapter 7
—"Peace on the Reservations; War Off of Them."—

[1] Keim, *Sheridan's Troopers*, 232; Nye, *Carbine and Lance*, 75-84.

[2] Keim, *Sheridan's Troopers* 254-55.

[3] Nye, *Carbine and Lance*, 89-91; Leckie, *Unlikely Warriors*, 161.

[4] Sheridan to Sherman, November 1, 1869, Letters Received, 1861-1870.

[5] Keim, *Sheridan's Troopers*, 279-80.

[6] Ibid., 280-81.

[7] Sherman, *Memoirs*, 926-27.

[8] Ibid., 927.

[9] Grant, First Annual Message, December 6, 1869, in Richardson, *Messages and Papers*, 3992.

[10] Tatum, *Red Brothers*, 23-24.

[11] Ibid., 24-26.

[12] Ibid., 28-30.

[13] Second Annual Report, Office of the Kiowa and Comanche Agency, Fort Sill, August 12, 1870, in Myers, Papers, Folder 10.

[14] Grierson to Tatum, September 30, 1869. Indian Archives, Kiowa-Military Relations.

[15] Second Annual Report, Office of the Kiowa and Comanche Agency, Fort Sill, August 12, 1870, in Myers, Papers, Folder 10.

[16] Leckie and Leckie, *Unlikely Warriors*, 171.

[17] Second Annual Report, August 12, 1870, in Myers, Papers, Folder 10.

[18] Foreman, "General Benjamin Henry Grierson," 203; Tatum, *Red Brothers*, 34-35.

[19] Austin *Weekly State Journal*, June 16, 1870; McConnell, *Five Years a Cavalryman*, 215-16; Robinson, "Kicking Bird," 16.

[20] Nye, *Carbine and Lance*, 112; Leckie, *Unlikely Warriors*, 179.

[21] Austin *Weekly State Journal*, April 28, 1870.

[22] Tatum, *Red Brothers*, 35-40.

[23] Ibid., 40-43; Tatum to Patrick Field, September 19, 1870, published in Austin *Weekly State Journal*, November 3, 1870; Leckie, *Unlikely Warriors*, 179.

[24] Tatum, *Red Brothers*, 47-48.

Chapter 8
—The Warren Massacre—

[1] Nye, *Carbine and Lance*, 127; Huckabay, *Ninety-four Years*, 170.

[2] J.W. Davidson to AAG, DptMo, July 10, 1871, RG 94 1305 AGO 1871, Letters Received, Main Series, 1871-1880, hereinafter referred to as Letters Received.

[3] Nye, *Carbine and Lance*, 123.

[4] The greeting "how?" appeared to have derived from the English "How do you do?"

[5] Myers, Papers, Folder 10.

[6] Nye, *Carbine and Lance*, 113-14; Huckabay, *Ninety-four Years*, 170.

[7] Morris, "Big Tree's Raid," 2-3.

[8] The following account of the Warren Massacre comes from two main sources: Nye's *Carbine and Lance*, 126-32, and Mrs. Huckabay's *Ninety-four Years in Jack County*, 170-72. Nye, who was stationed at Fort Sill when many old Kiowa warriors were still alive, heard a first-hand account from Yellow Wolf, the last survivor of the raiding party. He also visited the site of the raid accompanied by Hunting Horse, who did not participate but who remembered when it occurred, and by George Hunt, Old Satank's son-in-law who obtained his information from Big Tree and other warriors. Additional details were provided by Ay-tah, widow of Set-maunte who was on the raid. Mrs. Huckabay obtained her information from George Hunt in 1938.

[9] Carter, *On the Border*, 69.

[10] Huckabay, *Ninety-four Years*, 170-71; Nye, *Carbine and Lance*, 127-28.

[11] Quoted in Nye, *Carbine and Lance*, 128.

[12] Huckabay, *Ninety-four Years*, 171; Nye, *Carbine and Lance*, 128.

[13] Marcy, Journal, in Rister, "Documents," *Panhandle-Plains Historical Review*, 9:14-16, 18-19.

[14] Nye, *Carbine and Lance*, 128-30; Huckabay, *Ninety-four Years*, 171.

15 Quoted in Nye, *Carbine and Lance*, 130.

[16] Nye, *Carbine and Lance*, 130-31.

[17] Citizens of Jack County to Sherman, May 2, 1871, original document reproduced in Hamilton, *Sentinal*, 237-43.

[18] Huckabay, *Ninety-four Years*, 168; Sherman to Mackenzie, May 19, 1871, "Official Correspondence," *Museum Journal*, 9:23-24.

19 Grant, *Memoirs*, 2:541.

[20] Mackenzie's life and career are discussed in Robinson, *Bad Hand: A Biography of General Ranald S. Mackenzie*.

[21] Robinson, *Bad Hand*, 80.

[22] Quoted in Huckabay, *Ninety-four Years*, 168-69.

[23] Dr. Patzki's statement has been printed in many works. The quote here is from Nye, *Carbine and Lance*, 131.

[24] Huckabay, *Ninety-four Years*, 169; Robinson, *Bad Hand*, 80-81; Sherman to Mackenzie, May 19, 1871, "Official Correspondence," *Museum Journal*, 9:23.

[25] Sherman to General H.D. Townsend, May 24, 1871, RG 94 1305 ACP 1871, Letters Received, Main Series, 1871-1880.

[26] Ibid.

[27] Nye, *Carbine and Lance*, 132.

Chapter 9
—Arrest—

[1] Tatum, *Red Brothers*, 113-16.

[2] Sherman to E.D. Townsend, May 24, 1871, RG 94 1305 AGO 1871, Letters Received, Main Series, 1871-80; Butler, "Pioneer School Teaching," 503; Sherman to General John Pope, May 24, 1871, in Rister, "Documents," 10:52.

[3] Nye, *Carbine and Lance*, 132.

[4] Nye, *Carbine and Lance* 134; Tatum to Jonathan Richards, May 30, 1871, Indian Archive, Kiowa-Comanche Agency, Records Relating to the Trial of Satanta and Big Tree, 1871-78, hereinafter referred to as Kiowa File.

[5] Tatum, *Red Brothers*, 116-17; Tatum to Richards, Kiowa File; Nye, *Carbine and Lance*, 136.

[6] Nye, *Carbine and Lance*, 136.

[7] Tatum, *Red Brothers*, 117; Nye, *Carbine and Lance*, 136; Pratt, *Battlefield and Classroom*, 43-44; Butler, "Pioneer School Teaching," 504; Sherman to Sheridan, May 29, 1871, Letters Received.

[8] Pratt, *Battlefield and Classroom*, 44; Myers, Papers, Folder 10; Nye, *Carbine and Lance*, 136.

[9] Sherman to Sheridan, May 29, 1871, Letters Received; Tatum, *Red Brothers*, 117-18.

[10] Nye, *Carbine and Lance*, 137-38. As with the Warren massacre, Nye interviewed Indians who had been present as well as those who had heard it from now-deceased parents, particularly Andrew Stumbling Bear, son of the old chief. Many of the Indians he interviewed had understood what the chiefs said, including words exchanged among themselves as they dealt with Sherman. Therefore any work on the arrest of the chiefs must, again, rely heavily on Nye as the main source for the Indian side. Weems (*Death Song*, 133-34) has a lengthy statement supposedly made to Sherman by Satanta, whom he calls by the English "White Bear," but he is not specific as to source in his notes and it does not appear in any of the major historical works on the affair.

[11] Marcy, Journal, May 27, 1871, quoted in Wilbarger, *Indian Depredations*, 557-58; Sherman to Sheridan, May 29, 1871, Letters Received.

[12] Nye, *Carbine and Lance*, 138-41; Pratt, *Battlefield and Classroom*, 44.

[13] Myers, Papers, Folder 10; Nye, *Carbine and Lance*, 141-42; Marcy, Journal, May 27, 1871, in Wilbarger, *Indian Depredations*, 559. Nye's Indian informants (141) indicated that Lone Wolf did not want to be involved but was shamed into the demonstration by Kicking Bird who, through hand signals, had challenged him to take his place in the circle and prepare for possible death along with the rest of them.

[14] Nye, *Carbine and Lance*, 142; Sherman to Sheridan, May 29, 1871, Letters Received; Marcy, Journal, May 27, 1871, in Wilbarger, *Indian Depredations*, 559.

[15] Sherman to Townsend, May 28, 1871, Letters Received.

[16] Tatum to Sherman and Grierson, May 28, 1871, with endorsements, Letters Received.

[17] Sherman to Sheridan, May 29, 1871, Letters Received.

[18] Sherman to Mackenzie, quoted in Carter, *On the Border*, 88.

[19] Grierson to AAG, DptMo., June 1, 1871, Letters Received.

[20] Mackenzie to H. Clay Wood, June 5, 1871; Grierson to AAG DptMo., June 9, 1871, both in Letters Received; Nye, *Carbine and Lance*, 142; Pratt, *Battlefield and Classroom*, 47.

[21] Butler, "Pioneer School Teaching," 505-506.

[22] Butler, "Pioneer School Teaching," 506-507; Nye, *Carbine and Lance*, 144-45; Carter, *The Old Sergeant*, 78-79.

[23] Carter, *The Old Sergeant*, 81, and *On the Border*, 95-96.

[24] Carter, *On the Border*, 97-98; Jehu Atkinson to Ida Lasater Huckabay, October 18, 1947, in Huckabay, *Ninety-four Years*, 178. Atkinson, the last known survivor of that period, was sixteen at the time of the arrest and trial of the chiefs.

Chapter 10
—The Trial—

[1] Much of the trial record was lost over a century ago and is known mainly through bits and pieces which have been gathered and published over the years. The indictment is quoted in Huckaby, *Ninety-four Years*, 179-80. See footnote no. 7.

[2] Huckabay, *Ninety-four Years*, 138-39.

[3] Carter, *On the Border*, 99-101; Wilbarger, *Indian Depredations*, 561; Huckaby, *Ninety-four Years*, 178.

[4] McConnell, *Five Years a Cavalryman*, 282.

[5] Carter, *On the Border*, 100-101.

[6] Ibid., 101; Mackenzie to Tatum, June 25, 1871, Kiowa File; Tatum, *Red Brothers*, 121; "conducted their defense..." Wilbarger, *Indian Depredations*, 562.

[7] With much of the official record lost within a few years of the trial, and with two separate trials held on different days, events in the courtroom must be patched together from various sources. There is no way of knowing in which trial this speech, or the statements of the defense, was made. The order, therefore, is conjecture based on the most logical sequence. Lanham's speech has been reprinted many times and, in this case, comes from Wilbarger, *Indian Depredations*, 562-66.

[8] Quoted in Ledbetter, *Fort Belknap*, 277.

[9] Carter, *On the Border*, 101.

[10] Jack County, District Court Minutes, A:236.

[11] Corwin, *The Kiowas*, 64.

[12] Quoted by E.F. Gilbert, Austin *Weekly State Journal*, July 18, 1871.

[13] Austin *Weekly State Journal*, July 18, 1871.

[14] Jack County, District Court Minutes, A:237-38.

[15] Charles Soward to Edmund J. Davis, July 10, 1871, quoted in Wilbarger, *Indian Depredations*, 569-70.

[16] Edmund J. Davis, Proclamation, August 2, 1871, Texas Prison Papers.

[17] Quoted in Nye, *Carbine and Lance 147*.

[18] Headquarters, Department of Texas and Louisiana, Special Order No. 185, September 12, 1871, Letters Received. Sallie Reynolds Matthews (*Interwoven*, 85) says her husband, J.A. Matthews, rode part of the

way to Huntsville in a stagecoach with the chiefs and "almost smothered in tobacco smoke as the Indians kept their clay pipes going constantly." In view of the orders forbidding contact with civilians and the army's overall security precautions, this is highly unlikely. Mrs. Matthews did not marry her husband until five years after the trial and did not compile her memoirs for almost sixty years. Her account, therefore, is not first hand, and the recollections may have been slightly altered by time.

[19] Carter, *On the Border*, 103.

[20] Billy R. Ware, director, Bureau of Classifications and Records, Texas Department of Corrections, to Cecil Willis, June 30, 1976, Texas Prison Papers; Post Returns, Fort Richardson, Texas, October, November 1871; Huckabay, *Ninety-four Years*, 190; McConnell, *Five Years a Cavalryman*, 288-89.

Chapter 11
—Prison—

[1] Tatum, *Red Brothers*, 131.

[2] Ibid., 131-32.

[3] Ibid., 122-25.

[4] Ibid., 132.

[5] Augur to Sheridan, June 10, 1872, "Official Correspondence," *Musuem Journal*, 9:81.

[6] Sheridan, endorsement of June 19, 1872, to Augur, ibid., 9:82.

[7] Tatum, *Red Brothers*, 125.

[8] Ibid., 125-26; G.W. Greyson, to the President and Secretary of the Interior, May 1873, Day and Winfrey, *Texas Indian Papers, 1860-1916*, 341; Mooney, *Calendar History*, 190.

[9] Tatum, *Red Brothers*, 126-27.

[10] Ware to Willis, June 30, 1976, Texas Prison Papers.

[11] Wharton, *Satanta*, 200.

[12] Ibid., 200-201.

[13] Ibid., 201.

[14] Mooney, *Calendar History*, 190.

[15] Ibid., 190-92.

[16] *Galveston News*, September 20, 1872.

[17] Alvord's report is reprinted in Moony, *Calendar History*, 193-95.

[18] Carter, *On the Border*, 349-64.

[19] Probably a government official. Later in the talk Satanta mentioned Governor Davis, but there is no indication Davis was seriously involved at this point.

[20] *St. Louis Globe*, September 20, 1872, reprinted in *Galveston News*, October 5, 1872.

[21] Ibid.

[22] *McKinney Enquirer*, October 5, 1872, reprinted in *Galveston News*, October 12, 1872.

[23] *Army and Navy Journal*, October 26, 1872, 165.

[24] Secretary of the Interior Columbus Delano to Edmund Davis, March 22, 1873, Kiowa File; Leckie, *Unlikely Warriors*, 206.

[25] Leckie, *Unlikely Warriors*, 207.

[26] Tatum, *Red Brothers*, 131-33.

[27] Strong, *Frontier Days*, 22-23; Wilbarger, *Indian Depredations*, 573.

[28] Actually, he was about fifty-six or fifty-seven.

[29] *Scribner's Monthly*, 7:4 (February 1874):415, quoted in Mooney, *Calendar History*, 209.

Chapter 12
—Parole—

[1] Major G.W. Schofield to AAG DT, January 17, 1873, "Official Correspondence," *Museum Journal*, 9:159-60; Nye, *Carbine and Lance*, 164.

[2] Columbus Delano to Davis, March 22, 1873, Kiowa file.

[3] Hoag to Davis, April 9, 1873, Kiowa File.

[4] A detailed account of the Modoc War and the trial and execution of the Modoc chiefs is found in Paul I. Wellman, *Death in the Desert*.

[5] Delano to Davis, May 27, 1873, Kiowa File.

[6] Hoag to Haworth, June 3, 1873, ibid.

[7] Smith to Delano, May 22, 1873, Day and Winfrey, *Texas Indian Papers, 1860-1916*, 338-39.

[8] Smith to Haworth, June 26, 1873, quoted in Battey, *Life and Adventures*. 160-61.

[9] Hoag to Jonathan Richards, June 3, 1873; Delano to Smith, July 11, 1873, both in Kiowa File.

[10] Hoag to Haworth, July 15, 1873, ibid.

[11] Nye, *Carbine and Lance*, 167-69.

[12] Copy of telegram in Hoag to Haworth, August 12, 1873, Kiowa File.

[13] Davis to Davidson, August 14, 1873, ibid.

[14] Chauncey McKeever, AAG DT, to Commanding Officer, Fort Sill, August 23, 1873; Haworth to Richards, September 4, 1873, both ibid.

[15] Day and Winfrey, *Texas Indian Papers, 1860-1916*, entry 221, 342-48; Louis J. Valentine to Davis, September 14, 1873, ibid., 342-44.

[16] Hoag's reaction to Davis' accusations is in Hoag to Haworth, August 12, 1873, Kiowa File. Alvord's letter to Davis, dated September 22, 1873, is in Day and Winfrey, *Texas Indian Papers, 1860-1916*, 348-49.

[17] Davidson to AAG DT, October 8, 1873, RG 94 4447 AGO 1873; Nye, *Carbine and Lance*, 169.

[18] Davis, letter of October 5, 1873, Day and Winfrey, *Texas Indian Papers, 1860-1916*, 349-50.

[19] Day and Winfrey, *Texas Indian Papers, 1860-1916*, 350.

[20] Ibid., 351-53.

[21] Ibid., 353-61.

[22] Smith to Davis, October 7, 1873, RG 94 4447 AGO 1873.

[23] Battey, *Life and Adventures*, 202-03; Nye, *Carbine and Lance*, 174-75.

[24] Day and Winfrey, *Texas Indian Papers, 1860-1916*, 362-63; Nye, *Carbine and Lance*, 175.

[25] Sherman to Davis, February 17, 1874, Sherman, Unofficial Correspondence.

Chapter 13
—The Red River War—

[1] Wharton, *Satanta*, 283.

[2] Carlton to Haworth, May 8, 1874, Kiowa File.

[3] Wharton, *Satanta*, 220.

[4] Battey, *Life and Adventures*, 239-40

[5] Leckie, "Red River War," 80.

[6] Ibid., 79-80.

[7] Ibid., 80-81.

[8] Robinson, *Buffalo Hunters*, 84-85. The Red River War is covered in James L. Haley, *The Buffalo War*.

[9] Smith to Secretary of the Interior, July 18, 1874, RG 393, Special File, MilDivMo, Red River War, hereinafter referred to as "Special File—Red River War."

[10] Smith to Hoag, July 20, 1874, ibid.

[11] Wharton (*Satanta*, 220) states Satanta gave both the lance and the shield to a renowned warrior A'to-t'ain. In 1894, however, the shield was owned by Gray Goose, who passed it on to General Hugh Scott. Gray Goose's great-granddaughter, Betty Washburn, believes Satanta gave it

to Gray Goose when Satanta was sent to Texas for trial. The legality of Scott's acquisition, and the present (1997) ownership by the Phoebe Hearst Museum of Anthropology (formerly Lowie Museum and Anthropology) at the University of California at Berkeley, is disputed by the Kiowas. (Betty J. Washburn to Charles M. Robinson III, January 18, 1993)

[12] Haley, *Buffalo War*, 79-81; Captain B.K. Sanderson, November 26, 1874, endorsement to Sheridan to Belknap, November 17, 1874, Taylor, *Indian Campaign*, 97.

[13] Sanderson, November 26, 1874, endorsement to Sheridan to Belknap, November 17, 1874, Taylor, *Indian Campaign*, 97-98.

[14] Davidson to AAG DT, August 26, 1874, Special File—Red River War.

[15] Miles to General John Pope, commander, DptMo, September 14, 1874, Special File—Red River War; Nye, *Carbine and Lance*, 219.

[16] Kiowa informant: Betty Washburn, telephone conversation with the author; ibid., interview in Huntsville, Texas, April 19, 1991, Texas Prison Papers.

[17] Lieutenant Colonel Thomas H. Neill to Pope, September 30, 1874, Special File—Red River War; Nye, *Carbine and Lance*, 219.

[18] R. Williams, AAG DptMo to Colonel R.C. Drum, AAG, MilDivMo, October 2, 1874, Special File—Red River War.

[19] Neill to AAG, DptMo, October 1, 1874, ibid.

[20] Williams to Drum, October 7, 1874, quoted in Taylor, *Indian Campaign*, 87.

[21] Neill to AAG, DptMo, October 4, 1874, Kiowa File.

[22] William W. Belknap to U.S. Grant, October 5, 1874; Belknap to Sheridan, October 6, 1874; O.E. Babcock, secretary to the president, to Belknap, undated, all in Taylor, *Indian Campaign*, 90-92.

[23] James W. Forsyth, secretary, MilDivMo, to Carlton, October 30, 1874; Richard Coke to J.M.P. Campbell, inspector of penitentiary, November 5, 1874, both in Texas Prison Papers; Haworth to E.P. Smith, November 7, 1874, quoted in Taylor, *Indian Campaign*, 93.

[24] Smith to Delano, November 9, 1874, quoted in Taylor, *Indian Campaign*, 93-94.

[25] Delano to Belknap, November 9, 1874; Townsend to Sheridan, November 13, 1874; Sheridan to Belknap, November 17, 1874, with endorsement by Augur, November 24, 1874, all ibid., 94-97.

[26] Sanderson, November 26, 1874, endorsement to Sheridan, November 17, 1874, ibid., 99.

[27] Sheridan to Belknap, November 17, 1874, ibid., 96.

Chapter 14
—Death and Immortality—

[1] Nye, *Carbine and Lance*, 255; Wharton, *Satanta*, 234.

[2] Thomas J. Goree to P.B. Hunt, August 10, 1878, Kiowa File.

[3] Wharton, *Satanta*, 234; Nye, *Carbine and Lance*, 255; Huckabay, *Ninety-four Years*, 202.

[4] Billy R. Ware to Cecil Willis, June 30, 1976, Texas Prison Papers.

[5] Huckabay, *Ninety-four Years*, 202.

[6] Betty J. Washburn, telephone conversation with Charles M. Robinson III; videotaped interviews with various Kiowas, Huntsville, April 19, 1991.

[7] Huckabay, *Ninety-four Years*, 205-206.

[8] Nye, *Carbine and Lance*, 261; Scott, *Some Memories*, 169; Stanley, *Satanta*, 350.

[9] Scott, *Some Memories*, 170.

[10] Ibid., 165-66.

[11] Burton Benedict to David Boren, November 17, 1992, copy in possession of the author.

[12] Ibid.; Towana Spivey to Betty J. Washburn, October 6, 1992, and Betty J. Washburn to Burton Benedict, July 22, 1992, Texas Prison Papers. A possible legal conflict between the university's presumed title and the Native American Repatriation Act could raise interesting constitutional questions concerning Fifth Amendment protection of legally acquired property—assuming, of course, that the acquisition could be established as legal at the time it was made.

[13] State of Texas, House Concurrent Resolution No. 67, May 17, 1963, copy in "Satanta" file, Center for American History, University of Texas.

[14] Quoted in Stanley, *Satanta*, 351-52.

[15] House Concurrent Resolution No. 67, May 17, 1963, "Satanta" File, Center for American History, University of Texas.

[16] Quoted in Stanley, *Satanta*, 351.

[17] Quoted in ibid., 352-53.

[18] Dallas *Morning News*, June 19, 1963; Dallas *Times-Herald*, June 30, 1963.

Bibliography

There are many works on Satanta and his era. Unfortunately, they are scattered and much of the material is no longer in print.

During the first half of this century, Carl Coke Rister pioneered the study of Satanta and his times, although much of the work is now dated, as is Francis Stanley's 1968 book *Satanta and the Kiowas*. Benjamin Capps' book, *The Warren Wagon Train Raid*, while often accepted as factual history, is actually historical fiction and should be viewed as such.

Despite a certain amount of jingoism, Colonel W.S. Nye's *Carbine and Lance: The Story of Old Fort Sill* remains the best overall work on the last days of Kiowa military power, with much original material on Satanta. Nye, who was stationed at Fort Sill in the 1930s, was able to interview the last remaining Kiowas from that era and the immediate descendants of those already dead. His book, first published in 1937, has gone through three editions and remains in print to the good fortune of anyone interested in the period. James Mooney's *Calendar History of the Kiowa Indians* preserves much of what is known about the old Kiowa way of life.

I should also mention Clarence Wharton's *Satanta: The Great Chief of the Kiowas*. Wharton, who was born only two years before Satanta's death, compiled his work from the reminiscences of many who had known or fought Satanta, filling in the gaps with information from Mooney and other authorities.

Government Documents

Bourke, John Gregory. *Apache Medicine-Men*. Originally published as "The Medicine-Men of the Apache." *Ninth Annual Report of the American Bureau of Ethnology to the Secretary of the Smithsonian Institution, 1887-'88*. 1892. Reprint. New York: Dover Publications, 1993.

Day, James M. and Dorman Winfrey, eds. *Texas Indian Papers, 1825-1843*. Austin: Texas State Library, 1959.

___. *Texas Indian Papers, 1844-1845*. Austin: Texas State Library, 1960.

—. *Texas Indian Papers, 1860-1916*. Austin: Texas State Library, 1961.

District Clerk's Office, Jacksboro, Jack County, Texas. Minutes of the District Court, Cause No. 224, State of Texas vs. Satanta and Big Tree.

Hancock, Winfield Scott. *Reports of Major General W.S. Hancock Upon Indian Affairs, With Accompanying Exhibits*. Washington: U.S. Government Printing Office, n.d. (1867).

Mooney, James. *Calendar History of the Kiowa Indians*. 1898. Reprint. Washington: Smithsonian Institution Press, 1979.

—. "Kiowa." Frederick Webb Hodge, ed. *Handbook of American Indians North of Mexico*. Vol. 1. 1905. Reprint. Totowa, N.J.: Rowman and Littlefield, 1975.

—. "Satanta." Frederick Webb Hodge, ed. *Handbook of American Indians North of Mexico*. Vol. 2. 1905. Reprint. Totowa, N.J.: Rowman and Littlefield, 1975.

Richardson, James D. (comp.). *A Compilation of the Messages and Papers of the Presidents*. Vols. 5 and 6. Washington: Bureau of National Literature and Art, 1897.

Texas Prison Papers. Texas Prison Museum, Huntsville.

United States Department of the Interior. Bureau of Indian Affairs. Kiowa Agency, Federal, State and Local Court Relations, Trial of Satanta and Big Tree, May 30, 1871 to August 15, 1878. Indian Archives Division, Oklahoma Historical Society, Oklahoma City.

—. Kiowa-Military Relations. Indian Archives Division, Oklahoma Historical Society, Oklahoma City.

United States Department of War. Office of the Adjutant General. Record Group 94, Returns of U.S. Military Posts, Fort Richardson, Texas. Washington: National Archives Microfilm Publications. Vol. 617, Roll 1008.

——. Record Group 94 Adjutant General's Office File R 1870. Letters Received, Main Series, 1861-1870. Reports by Generals Sheridan and Custer and Others Officers Regarding Activities Against Indians in the Military Division of the Missouri, 1868-1869. Washington: National Archives Microfilm Publications. Vol. 619, Roll 812.

___. Record Group 94 1305 Adjutant General's Office, Letters Received, Main Series, 1871-1880. Washington: National Archives Microfilm Publications. Vol. 660, Roll 10 (1871).

——. Record Group 94 4447 AGO 1873. Letters Received. National Archives. Electrostatic copy in possession of the author.

___. Record Group 393, Special File, Military Division of the Missouri, as follows:

Hancock's War. Washington: National Archives Microfilm Publications. Vol. 1495, Roll 7.

Red River War. Washington: National Archives Microfilm Publications. Vol. 1495, Rolls 8 and 9.

——. *War of the Rebellion: A Compilation of the Official Records of the Union and Confederate Armies*. 130 vols. Washington: U.S. Government Printing Office, 1891-1898.

United States Indian Peace Commission. *Report to the President by the Indian Peace Commission, January 7, 1868.* N.p. N.d. (Washington, 1868).

Books, Articles and Manuscripts

Battey, Thomas C. *The Life and Adventures of a Quaker Among the Indians*. 1875. Reprint. Williamstown, Mass.: Corner House Publishers, 1972.

Brown, Dee. *Bury My Heart at Wounded Knee*. New York: Holt, Rinehart and Winston, 1970.

Butler, Josiah. "Pioneer School Teaching at the Comanche-Kiowa Agency School 1870-3." *Chronicles of Oklahoma*. Vol. 6, No. 4 (1928).

Carter, Robert G. *The Old Sergeant's Story: Fighting Indians and Bad Men in Texas from 1870 to 1876*. 1926. Reprint. Mattituck, NY, and Bryan, Tex.: JM Carroll and Company, 1982.

——. *On the Border with Mackenzie, or Winning the West from the Comanches.* 1935. Reprint. New York: Antiquarian Press, 1961.

Catlin, George. *Letters and Notes on the Manners, Customs and Conditions of North American Indians.* 4th edition. 2 vols. 1844. Reprint. New York: Dover Publications, Inc., 1973.

Connelley, William E. "The Treaty Held at Medicine Lodge Between the Peace Commission and the Comanche, Kiowa, Arapahoe, Cheyenne and Prairie Apache Tribes of Indians, in October, 1867." *Collections of the Kansas State Historical Society.* Vol. 17 (Winter 1926-27).

Continental Publishing Co. (comp.). *Wild Life on the Plains and the Horrors of Indian Warfare.* 1891. Reprint. New York: Arno Press, 1969.

Corwin, Hugh D. *The Kiowa Indians: Their History and Life Stories.* Lawton, Okla.: Privately Printed, 1958.

Custer, George Armstrong. *My Life on the Plains.* 1952. Reprint. Lincoln: University of Nebraska Press, 1966.

"Diary of Samuel A. Kingman at Indian Treaty in 1865." *Kansas State Historical Quarterly.* Vol. 1 (November 1932).

Doan, C.F. "Reminiscences of the Old Trails." J. Marvin Hunter (comp.). *The Trail Drivers of Texas.* 1925. Reprint. Austin: University of Texas Press, 1985.

Dodge, Richard Irving. *Our Wild Indians: Thirty-Three Years' Personal Experience Among the Red Man of the Great West.* Hartford: A.D. Worthington and Co., 1882.

Douglas, C.L. *Cattle Kings of Texas.* 1939. Reprint. Austin: State House Press, 1989.

Foreman, Carolyn Thomas. "General Benjamin Henry Grierson." *Chronicles of Oklahoma.* Vol. 24, No. 2 (Summer 1946).

Grinnell, George Bird. *The Fighting Cheyennes.* 1915. Reprint. Norman: University of Oklahoma Press, 1956.

Guild, Thelma S. and Harvey L. Carter. *Kit Carson: A Pattern for Heroes.* Lincoln: University of Nebraska Press, 1984.

Haley, James L. *The Buffalo War: The History of the Red River Indian Uprising of 1874.* 1976. Reprint. Norman: University of Oklahoma Press, 1985.

Hamilton, Allen Lee. *Sentinel of the Southern Plains: Fort Richardson and the Northwest Texas Frontier, 1866-1878.* Fort Worth: Texas Christian University Press, 1988.

Hazen, William B. "Some Corrections of 'Life on the Plains.'" 1874. Reprint. *Chronicles of Oklahoma*, Vol. 3, No. 4 (December 1925).

Hoig, Stan. *The Battle of the Washita: The Sheridan-Custer Indian Campaign of 1867-69*. Garden City: Doubleday & Company, 1976.

—. *Tribal Wars of the Southern Plains*. Norman: University of Oklahoma Press, 1993.

Huckabay, Ida Lasater. *Ninety-four Years in Jack County, 1858-1948*. 1949. Centennial Edition. Waco: Texian Press, 1979.

Hutton, Paul Andrew. *Phil Sheridan and His Army*. Lincoln: University of Nebraska Press, 1985.

Jacob, Richard Taylor, Jr. "Military Reminiscences of Captain Richard T. Jacob." *Chronicles of Oklahoma*, Vol. 2, No. 1 (March 1924).

Jones, Douglas C. *The Treaty of Medicine Lodge: The Story of the Great Treaty Council as Told by Eyewitnesses*. Norman: University of Oklahoma Press, 1966.

Keim, De Benneville Randolph. *Sheridan's Troopers on the Border: A Winter Campaign on the Plains*. 1885. Reprint. Freeport, New York: Books for Libraries, 1970.

Knight, Oliver. *Following the Indian Wars: The Story of the Newspaper Correspondents Among the Indian Campaigners*. 1960. Reprint. Norman: University of Oklahoma Press, 1993.

Kroeker, Marvin E. *Great Plains Command: William B. Hazen in the Frontier West*. Norman: University of Oklahoma Press, 1976.

Lavender, David. *Bent's Fort*. Garden City: Doubleday & Company, Inc., 1954.

Leckie, William H. "The Red River War of 1874-1875." *Panhandle-Plains Historical Review*. Vol. 29 (1956).

—, and Shirley A. Leckie. *Unlikely Warriors: General Benjamin H. Grierson and His Family*. Norman: University of Oklahoma Press, 1984.

Ledbetter, Barbara A. Neal. *Fort Belknap, Frontier Saga: Indians, Negroes and Anglo-Americans on the Texas Frontier*. Burnet, Texas: Eakin Press, 1982.

Lowe, Percival. *Five Years a Dragoon ('49 to '54) and Other Adventures on the Great Plains*. Kansas City: The Franklin Hudson Publishing Co., 1906.

McConnell, H.H. *Five Years a Cavalryman*. Jacksboro, Tex.: J.N. Rogers & Co., 1889.

Matthews, Sallie Reynolds. *Interwoven: A Pioneer Chronicle*. 4th ed. College Station: Texas A&M University Press, 1982.

Mayhall, Mildred. *The Kiowas*. Norman: University of Oklahoma Press, 1971.

Miller, James E., Jr., et. al. *America Reads: The United States in Literature*. Classic Edition. Glenview, Ill.: Scott, Foreman and Company.

Moore, Horace. "The Nineteenth Kansas Cavalry in the Washita Campaign." 1897. Reprint. *Chronicles of Oklahoma*. Vol. 2, No. 4 (December 1924).

Morris, W.A. "Big Tree's Raid in Montague County." *Frontier Times*, Vol. 5, No. 1 (October 1927).

Myers, James Will. Papers. Panhandle-Plains Historical Society, Canyon, Texas.

Nye, Wilbur S. *Carbine and Lance: The Story of Old Fort Sill*. 1937. Reprint. Norman: University of Oklahoma Press, 1969.

Pratt, Richard Henry. *Battlefield and Classroom: Four Decades with the American Indian, 1867-1904*. New Haven: Yale University Press, 1964.

O'Neal, Bill. *Fighting Men of the Indian Wars: A Biographical Encyclopedia of the Mountain Men, Soldiers, Cowboys, and Pioneers Who Took Up Arms During America's Westward Expansion*. Stillwater, Okla.: Barbed Wire Press, 1991.

Rister, Carl Coke, ed. "Documents Relating to General W.T. Sherman['s] Southern Plains Indian Policy 1871-1875." *The Panhandle-Plains Historical Review*. Vol. 9 (1936).

——. Papers. Southwestern Collection. Texas Tech University. Lubbock, Texas.

Robinson, Charles M., III. *Bad Hand: A Biography of General Ranald S. Mackenzie*. Austin: State House Press, 1993.

——. "Blundering on the Plains: Hancock's War." *Old West*, Vol. 29, No. 4 (Summer 1993).

——. *The Buffalo Hunters*. Austin: State House Press, 1995.

——. *A Good Year to Die: The Story of the Great Sioux War*. New York: Random House, 1995.

——. "Kicking Bird: Kiowa Martyr for Peace." *True West*. Vol. 40, No. 1

(January 1993).

___. "Kit Carson's Last Fight." *True West*, Vol. 40, No. 11 (November 1993).

Russell, Don. "Jeb Stuart's Other Indian Fight." *Civil War Times Illustrated*, Vol. 12, No. 9 (January 1974).

"Satanta (White Bear)" File. Center for American History, University of Texas, Austin.

Scott, Hugh Lenox. *Some Memories of a Soldier*. New York: The Century Co., 1928.

Sheridan, Philip Henry. *Personal Memoirs*. 2 vols. New York: Charles L. Webster & Co., 1888.

Sherman, William Tecumseh. *Memoirs of General W.T. Sherman*. Rev. ed. 1886. Reprint. New York: Library of America, 1990.

——. Unofficial Papers. Library of Congress, Washington, D.C.

Spotts, David L. *Campaigning With Custer and the Nineteenth Kansas Volunteer Cavalry on the Washita Campaign, 1868-'69*. 1928. Reprint. New York: Argonaut Press, 1965.

Stanley, F. (Francis). *Satanta and the Kiowas*. Borger, Texas: Jim Hess Printers, 1968.

Stanley, Henry M. *My Early Travels and Adventures in America*. 1895. Reprint. Lincoln: University of Nebraska Press, 1982.

Strong, Henry W. *My Frontier Days and Indian Fights*. Dallas: Privately printed, 1926.

Tatum, Lawrie. *Our Red Brothers and the Peace Policy of President Ulysses S. Grant*. 1899. Reprint. Lincoln: University of Nebraska Press, 1970.

"Tsait-ante's Shield." Transcript of sign language conversation between Taybodl and Hugh L. Scott, 1897. Copy in possession of the author.

Taylor, A.A. "Medicine Lodge Peace Council." *Chronicles of Oklahoma*. Vol. 2, No. 2 (June 1924).

Taylor, Joe F. (comp.) *The Indian Campaign on the Staked Plains, 1874-1875: Military Correspondence from War Department Adjutant General's Office, File 2815-1874*. Canyon, Texas: Panhandle-Plains Historical Society, 1962.

Utley, Robert M. *Cavalier in Buckskin: George Armstrong Custer and the Western Military Frontier*. Norman: University of Oklahoma Press, 1988.

___, ed. *Life in Custer's Cavalry: Diaries and Letters of Albert and Jennie Barnitz, 1867-1868*. New Haven: Yale University Press, 1977.

Wallace, Ernest, ed. "Ranald S. Mackenzie's Official Correspondence Relating to Texas, 1871-1873." Vol. 9, *The Museum Journal*. Lubbock: West Texas Museum Association, 1968.

Washburn, Betty J. [*At-me-ponyah Sankadota*]. "Chief Satanta (White Bear) Celebration and Honoring Clarence (Set'tain-te/Satanta)" Mimeographed program. N.d. N.p.

Weems, John Edward. *Death Song: The Last of the Indian Wars*. New York: Indian Head Books, 1991.

Wellman, Paul I. *Death in the Desert: The Fifty Years' War for the Great Southwest*. 1935. Reprint. Lincoln: University of Nebraska Press, 1987.

Wilbarger, J.W. *Indian Depredations in Texas*. 1889. Reprint. Austin: Eakin Press and State House Press, 1985.

Wharton, Clarence. *Satanta, the Great Chief of the Kiowas and His People*. Dallas: Banks Upshaw and Company, 1935.

Worcester, Donald. "Satanta." R. David Edmunds, ed. *American Indian Leaders: Studies in Diversity*. Lincoln: University of Nebraska Press, 1980.

Newspapers and Periodicals

Army and Navy Journal and Gazette of the Regular and Volunteer Forces, Vol. 10, October 26, 1872.

Austin *Weekly State Journal*, November 3, 1870, July 18, 1871.

Cincinnati Commercial, October 19, October 21, October 28, November 4, 1867.

Chief Satanta (White Bear) Descendants Newsletter. Vol. 8, No. 2 (February 8, 1995).

Dallas *Morning News*, June 19,1963.

Dallas *Times-Herald*, June 30, 1963.

Galveston News, September 20, October 12, 1872.

New York Herald. October 23, 1868.

New York Times. October 30, November 4, 1867.

St. Louis *Daily Republican*, October 18, October 24, October 25, October 27, October 28, 1867.

St. Louis *Missouri Democrat*, November 2, 1867.

Index

Adobe Walls, Tex., 36-39, 184-85

Alvord, Capt. H.E., 159-61, 163, 173-74

Anadarko, Okla., 169, 195

Apache Indians, 3, 20, 23, 36, 41, 53, 77, 79, 80, 82, 84, 108, 111, 159

Apache, Okla., 198

Arapaho Indians, 19, 20 41, 51, 53, 60, 64-65, 77, 78, 80, 84, 174, 185

Armijo, Jose, 29

At-me-ponyah (Kiowa), 198

Atkin, John A., 52

Auchiah, James (Kiowa), 196-97, 198

Auchiah, Mark (Kiowa), 195, 196

Augur, Gen. Christopher C., 60, 155-56, 172, 191

Ball, Thomas, 142-43, 146, 149

Barnitz, Capt. Albert, 80

Battey, Thomas, 7, 183-84

Baxter, N.J., 141

Bear Lying Down (Kiowa), 73

Beede, Cyrus, 157

Belknap, William W., 189, 190

Benedict, Burton, 196

Bent's Ranch, Colo., 33-35

Bent, William, 33, 34, 40

Big Bow (Kiowa), 129, 130, 148, 155, 160

Big Tree (Kiowa), 116, 119, 127, 128, 130, 131-40, 141-52, 153-55, 158-64, 165, 167-72, 174-80, 183-84, 187-88, 192, 194-95

Black Bird (Kiowa), 51, 59

Black Bonnet (Kiowa), 12

Black Eagle (Kiowa), 65, 73, 94-95, 132

Black Horse (Kiowa), 24

Black Kettle (Cheyenne), 35, 51, 84, 86-87, 89, 137

Blackwater Springs, Nebr., 27

Blinn, Clara, 83, 88-89

Blinn, Willie, 83, 88-89

Blunt, Maj.Gen. James G., 34

Border Regt., Texas Cavalry, 35

Boren, David, 196

Bowman, James, 141

Box, James & family, 48, 57, 68, 82

Brazeal, Thomas, 122, 132, 142, 146

Brown, Dee, xix-xx

Brown, George, 64, 73, 76

Butler, John, 103-104

Butler, Josiah and Lizzie, 109, 139

Butterfield, Dave, 52

Byrd, Capt. Joe, 197-98

Byrne, Thomas E., 194

Callway, Wesley, 142

Camp Supply, Okla., 108, 155

Canby, Brig.Gen. Edward, 168-69

Carlton, Capt. C.H., 181-82, 190

Carson, Col. Christopher, 36-40, 59-60

Carter, Lt. Robert, 124, 140, 146, 161

Catlin, George, 5-6

Charlton, John 139-40

Cherokee Indians, 125

Cheyenne Indians, 3, 16, 17-20, 27, 35, 41, 43, 49-51, 53-54, 60, 64-65, 77, 78, 80, 84, 127, 184, 188

Chilton, Maj. Robert H., 22-23

Chipman, Capt. H.L., 151-52

Chivington, Col. John, 32, 35, 59

Cimarron Crossing, Colo., 33, 34

Civil War, 27-28, 35, 74, 80, 81

Clous, Capt. J.W., 97

Cohen, B.R., 163-64

Coke, Richard, 190

Colley, S.G., 32-35

Comanche Indians, 3, 16, 21, 23, 27-28, 31-31, 35, 39, 41, 51, 53, 60, 71, 73, 77, 79, 80, 82, 84, 108, 159, 162, 167, 169, 174, 179, 184-85, 193

Connally, John, 197

Cooke County, Tex., 48
Cotton, James, 197
Cowen, B.R., 163, 189
Crawford, Samuel, 61, 71, 84
Creek Indians, 125
Crosby, Lt.Col. J. Schuyler, 91
Crow (Apache or Kiowa), 62, 73
Curtis, Maj.Gen. Samuel R., 32-34
Custer, George A., 12, 49-50, 84-96, 126, 127, 148

Dangerous Eagle (Kiowa), 172-73
Davidson, Lt.Col. John W., 170, 172, 174, 181, 187, 190
Davis, Gov. Edmund J., 149, 161, 167, 169, 170-80, 190
Davis, Jefferson, 28
Delano, Columbus, 167-69, 170, 185, 190, 191
Denson, Albert, 158
Denton, Tex., 161
Doan, C.F., xvii
Dodge, Richard I., 29
Dohasen the Elder (Kiowa), 4, 5-6, 19, 36, 37, 41-44, 45, 94
Dohasen the Younger (Kiowa), 33, 38-39
Double Vision (Kiowa), 187
Douglas, Jack, 193
Douglass, Maj. Henry, 48, 68

Eagle Heart (Kiowa), 116, 127, 128, 130, 134, 148
Eleventh Infantry, 151, 186
Elliott, Maj. Joel H., 64, 88
Elliott, Samuel, 120, 123, 124, 132, 141
Evans, John, 32, 33

Fast Bear (Kiowa), 127, 130, 148
Fayel, William, 62-63, 67, 69
Fetterman, Capt. William J., 48
Field, Mrs. Dorothy, 32, 111
First Cavalry, 27
First Colorado Cavalry, 34
First New Mexico Volunteer Cavalry, 36-40
Fishermore (Kiowa), 65, 73, 108
FitzPatrick, Elizabeth Ann, 35-36
Fitzpatrick, Thomas, 23-24
Five Civilized Tribes, 156-57, 159
Forsythe, 97
Fort Arbuckle, Okla., 97
Fort Atkinson Treaty Conference, 21-24
Fort Bascomb, N.Mex., 36
Fort Belknap, Tex., 114, 116
Fort Chadbourne, Tex., 2, 26
Fort Cobb, Okla., 80, 82-83, 84, 92-93, 97-98, 156
Fort Concho, Tex., 117, 167, 168, 169
Fort Dodge, Kans., 48, 51, 58, 77, 91
Fort Griffin, Tex., 109, 118, 155
Fort Hays, Kans., 155
Fort Laramie, Wyo., 41, 61
Fort Larned, Kans., 12, 29, 31-32, 48, 49, 52, 61, 63, 77, 82
Fort Leavenworth, Kans., 28 49, 126
Fort Lyon, Colo., 26, 32, 33, 34
Fort Marion, Fla., 193

Fort Mason, Tex., 45
Fort Richardson, Tex., 109, 114, 116, 117, 118, 122, 124, 126, 138, 140, 141, 149, 150-51, 173
Fort Sill, Okla., 97, 103, 108, 109, 114, 123-24, 125, 130, 137, 138, 160, 163-64, 168, 170, 172, 174, 179, 181, 186-87, 189, 190, 195, 196, 198
Fort Snelling, Minn., 189
Fort Union, N.Mex., 28
Fort Zarah, Kans., 43, 52-53
Fourth Cavalry, 116-17, 120-23
Fredericksburg, Tex., 45

Gainesville, Tex., 48, 161
Godfrey, Lt. E.S., 88
Goree, Thomas J., 193-94
Grant, U.S., 100-101, 122, 190, 191
Gray Goose (Kiowa), 12, 92-96, 99-100, 195, 198
Grierson, Col. Benjamin, 97, 103, 106, 108, 110, 111, 130-39, 147-48, 155, 162, 164
Grinnell, George B., 18-19
Griswold, Gillette, 198

Hancock's War, 48-58; council after, 51-58, 60, 86
Hancock, Gen., W.S., 12-13, 48-58, 68, 77
Harney, Maj.Gen. William S., 40, 59, 60, 61-62, 64, 68
Hau-tau (warrior), 120, 124, 127
Haworth, James M., 164, 169, 173, 174, 178, 184, 189

Hazen, Col. William B.,
  78-79, 80-83, 90, 93,
  97, 126, 129, 156
Heap of Bears (Kiowa),
  41, 51, 80
Henderson, John B., 59,
  69, 72-73
Hoag, Enoch, 102, 153,
  157, 160-64, 167-71,
  173, 174, 177-78, 186
Horseback (Comanche),
  99, 138
Hunt, P.B., 193
Huntsville, Tex., 150-52,
  153, 163, 172, 190,
  192, 198

Isa-tai (Comanche), 184-85

Jack County, Tex., 104,
  110, 122, 173
Jacksboro, Tex., 109, 122,
  140, 141, 149, 173,
  183
Jacob, Richard T., 9
Jenkins, Johnny, 46, 158
Johnson, Andrew, 59, 77
Johnson, Britt, 114
Jones, Frederick, 52
Jones, Horace, 130-31,
  134, 139, 142, 147,
  155, 174

Kaw Indians, 78
Keim, DeB. Randolph, 12,
  91, 97-100
Kicking Bird (Kiowa), 6,
  41, 44, 45, 47, 51-52,
  54, 65, 69, 73, 84, 88,
  89, 95, 108, 109, 111,
  125, 127, 131-38, 148,
  150, 153-55, 157, 181-
  83, 186, 193
Kidd, Maj. M.H., 108
Kilgore, Martin, 110, 111-
  12
Kincaid (interpreter), 52

King, Edward, 165-66
Kiowa Indians
  battles/raids of, 18-19,
    20-21, 31-34, 35, 36-
    39, 77, 80, 109, 115-
    19, 155, 187;
  history & society of, 1-14;
  relations with Texans, 17-
    18, 21, 28, 31, 74-75,
    82
  treaty conferences of, 22-
    24, 53-58, 62-76, 90-
    95, 125, 159-64, 174-
    79
Koozier, Gottlieb, 109,
  111-12
Lanham, S.W.T., 142-46
Lavender, David, 18-19
Leavenworth, Jesse H., 40,
  41, 48, 52-54, 57, 71-
  72, 104
Lee, Abel & children, 155,
  157-58
Leeper, Matthew, 127, 142
Light, Evander, xvi-xvii
Light-Haired Young Man
  (Apache), 119
Little Arkansas Treaty, 40-
  44, 45, 48, 59, 70-71,
  82
Little Buffalo (Comanche),
  35
Little Heart (Kiowa), 51
Little Raven (Arapaho),
  62, 65, 70, 84, 137
Little Robe (Cheyenne),
  184
Lone Bear (Kiowa), 73
Lone Wolf (Kiowa), 29, 41,
  43-44, 45, 47, 51, 54,
  83, 84, 90-91, 92-95,
  98-99, 111, 127, 134-
  35, 148, 155, 157, 160,
  170, 175, 177, 186-88,
  190, 191, 192, 193
Long, Nathan S., 119, 141

Lowe, Percival G., 9, 21-
  22, 28-29, 32
Lyman, Maj. Wyllys, 187,
  188, 190, 192

Mackenzie, Col. Ranald,
  122-24, 126, 136-38,
  142, 145, 150, 167,
  187-88
Mah-wis-sa (Meot-si)(Chey-
  enne), 88, 89
Maman-ti (Kiowa), 113-
  20, 127, 137, 153-55,
  186-88, 193
Man-That-Moves (Kiowa),
  51
Marcy, Gen. Randolph B.,
  118, 132
McCusker, Philip, 81-82,
  174
Medicine Arrow (Chey-
  enne), 84
Medicine Lodge Council
  & Treaty, 61-76, 77,
  98, 159
Menard, Tex., 32
Miles, Col. Nelson, 187,
  192
Miles, John D., 174, 184
Milky Way (Comanche),
  163
Mobeetie, Tex., 18
Modoc Indians, 168-69,
  170
Montague County, Tex.,
  109, 110, 116
Moore, Lt.Col. Horace, 94-
  95
Mow-Way (Comanche),
  108
Mullins, John, 141
Murphy, Thomas, 40
Myers, Lt. James Will, 3,
  13, 14, 15-16, 114

Nap-a-wat (medicine
  man), 186

Neill, Col. Thomas H., 188-89
Nineteenth Kansas Volunteer Cavalry, 84, 88, 93, 94
Nye, Col. W.S., xix, 91, 95, 99, 129, 188

Or-dlee (Comanche), 119, 122, 127
Osage Indians, 20, 21, 86

Page, Capt. John H., 63
Palo Duro, battle of, 188
Palo Pinto County, Tex., 104
Parker County, Tex., 104, 110, 149
Parker, Quanah (Quahadi Comanche), 155
Parra-o-coom (Comanche), 148
Patzki, Dr. Julius, 123
Pawnee Indians, 20-21
"Peace Policy" (Quaker), 100-104
Pettis, Lt. George, 36, 38
Pierce, Dr. Robert, 198
Pike, Brig.Gen. Albert, 27-28
Poor Bear (Kiowa/Apache), 65
Poor Buffalo (Kiowa), 187
Pope, Gen. John, 126, 188
Price, Col. William R., 187
Pugh, Achilles, 103-104
Pyle (mountain man), 23

Quahadi Comanches, 111
Quakers, 100-104, 110, 112, 153, 164, 168
Quirts Quip (Comanche), 177
Quitan (Kiowa), 114

Red Cloud War, 48-58, 59, 61

Red Otter (Kiowa), 187
Red River War, 185-89
Red Tipi (Kiowa), 1, 2, 6, 11, 24, 134, 175
Red Warbonnet (Kiowa), 119
Rees Indians, 4
Reynolds, Col. J.J., 150, 152
Reynolds, Milton, 62
Richards, Jonathan, 169, 174, 187
Roessler, Prof., 109
Romero, Rafael, 89, 92
Rood (family), 33, 34
Ross, Edmund G., 61, 71
Russell, Don, 27

San Angelo, Tex., 167
Sanborn, John B., 59, 68
Sand Creek Massacre, 35, 41, 49, 59, 60, 67-68, 70
Sanderson, Capt. B.G., 186-87, 191-92
Sankadota, Clarence (Kiowa), 198-99
Satank (Kiowa), 8-9, 10, 18, 19, 26, 27, 32, 51, 69, 73-76 (speech), 83, 84, 116, 127, 128, 130-40, 146
Satanta (Kiowa)
  early life of, 1-14
  name, 2, 198-99
  battles/raids of, 19-20, 26, 36-40, 45, 108, 115-24, 183-84, 187
  discourses of, 53-55, 63-73, 91, 104, 114-15, 127-30, 132-33, 147-48, 162-63, 175, 189
Satanta, Kans., 197
Schofield, Maj. G.W., 161
Scott, Capt. Hugh L., 24, 26, 195, 196
Sedgwick, John, 27
Set-maunte (Kiowa), 120
Seventh Cavalry, 24, 49-

50, 51, 64, 80, 84, 98, 195
Shawnee Indians, 20-21
Sheridan, Maj.Gen. Philip H., 77-78, 80-82, 85-95, 97-100, 126, 137, 148, 156, 189, 191, 192
Sherman, Maj.Gen. W.T., 59-60, 61, 77, 98, 118-24, 126, 130-37, 145, 147, 150, 179-80
Sioux, 60
Sioux, Burnt Thigh, 20
Sioux, Lakota, 3, 16, 17, 41
Sioux, Oglala, 48-49, 59
Sixth Cavalry, 109, 122
Smith, Col. A.J., 51, 52, 58, 85
Smith, Edward P., 169, 170, 173, 174, 177, 178, 179, 184-86, 190, 191
Smith, John B., 83
Soward, Charles, 142, 146-47, 14950
Spivey, Towana, 196
Spotts, David L., 93, 95
St.Louis, Mo., 159, 161, 164
Stanley, Henry Morton, 10, 41, 49-51, 52, 58, 61, 63, 64, 71, 73, 76
Steele, William, 27
Stuart, J.E.B., 27
Stumbling Bear (Kiowa), 39, 41, 45, 51, 54, 57, 73, 88, 127, 131-35
Sturgis, Col. Samuel, 85
Sun Boy (Kiowa), 159
Sun Dance, 3, 4, 7, 16-19, 24, 109, 185, 186
Sun shields, 24-26, 195-96

Tall Bull (Oglala Sioux), 49
Tappan, Col. Samuel, 59, 62, 72
Tappan, John, 72, 79